The Practical Critical Educator
Critical Inquiry and Educational Practice

Edited by

KARYN COOPER
University of Toronto, Ontario, Canada

and

ROBERT WHITE
St. Francis Xavier University, Nova Scotia, Canada

 Springer

A C.I.P. Catalogue record for this book is available from the Library of Congress.

ISBN-10 1-4020-6648-1 (PB)
ISBN-13 978-1-4020-6648-1 (PB)
ISBN-10 1-4020-4472-0 (HB)
ISBN-13 978-1-4020-4472-4 (HB)
ISBN-10 1-4020-4473-9 (e-book)
ISBN-13 978-1-4020-4473-1 (e-book)

Published by Springer,
P.O. Box 17, 3300 AA Dordrecht, The Netherlands.

www.springer.com

Printed on acid-free paper

DEDICATION

To
Jamilla Arindell, Cindy Bird,
Dianne Riehl, Suzanne Thomson,
and Robert White
who formed the
Critical partnership that was the inspiration for this book -
and to Dr. Sandra Monteath for her unflinching support

- Karyn

and

To
Robert, Alexander, Elizabeth, Callie
and Melanie
for helping to teach me throughout the years.
It was your powers of observation that helped me to become more critical.
Thank you.

- Robert

CONTENTS

LIST OF CONTRIBUTORS

Richard A. Brosio
University of Wisconsin Milwaukee
P.O. Box 413
2200 E. Kenwood Blvd.
Milwaukee, WI 53201-0413

The author's Ph.D. is in the Social Foundations of Education (focus on philosophical aspects) from the University of Michigan (1972). Dr. Brosio taught at Ball State University from 1972-2000 and is professor emeritus from that institution. He currently is a lecturer at the University of Wisconsin Milwaukee and continues to teach within the Foundations fields of inquiry.

Meredith Rogers Cherland
Professor of Education
Faculty of Education
University of Regina, Saskatchewan
S4S 0A2 Canada
Meredith.Cherland@uregina.ca

Meredith Rogers Cherland is Professor of Literacy Education at the University of Regina, Saskatchewan, Canada. Formerly a junior high school English teacher, she has worked in teacher education since 1978. She is the author of *Private Practices: Girls Reading Fiction and Constructing Identity* (Taylor and Francis, 1994), and of many articles about gender, justice, literature and teaching.

Barbara Comber
Centre for Studies in Literacy, Policy and Learning Cultures
School of Education
University of South Australia
Underdale, South Australia, 5032
Email: Barbara.Comber@unisa.edu.au

Barbara Comber is Director of the Centre for Studies in Literacy, Policy and Learning Cultures, School of Education, University of South Australia. Her main research interests are teachers' work, literacy and social justice, poverty and education and critical literacies. She is co-editor of *Negotiating critical literacies in classrooms*.

Karyn Cooper
Curriculum, Teaching and Learning
Ontario Institute for Studies in Education
of the University of Toronto
252 Bloor Street West
Toronto, Ontario
M5S 1V6
kcooper@oise.utoronto.ca

Karyn Cooper is an assistant professor in Teacher Education, Literacy, Language and Culture at the Ontario Institute for Studies in Education of the University of Toronto. Her research focuses on the sociocultural dimensions of literacy and teacher education.

Noah De Lissovoy
Department of Educational Leadership & Policy Studies
The University of Texas at San Antonio
6900 North Loop 1604 West
San Antonio, Texas 78249-0654
noah.delissovoy@utsa.edu

Noah De Lissovoy is an Assistant Professor in the Department of Educational Leadership and Policy Studies at the University of Texas at San Antonio. His research interests include the investigation of processes of oppression and resistance in public schooling and society, as well as the development of contemporary theories of liberatory pedagogy. His articles have appeared in *The Journal of Education Policy, The Journal of Postcolonial Education, Equity & Excellence in Education, Educação Unisinos,* and other journals, as well as in several edited collections on pedagogy and politics.

Carole Edelsky
Curriculum & Instruction
Arizona State University
Tempe, AZ 85287-0911
USA
edelsky@asu.edu

Carole Edelsky, Professor of Curriculum and Instruction at Arizona State University, is the author of *With Literacy and Justice for All, Writing in a Bilingual Program, Whole Language: What's the Difference* and the editor of *Making Justice our Project* and *The Fate of Progressive Language Policies and Practices.*

Sharon Fillion
Texas State University-San Marcos
College of Education
601 University Drive
San Marcos, TX 78666
sfillion@txstate.edu

Sharon E. Fillion, M.Ed., is a doctoral student at Southwest Texas State University with a focus in school improvement. She has extensive international life experiences leading to current employment as a foreign language teacher in the public school system in Austin, Texas.

Patrick Inglis
City University of New York
Graduate Centre
365 Fifth Avenue
New York, NY 10016-4309
pinglis@gc.cuny.edu

Patrick Inglis is a doctoral student in Sociology at the City University of New York Graduate Center. He recently finished a Master of Arts degree at the University of British Columbia in which he developed a critique of the popular writing workshop approach to writing instruction and made a case for how it might better address demands for democratic citizenship. He taught four years of high school English, Drama and Humanities in Vancouver, British Columbia.

Hilary Janks
University of the Witwatersrand
Private Bag 3, WITS, 2050, South Africa
janks@languages.wits.ac.za

Hilary Janks is a Professor in Applied English Language Studies at the University of the Witwatersrand, Johannesburg, South Africa and an adjunct Associate Professor at the University of South Australia (UniSA). Her teaching and research are in the areas of language education in multilingual classrooms, language policy and critical literacy. She is best known for the *Critical Language Awareness Series* in which she was both a contributing author and the series editor. Her work is committed to a search for equity and social justice in contexts of diversity.

Peter McLaren
University of California, Los Angeles
Graduate School of Education and Information Studies (GSE&IS)
1009 Moore Hall
Box 951521
Los Angeles, CA 90095-1521
mclaren@gseis.ucla.edu

Peter McLaren is a Professor in the Urban Schooling Division of the Graduate School of Education and Information Studies at the University of California, Los Angeles. He is author and editor of over 35 books on a variety of topics in education. He was the recipient of the inaugural Paulo Freire Social Justice Award, presented by Chapman University. His most recent books are *Che Guevara, Paulo Freire, and the Pedagogy of Revolution* (Rowman & Littlefield, 2000) and (with Dave Hill, Mike Cole, and Glenn Rikowski) *Marxism Against Postmodernism in Educational Theory* (Lexington Press, 2002).

William Pinar
Curriculum & Instruction
223 Peabody Hall
Louisiana State University
Baton Rouge, LA 70803
wpinar@lsu.edu

William F. Pinar teaches curriculum theory at Louisiana State University, where he serves as the St. Bernard Parish Alumni Endowed Professor. He has also served as the Frank Talbott Professor at the University of Virginia and the A. Lindsay O'Connor Professor of American Institutions at Colgate University; he taught at the University of Rochester (New York) 1972-1985. Pinar is the founding editor of the scholarly journal JCT and is now President of the International Association for the Advancement of Curriculum Studies. Pinar is the author of *Queer Theory in Education* (Lawrence Erlbaum, 1998), *The Passionate Mind of Maxine Greene* (Falmer, 1998), *Contemporary Curriculum Discourses* (Peter Lang, 1999) and the *International Handbook of Curriculum Research* (Lawrence Erlbaum, in press).

Maselela Paulina Sethole
PO Box 61, Atteridgeville 0008,
South Africa
Fax +2712 375 5250

Maselele Paulina Sethole joined the staff of Phepo School in 1976, became a head of department in 1994, acting principal in 1998 and principal in 1999. Since she assumed the principalship the school has won awards for improvements in teaching and learning and for its work in the area of environmental awareness. Sethole has personally won national recognition for her S.E.E.D garden project, which provides enough vegetables to provide a hot meal a day for all its students, and for school leadership. Two of her most prestigious awards are the Gauteng Women of the Year award for her outstanding performance in the building and shaping of our society, received in 2003 and the Department of Education National Lifetime Achievement Award, received in 2004.

David G. Smith
Faculty of Education
University of Alberta
114 St - 89 Ave
Edmonton Alberta
Canada T6G 2E1
davidg.smith@ualberta.ca

David Geoffrey Smith was born in China (Szechuan) and grew up in Africa (Northern Rhodesia/Zambia). He is currently a Professor in the Faculty of Education, University of Alberta, Canada. His published papers have been collected into two volumes, *Pedagon: Interdisciplinary essays in the Human Sciences, Pedagogy and Culture,* and *Teaching in Global Times.*

Barbara J. Thayer-Bacon
Cultural Studies in Education
A535 Claxton Complex
1126 Volunteer Blvd.
University of Tennessee
Tennessee 37996-3456 USA
bthayer@utk.edu

Barbara Thayer-Bacon is a professor in the Program of Cultural Studies in Education, University of Tennessee. Her primary areas of scholarship as a philosopher of education are feminist theory and pedagogy, pragmatism, and cultural studies in education.

Duncan Waite
Texas State University-San Marcos
Educational Administration and Psychological Services
College of Education, EDA
601 University Drive
San Marcos, TX 78666
dw26@txstate.edu

Duncan Waite is a professor of educational leadership, Editor of *The International Journal of Leadership in Education*, and Director of The International Center for Educational Leadership and Social Change (http://edlchange.org). He is the author of *Rethinking Instructional Supervision: Notes on Its Language and Culture* (Falmer Press, 1995) and *Research in Schools: A Reflective Ethnography for Educators* (Garland Press, forthcoming).

Susan Field Waite
Texas State University-San Marcos
Department of Curriculum and Instruction
College of Education
601 University Drive
San Marcos, TX 78666
sw22@txstate.edu

Susan Field Waite is Assistant Professor of Curriculum and Instruction at Southwest Texas State University. Her interests include teacher development, democratic education, and technology.

Robert E. White
School of Education
St. Francis Xavier University
P.O. Box 5000
Antigonish, Nova Scotia
Canada, B2G 2W5
rwhite@stfx.ca

LIST OF CONTRIBUTORS

Robert E. White has taught extensively in public school systems across Canada and is currently Assistant Professor of Inclusion at St. Francis Xavier University in Nova Scotia. Research interests include critical aspects of literacy, learning and leadership, globalization and social justice.

John Willinsky
Department of Language & Literacy Education
Faculty of Education
University of British Columbia
2125 Main Mall, Vancouver, BC V6T 1Z4
john.willinsky@ubc.ca

John Willinsky is currently the Pacific Press Professor of Literacy and Technology and Distinguished University Scholar in the Department of Language and Literacy Education at the University of British Columbia. He is the author of *Learning to Divide the World: Education at Empire's End* and more recently, *Technologies of Knowing* and *If Only We Knew: Increasing the Public Value of Social Science Research*. Examples of his work, including open source publishing software designed to improve the access and quality of research, are available at the Public Knowledge Project (http://pkp.ubc.ca) which he directs at UBC.

Terry Wrigley
Education Studies
Faculty of Education
University of Edinburgh
Old College
South Bridge
Edinburgh, EH8 9YL
Terry.Wrigley@ed.ac.uk

Terry Wrigley teaches at the University of Edinburgh, Scotland. His teaching, research and writing connects diverse fields of interest: school development, pedagogy, curriculum studies, social justice. He has worked in education for over thirty years, as a secondary school teacher, staff development manager, inspector and university lecturer. He edits the journal *Improving Schools*, and has written two books. *The Power to Learn* (2000) and *Schools of Hope: A New Agenda for School Improvement* (2003).

FOREWORD

I am delighted to have the opportunity to write this foreword for Karyn Cooper's and Robert White's splendid and compelling edited text on *The Practical Critical Educator*.

Critical practice in education is grounded in two bodies of thought and action: *critical theory* and *critical pedagogy*. Drawing on classical Marxism and its articulation of how oppression and injustice arose through capitalism's economic exploitation of labour, *critical theories* of society took a cultural turn in the writings of Adorno and Horkheimer, European Jewish refugees who fled to America, where they articulated how the power relations and oppressive forces of capitalism expressed themselves in the alienating symbolic forces of culture, music and art.

When booming demographics and an economic surplus fuelled the student movement of the late 60s, and in to the 70s, in many Western nations, new forms of cultural Marxism were added to this body of critical theory, extending beside but also far beyond the classical Marxist preoccupations with economic equalities of social class. British writers, such as the articulate and elegant cultural Marxist Raymond Williams, revived and refined the "lost" work of Italian Marxist, Antonio Gramsci from the 1920s, and his concern with the influence of what he called hegemony – the force through which ruling classes could maintain existing structures of domination by defining, through language, media and culture, what was normal, natural, true, beautiful and defensible, and what was eccentric, unreasonable, or unworthy of serious consideration.

French sociologists, such as Louis Althusser argued that the modern state (and its educational system) had a degree of "relative autonomy" from the economic base of capital accumulation and exploitation, and could "act back" on it and modify it from time to time, yet it still supported the interests of this economy "in the last instance". British and French writers Ralph Miliband and Nicos Poulantzas debated whether the state served the interests of capital because of how privileged elites were recruited into top state positions, or whether this relationship was a structured inevitability irrespective of who occupied powerful state positions – since the state was always necessarily destined to serve the interests of capital. Another French sociologist, Pierre Bourdieu, in work of lasting educational impact, presented arguments and evidence that social class structures and inequalities were perpetuated from generation to generation not just because of sheer differences of *economic* capital, of income, property and wealth; but also because of differences of *cultural* capital – of people's differential access through the family, then through education, of what dominant groups counted as being the legitimate symbolic tools of culture, taste, distinction and discernment that subtly distinguished and demarcated powerful groups from powerless ones in capitalist societies.

In the 1970s, British sociologists of education such as M.F.D. Young drew on many of these cultural and critical theories, and combined them with studies of classroom interaction, as well as investigations into how social groups created different kinds of knowledge together, to develop critical theories of classrooms, cultures, and curriculum in schools. The school curriculum, they argued, presumed and perpetuated elitist forms of cultural capital in valuing those forms of knowledge in which elites excelled – knowledge that was abstract, impersonal, hierarchically organized and separated from commonsense everyday life. Historians of education like Ivor Goodson in the United Kingdom and Barry Franklin in the United States subsequently provided empirical reinforcement for these claims by demonstrating that what counted as valid school subjects (chemistry, rather than astronomy, for example), what counted as valid content for school subjects (such as abstract and decontextualized laboratory experiments rather than studying the science of "common things"), and what counted as valid realizations of school knowledge (paper and pencil tests and arguments, rather than projects or performances), were the subject and the outcome of struggles between dominant and subordinate groups in society, and the kinds of knowledge and understanding that each of them valued. Weaken the boundaries between subjects, said curriculum theorist Basil Bernstein – soften the destruction between school knowledge and non-school knowledge – and you began to threaten the fundamental structures of power and control in society by challenging the privileged forms of knowledge in which dominant groups excelled.

In subtle and less subtle ways, critical theorists and their fellow travellers in educations showed how schools "reproduced the social relations of production" in capitalist societies, perpetuating class inequalities and the long standing opposition between capital and labour. For some, this process was all encompassing and inescapable. Others, most notably Paul Willis, who authored a compelling critical ethnography of a dozen working 'lads' in the English Midlands, which documented their inarticulate and sometimes offensively expressed capacity to "see through" the inequalities of the secondary school experience that was inflicted upon them, pointed to the ability of working class students, (and later the teachers of such students) to become 'resistant' to educational oppression and exploitation.

Inspired and influenced by the work of the Europeans, North American writers like Michael Apple, Peter McLaren and Henry Giroux developed critical perspectives in education by showing how the curriculum-in-theory and the curriculum-in-everyday use were suffused with the ideological influences of capitalist societies, and how youth cultures and teachers could create pedagogies and practices of resistance in response to these ideological and hegemonic forces.

Lacking the research resources of more liberal European academic and government regimes, American critical theory in education was not strongly supported by an empirical research base. Apart from just a few exceptions of published critical ethnographies by Jean Anyon and others, arguments were developed largely at the level of theory itself or were occasionally connected to individual ethnographic studies of the authors' doctoral students. This made a lot of the work in critical theory intellectually invigorating – but it also lent it a tendency to become disconnected from and insufficiently informed by the complex and mundane everyday realities of ordinary schools and their teachers.

The sometimes opaque and impenetrable language of critical educational theory often seemed to be addressed more to intellectual peers and associates, than to the practical needs and discourse of educators in schools. Like in most intellectual communities, bibliographies contained a high degree of self-referencing of fellow critical theorists, with insufficient acknowledgements of related work elsewhere. Many analyses seemed susceptible to the 'left sectarianism of intellectual as well as political certainty and superiority which Paulo Freire attributed to much critical theory and which had driven critical change theorist Seymour Sarason out of the American Socialist Workers Party in his early adulthood, long before critical theory itself had been invented. Some of the claims of critical theory did seem overextended – as when theorists interpreted every act of teacher skepticism or pupil misbehavior as resistance to capitalist domination, for example.

Over time, critical educational theory addressed many of these shortcomings. As it matured, the writing of its most senior proponents became increasingly accessible. Postmodernism and post-structuralism also lent critical theory greater openness and complexity, acknowledging other significant sources of inequality and injustice as well as social class – especially race, gender, sexual orientation and disability.

In the 1980s and 90s, a number of critical educational theorists in the areas of language and policy discourse, as well as action research further broadened the understanding of power imbalances in education by drawing on the critical theory of German sociologist Jürgen Habermas who explained how social action was guided by three different kinds of interest – *technical interests* directed at improving efficiency (as in the school effectiveness movement), *human or communicative interests* directed at increasing mutual understanding (as in the field of school improvement), and *critical or emancipatory interests* directed at rectifying injustice and transforming power relationships. In some cases, the search for other theoretical interpretations became so broad as to lose its usefulness – as in widespread intellectual adoptions of Michel Foucault's argument that power was diffused everywhere through discourse and society, rather than being embodied in particular positions and relationships. In this interpretation, power was everywhere and also nowhere – at a time when capitalism began closing in on public education and public life in the 1990s, postmodernism and poststructuralism avoided rooting power in groups, interests and systems that were widening inequalities between people in the world, and between different social groups of pupils and their achievements in schools.

If *critical educational theory* addressed and articulated the widespread nature of oppression, injustice and imbalance of power in education, the *critical pedagogy* movement developed and applied strategies of teaching and learning to rectify these imbalances. Working with illiterate peasants in South America, Paulo Freire advocated a program and practices of conscientization in which learning would be rooted in and connected to deep-seated contradictions in the lives and experiences of the people. While, as Elisabeth Ellsworth argued, any contemporary applications of Freire's critical pedagogy have been more haranguing than empowering – horrible examples of the Left Sectarianism of which Freire complained – Freire himself saw critical pedagogy as being absolutely connected with pedagogies of collaboration, love and hope.

Cooper and White's inspiring and imposing collection brings together and publishes for the first time some of the best writers and writing from across the world in critical theory and critical pedagogical practice. In large part, this writing is accessible, not impenetrable. The worlds of critical practice it portrays seem ordinary and achievable, not outrageous or extreme. The empirical papers in particular, reveal critical pedagogy to be not just a litany of intellectual dissatisfaction enunciated from the sidelines, nor a call to martyrdom and self-denial in a world bereft of pleasure. Critical pedagogy, rather, is presented as a field of theory and practice which can and does inspire thoughtful and morally committed teachers to make real differences for their most vulnerable students, and to extend the impact of their social justice agenda beyond their students.

Edelsky and Cherland provide actual examples of outstanding teaching to push our understanding of what distinguishes good and even great teaching, from the still greater teaching that addresses and embeds social justice concerns within the everyday literacy practices of the classroom. Barbara Comber movingly describes how making movies about "Cooking Afghani style" can present cultural difference as a source of strength and empowerment, not as a bunch of deficits which portrays refugees as pitiable, and asylum seekers as trouble. Patrick Inglis and prize-winning author John Willinsky show how student acts of community service in a soup kitchen can also be used as an opportunity to teach about democracy. And in post-apartheid, but still profoundly poor South Africa, Hilary Janks and Paulina Sethole, tell the inspiring story of a school principal who overcame teacher resistance and even death threats, by then working with her staff, her community and even a high class business partner, to transform her school by building a vegetable garden and demonstrating principles of sustainable development that spread throughout her school and community.

Theoretical giants like Bill Pinar and Peter McLaren, and a number of other authors such as philosopher Richard Brosio, leadership theorist Duncan Waite and school improvement critic Terry Wrigley, add theoretical introspection and exploration to these activist examples – giving us examples of scholars and specialists at the leading edge of their latest thinking as they push the field further forward.

Karyn Cooper's and Robert White's book makes critical theory practical for any and all teachers who are authentically concerned about promoting social justice among their students and in their world. Modest, not messianic in personality, witty not weary in disposition, compassionate rather than cutting in their engagements with those around them, Cooper and White have produced a book that reflects their vision as professionals and their values as people. If you want to make a difference, and want to change the world, this is the book that will get you started and keep you going.

Andy Hargreaves
Boston College
May 2005

PROLOGUE

This text is about being sensitive to, respecting and honouring differences among individuals and groups of individuals. But how are professionals — pre-service and in-service educators as well as teacher leaders and educational administrators — able to bridge the gap between democratic educational practice and Critical pedagogic theory? We ask how one begins to connect the professional lives of educators with a Critical democratic practice for the pluralistic milieu of the twenty-first century. The following quotation from Chambers may be an appropriate place to begin this text.

> To inhabit the multiplicity of cultural borders, historical temporalities and hybrid identities calls for a state of knowledge, an ethics of the intellect, an aperture in politics, able to acknowledge more than itself; a state of knowledge that is prepared to suffer modification and interrogation by what it neither possesses nor can claim as its own...and permits us to lend our ears to what is unsaid in the discourses we employ (Chambers, 1996, 50).

What Chambers refers to as a "state of knowledge" reveals a growing critical awareness of one's self and one's relationships to others within any enclosed system, educational systems not excepted. This critical perspective may be characterized by Habermas's (1990) ideal speech situation, in which any conversation must be able to be intelligible, truthful, sincere and justified. As a result, in essence, "Critical" has as its earmarks not only an ability to think Critically, but also a disposition to do so (Capper, 1993). The result of this process of Critical pedagogy is the development of voice – a voice that is not only heard, but also listened to and acted upon (Vibert, Portelli, Shields, LaRoque, 2002). The emergence of such a voice would acknowledge 'the multiplicity of cultural borders, historical temporalities and hybrid identities.' Such a voice, to be truly Critical, must be an ethical voice and must therefore recognize the politics of power in any given situation. This voice extends to the examination of one's own life and to the roles that one plays in emancipation and other issues of social justice.

While the editors of this volume come from different educational disciplines – that is, literacy and educational administration - they share common philosophies, common educational practices and common educational goals premised upon a democratic Critical education. However different these vantage points may appear, they are both rooted in the desire for positive social change. This blended view regards the opportunity to challenge educational policies and practices that are becoming increasingly less democratic in these globalizing times. The two vignettes that follow serve to situate our vantage point(s).

Karyn Cooper: Education is not Always Democratic

I grew up in a remote part of Northern Alberta, Canada, populated predominantly by French, Aboriginal, and English families. Not unlike most of the children I went to school with, I was born into a working class family; yet unlike many of my classmates, I went on to pursue a post-secondary education. I am not altogether certain why I was one of the few who went on to a post-secondary education or even whether this is necessarily a good or bad thing. I do know that my father, like many immigrants, dreamed of a better life for his children and education was the vehicle, or so I was told. When I was thirteen and in grade nine my father's dream nearly vanished when I very narrowly escaped being streamed into vocational education. I had failed the mathematics component of a province-wide examination, and at that time in Alberta, Canada, this exam determined it all. Needless to say, my father was devastated. My mother courageously took on the role of advocate, determined to prove that her thirteen-year-old daughter would be more than able to handle the "academic stream". Her argument focused on my strengths; the fact that I had scored well on the English standard of the examination, my track record (old report cards) and strong test results from other standardized examinations in elementary school. My mother ended up persuading the "powers that be" and so I was able to eventually go on to pursue a career in teaching.

At the time, I don't remember discussing the outcome of this provincial exam with any of my classmates other than Luc, someone who challenged my every thought. Luc was surprised to learn that I had plans to go on to attend university and was puzzled as to why my mother should challenge the examination. I can still remember his keen dark eyes and his fresh young face as he said, "only *really* smart people get to go university, Karyn". I was stunned; Luc was one of the smartest people I have ever known. Critiques such as those of Baker & Freebody (1989) serves to remind us that a democratic education entails freedom of choice. Looking back at this incident, I believe that what was so tragic was that Luc did not even know he *also* had a choice to go on to post-secondary education.

As a special education teacher and reading specialist, I have learned first-hand that education is not always democratic with large numbers of children, particularly ESL, indigenous, and the poor continuing to be limited by second-hand dreams of a normative education. Fortunately, I believe, many dedicated educators and teachers, such as those who have contributed to this book, are challenging educational policies and practices that are increasingly less democratic in globalizing times.

Robert E. White: "Trickle Down" Globalization

During my more than thirty years as parent, teacher, consultant and professor spent in the halls of schools and school board offices in Canada, I have often been impressed by the quality of teaching and learning that I have witnessed. Not only is this true of the classrooms dedicated to the exploration of Science and Math, English and History, but it is also true of the more "practical" aspects of schooling. Take for example, the machine shop where I often took my car to be serviced or the teaching cafeteria where the meals were nutritious and delicious, as well as beautifully presented. Over the years, however, changes have occurred. In the aforementioned school districts, the machine shop has become interested in not just servicing automobiles, but aircraft. The school cafeteria is no longer a teaching cafeteria but is now run by a company external to the school. The chef has gone to work in a commercial restaurant and the students who want to learn culinary arts must travel to the only school in the district that still provides a culinary arts program. In other schools, the only available nutrition, to use the word loosely to connote the notion of "food", is frequently dispensed from vending machines.

It was simply more *efficient* to have a teaching cafeteria in a central location where students were expected to transport themselves, than to have such cafeterias in every school where there was a significant proportion of students who aspired to a culinary arts background. The social, educational and nutritional benefits of such programs, although costly, were overlooked in an attempt to become more efficient and, in a sense, more global. The hidden costs in terms of students not having access to the centralized programs as a result of transportation or other issues, the social costs of students identifying vending machine wares with actual meals and the long term health costs of such misguidance were largely ignored in a rush to greater efficiency and "effectiveness" in schooling.

As I travelled from school to school, district to district and, ultimately, province to province over the past quarter century, I began to notice similar kinds of transformations occurring. Not only were recognizable market forces becoming more clearly integrated with schools and school districts, it appeared to be the same major corporations that were recognizable time and time again. This led to the idea that this was not a random occurrence or a coincidence, but a pattern.

But what about this pattern – the "big picture" – and how does this "big picture" relate to a democratic education, especially in this pluralistic milieu of the twenty-first century? After numerous attempts to identify a conspiracy in all of this marketization and commodification of schooling, I began to feel that it was a trend rather than a plot. As my doctoral research proceeded, it became clear to me that these effects in our schools were caused by a "trickle down effect" of the world-wide trend towards globalization. What I was looking at seemed to be a pattern, part of the trend towards a more globalized economy, one than stressed effectiveness and efficiency over individual needs, wants and desires. As Jonathan Hale (1994) suggests:

> People do have innate standards, but most do not know how to get at them. It is hard for people to separate the important from the unimportant, the primary geometry from the secondary applied symbol, if they do not know about pattern. (Hale, 1994, 25).

Why are Hale's words so important here? Simply put, it is important for citizens in a democratic society to be *Critical* of patterns such as the trend towards globalization, and the possible harmful effects on schooling particularly for disadvantaged students if one wants to view education in a more democratic and equitable fashion.

Our two vantage points merge, change, and are changed in and through the writing of this book. Yet, "patterns" emerge, which allow for a synthesis of three huge and separate areas: literacy, learning, and leadership framed through a Critical lens in each section of the book, pulled together in the epilogue. While these sections are not mutually exclusive, it is perhaps helpful for organizational purposes to group similar chapters together. As a result, this book is divided into three sections. The first section, entitled "Critical Literacy for a Democratic Education", focuses on the importance of a Critical language capable of developing an awareness that not only needs to question but seeks to emancipate the questioner. The second section, entitled "Critical Learning for a Democratic Education," serves to connect the individual's 'state of knowledge' to the broader problematics in society. Issues are brought forward, examined and discussed in order to establish, develop and promote the realization that we are learning, functioning and interacting within the larger societal context. But it is this very literacy that is essential to promote learning. But this raises another question. Who teaches and who learns? It is from this perspective that the issue of being *Critically* aware, in the political sense rather than the literal sense, must be addressed. Why? Teaching and learning implies a power differential, if not a power hierarchy. There is an adage in the culture of teaching that suggests the best way to learn something is to teach it. Taking this as another starting point, we arrive at the delicacy of a leadership style that is at once just, democratic and relatively free of issues of power. This is discussed in the third section of this volume, and is entitled "Critical Leadership for a Democratic Education" This section examines effective practical strategies in the continuous development of the leader, formal or informal; who is at once Critical, reflective and democratic.

Perhaps it is *process wisdom* that sets leaders apart from their colleagues. However, leadership still needs to benefit from the learning that is born of a variety of literacies in evidence during each and every day. This then, is how we have conceived of the integrated framework of literacy, learning and leadership. But is this enough in this pluralistic milieu of the twenty-first century? Is this sufficient to be able to meet the needs of the students who we teach, the teachers who we influence and the members of the society who we come into contact with each day? Perhaps not.

It is for these reasons that we felt it essential to build in a critical component to this integrated framework. It is this critical component that continuously asks who benefits? In whose interests are changes being effected? What are the power differentials? Are there hidden agendas? Hidden curriculums? Null curriculums? This critical framework has been developed in order to question issues of power and to promote voice and human agency in the pursuit of social justice and positive social change. It is hoped that on each and every page of this volume, these concerns will be addressed through lived experiences of those involved in creating positive social change. Through an integrated framework of Critical literacy, Critical learning and Critical leadership, it is hoped that some of the more prevalent and pernicious problems of humanity can be identified, engaged and rectified for the betterment of all human beings. It is hoped also that, in these times of increased global injustices, the idea of such an integrated framework may serve educators and their students well.

Parts One, Two and Three of this volume build on each of these themes of Critical literacy, learning and leadership. While they do not necessarily represent a conception of linear progressions, nor stages of advancement on a hierarchical construct, they are presented in the order in which these skills are for the most part, learned, developed and practiced. Furthermore, these three themes of literacy, language and leadership are not mutually exclusive domains in that the strands that unite them are suffused throughout the entire process of learning and do not necessarily exist independently of one another. Finally, we tend to develop these skills in a relatively simultaneous fashion. Represented here, then, is the work of contributors to the practice of Critical education. Through concrete examples, the editors promote the concept that every educator, including students, can become agents of change. The general purpose of this book is

- To provide individuals with opportunities for developing greater capacity for Critical inquiry wherever an individual is, within any given educational system:
- To examine the recognition of not only a vocabulary but also the recognition of a context within which to use the vocabulary in order to be eternally vigilant to protect one's democratic rights.
- To encourage participants in greater understandings of themselves, the students they teach and the broader cultural framework within which educators teach, learn and lead.
- To incorporate change for social action. Without the means of becoming agents for social change, Critical educators may lose an opportunity for the promotion of social justice.

New directions in Critical educational thought and tremendous potential for social change may be realized through this process of Critical inquiry. Based on the concept that inquiry fosters understanding, the contributors highlight the role of ongoing Critical inquiry into the role of language, its connection to and its potential for learning and emancipation within and among individuals and groups. This text seeks to bridge perceived gaps and silences between theoretical and practical aspects of literacy, learning and leadership, based on relevant theoretical concepts. Critical inquiry is a frequently neglected aspect of education, yet there is the need for such a focus in the pluralistic milieu of the twenty-first century.

REFERENCES

Baker, C. D. and Freebody, P. (1989). *Children's first school books: Introduction to the culture of literacy*. Oxford, UK; Cambridge, MA: Blackwell.

Capper, C. (1993). Educational administration in a pluralistic society: A multiparadigm approach. In C. Capper (ed.) *Educational administration in a pluralistic society*, (7-35). New York: SUNY Press.

Chambers, I. (1996). *The post-colonial question: Common skies, divided horizons*. London: Routledge.

Habermas, J. (1990). *The philosophical discourse of modernity*. MIT Press: Cambridge MA.

Hale, J. (1994). *The old way of seeing*. New York: Houghton Mifflin.

Vibert, A., Portelli, J., Shields, C. and Larocque, L. (2002). Critical practice in elementary schools: Voice, community and curriculum of life. *Journal of Educational Change*. 3(2), 93-116.

PART ONE:

CRITICAL LITERACY FOR A DEMOCRATIC EDUCATION

When this volume was in its planning stages, it soon became abundantly evident that there was a significant interrelationship between literacy and learning, learning and leadership, and leadership and literacy. Simply put, in order to learn, one must have the tools available to learn with. That is to say, literacy is the basic tool that we use in order to demystify and demythologize our daily, lived experiences. Needless to say, there are a multiplicity of literacies, among them are decoding and encoding skills such as reading and writing, oracy, numeracy, encryption and logo literacy, to mention only a few. Multiple and interconnected literacies form an essential part of daily life. Imagine being in a foreign country and not having access to the taken-for-granted literacy required to make a telephone call. First of all, recognizing a telephone station may be relatively simply, but does one dial the number first, or insert the coins first? Which coins do you use? How many? There may be pictures of the coins that can be inserted on the telephone box itself, but even this process may be open to interpretation. Once you have weathered these problems of literacy and logic, do you include the area code? The city code? Only the last four digits? Which language will you use? Even when one is able to ask questions in a different language, which presumes a certain literacy, the answers also tend to be provided in the language in which the questions were asked. It can be a bit of a shock to find that one is not so literate as had been originally presumed. In sum, one tends to take literacy for granted, especially if one is (relatively) literate in whichever form(s) of literacy within which one is operating.

This section focuses on the importance of a Critical literacy capable of developing an awareness of the underlying assumptions regarding the nature of language. This section begins with a discussion of some of the concepts involved in Critical inquiry. The first chapter in section one, entitled "Critical literacy in action: Action Research in a grade three classroom", written by Karyn Cooper and Robert White, evolved out of a small scale Social Science Humanities Research Council grant the co-editors were engaged in. This exploratory action research account on Critical literacy, examined in greater detail through the lens of Critical pedagogy is reported in this chapter. It is our belief that it would be helpful to contextualize Critical pedagogy in a practical school context, with a student population comprised mainly of ESL, indigenous and poor students because it is these students who are often the subject of our conversations but are seldom the subjects who are engaged in the conversation. What we are saying of students here can often equally be true of teachers and school leaders as well.

The idea for this book was born out of the experience of trying to envision Critical literacy in practice. In concert with arguably some of the most distinguished

1

scholars in education, we have the great honor of exploring the linkages between Critical literacy, Critical learning and Critical leadership in democratic practice.

Chapter 2 in this section, written by Carole Edelsky and Meredith Cherland, entitled "A critical issue in critical literacy: The 'Popularity Effect'" provides poignant and provocative accounts of teachers in action. At the heart of this chapter lies the etymology of the concept "Critical literacy." The authors claim that while all six of the teaching accounts can be said to be excellent, only two can be called *Critical* according to the authors' criteria. Edelsky and Cherland, speak to this by claiming that the popularization of the term "critical" tends to trivialize what Critical literacy—and pedagogy—really mean. The position taken by these researchers is simultaneously definitional and political, linked to the lens of emancipation through Critical literacy.

In support of the previous two chapters, Patrick Inglis and John Willinsky describe a class field trip, working in a downtown Vancouver soup kitchen, to explore what can be done to increase the educational value and service of such important experiences for students and teachers. Chapter 3, entitled "Soup-Kitchen democracy: Practical, Critical lessons in theory" draws on four theories of democracy – constitutional, procedural, deliberative, and rhetorical in order to construct a twelve-step program for democratic inquiry, skill development, and community service. This schematic approach toward exercising and practicing democratic rights is intended to demonstrate to students a broad range of practical, Critical activities which can be undertaken to address issues of democracy and social justice.

Chapter 4 begins with a discussion by Barbara Comber about how Critical literacy educators go about their work. Entitled " Critical literacy educators at work: Dispositions, discursive resources and repertoires of practice", this chapter probes how teaching democratically in increasingly undemocratic and globalized times is seriously challenging work. The ethical commitments, professional knowledges and pedagogical repertoires that facilitate or circumscribe teachers' practices are considered. The dispositions, discursive resources and practices of teachers who take a Critical literacy standpoint are also discussed in terms of different approaches to Critical language awareness. Comber's analysis through studies of practical Critical educators at work in literacy classrooms draws on her observations, educators' writings and other professional artifacts. A key to fostering Critical literacy in educational institutions is the democratization of research and knowledge producing practices.

KARYN COOPER AND ROBERT WHITE

CRITICAL LITERACY IN ACTION[1]:

Action Research in a Grade Three Classroom

Abstract. This paper discusses the implications of critical literacy as it impacts upon educational practices, procedures and policies. The study detailed here is a multi-year project that employed action research to develop capacity among the entire research team in order to make inroads in critical literacy with a grade three class at Sir Simon George Elementary School in Canada. This action research project on critical literacy in a high poverty area in Toronto becomes the practical backdrop for examining how critical literacy can be developed and applied in regular classroom situations. Educators are encouraged to look for patterns within classrooms that serve to prevent students from participating fully in all aspects of a democratic society.

1. THE PROJECT

The action research project, reported here, offers promise for on-going collaborative research into critical literacy for urban students who continue to be at a disadvantage. The research team consisting of the co-authors, a graduate research assistant, one grade three teacher, a school literacy co-ordinator and a district primary literacy consultant. In the Fall of 2001, we were invited to participate in a multi-year action research project at Sir Simon George Elementary School, the focus of which was school wide literacy improvement. This chapter reports on an exploratory action research project on critical literacy that grew out of this initiative.

Sir Simon George Elementary, an urban K-6 school in Toronto, Canada, is a diverse school with a rich tapestry of languages and cultures. Unfortunately, like many urban schools in lower-socio-economic areas, Sir Simon George's literacy levels are characteristically low. Recent new administration at Sir Simon George has seen new visions for that school. Having the "courage to take a stand for one's vision", not unlike Principal Maselele Paulina Sethole in this volume, the administration began a school-wide change process in the hopes of not only reversing this school's low educational ranking in literacy but in promoting the vision of the school as a community of reflective and critical learners. In the first year of this project much time was invested in outlining the parameters of the research project, including serious school-wide discussion, culminating in a joint initiative on the methods of literacy instruction for primary students (kindergarten through grade three) in the school. The program of research was based on the action research methodology loop, "act-reflect-revise" (Mills, 2000), with teachers and their students as they engaged in action research to select and implement suitable and appropriate practices for critical literacy, as defined by the teachers themselves.

K. Cooper and R. White (eds.), The Practical Critical Education, 3–16.

At the school level, all research members participated in sessions to decide upon the foundations for the research project based on suitable and appropriate practices for building critical literacy capacities relating to primary urban students and their teachers (see Comber, Thomson, Wells, 2001). All stages in the process were developed through consensus. Learning strategies such as KWL (Thompkins, 1998) and other reflective practices were included.

The "K-W-L" (what we KNOW–what we WANT to learn–what we have LEARNED) strategy for reflective thinking (Thompkins, 1998) is outlined below.

K   What we KNOW (One's preconceptions)

Based on my experience, I believe critical literacy can be described as.....
I am now thinking.....

W   What we WANT to learn

Lately, I've noticed.....
I wonder.....
What would happen if.....
It's funny how my students.....
How can I.....

L   What we have LEARNED

Developing critical literacy capacities of students and teachers
Practice or strategy for developing critical literacy capacities within this component.....
When students are engaged in developing critical literacy capacities, it looks like.....
When students are engaged in developing critical literacy capacities, it sounds like.....
Perhaps (specific student) demonstrates the best response to this strategy because.....
Perhaps (specific student) demonstrates the weakest response to this strategy because...
For this student to assess his/her critical literacy capacity, what needs to happen?
The opportunity for revision ("Are revisions needed to be made to the action plan itself at this time?") follows this reflection, which in turn produces a new action plan.

At the end of the school year, all research participants reflected upon the action research to date, and planned for revision to the research process for the next year. The previously described K-W-L strategy provided the basis for the structure of the focus group reflections within the project. The Debbie Miller (2002) book, *Reading with Meaning*, was chosen by the participants in this project for its attention to establishing a framework for creating a culture and climate for critical thinking. This book is written by a teacher-researcher and reflects goals similar to the objectives of this critical action research project, providing goals both for teachers and students regarding how to think more deeply while at the same time working towards esteem and agency. After one of the teachers in the project highly endorsed the book, everyone in the project read sample chapters and agreed that it fit into an operative framework for beginning the project. The research team particularly liked the way in which Miller (2002) worked at enabling her students to become more experienced at making meaningful and thoughtful connections to the stories of their own lives so that they might become more adept at reading the broader context within which they live. Like Miller, it was the group's belief, that the only way to develop responsibility in students is to allow them to practice it.

The critical literacy action research project began with that premise, and in September the following questions were asked of the students of the grade three teacher who was part of the research team: "Why do people read?" "What do you see readers doing?" "Where do you see people reading?" These questions and other questions were used to establish some connection with students' lives and to develop a greater understanding of their own reading worlds in order to make the context of the project relevant to them.

Responding to the first question entailed brainstorming with the large group and recording students' thinking. In this way, the project began to be outlined with the grade three students by the primary literacy consultant in collaboration with the grade three teacher and the research team. These questions, which framed the beginning work with our students, not only told us much about the children's perspectives about reading but assisted in the selection of relevant teaching materials.

In October, focus meetings followed the K-W-L format as previously described. For purposes of framing the discussion, one example from each KWL strategy for reflective thinking is presented below.

2. "K" REPRESENTS THE RESEARCH TEAM'S CURRENT UNDERSTANDING OF CRITICAL LITERACY

As a research team we realized early on that we needed to unravel our understanding of the term critical literacy. The research team's first discussion regarding our preconceptions of what critical literacy means was timely, given Edelsky and Cherland's (in this volume) concern about the popularization and appropriation of the term "critical" and the tendency to trivialize what critical literacy — and critical pedagogy — really means.

From the first meeting: On our preconceptions around the meaning of critical literacy:

Jamilla: Whatever we are doing needs to be important to us and our belief structures. Otherwise, what are we doing it for? There needs to be some connection to ourselves for it to be meaningful practice.

Karyn: Critical literacy is a way to view the world. It's a key to a democratic education. It's basic in terms of being critical oneself.

Jamilla: We all have different ideas of things in our own heads.... We might think that we are talking about the same thing, but we're talking about different things altogether.

Dianne: ...sharing ownership and trusting...and trusting the students to be able to be responsible and to think

Suzanne:If teachers don't ask themselves why, then how do they expect students to ask why? Many of the students in this particular situation are ESL students. We have had grade three students whom teachers were bringing forth as having difficulties. They were Canadian-born but were receiving ESL instruction and couldn't be considered ESL students any more. We're masking a problem that could be deeper than we realize.

This brief snippet taken from our first discussion concerning the need to define our critical literacy stance perhaps points to the notion that "critical literacy" needs to be understood in terms of the dynamics of identity, context and teaching practices employed. For example, Jamilla acknowledges how one's own belief structures are connected to classroom practice. In speaking about her own identity as a young black teacher, she can begin to see traces of her identity rooted in and through her teaching practices in both explicit and implicit ways. Dianne connects this thought to the all important roles that teachers play in helping to construct their students' identities through the beliefs they carry about who the students are and what they believe the students are capable of. Suzanne reminds us of the need to understand the politics of the 'local' literacy context when she states that "Many of our students in this particular situation are ESL students". Suzanne is speaking to the idea that the cultural and political run deep in literacy and that teachers need to be aware of these factors, particularly if they are concerned with all students, including "minority" students, gaining a chance to define themselves. Through this discussion we began to consider more deeply just how literacy practices used in educational settings serve to affirm or disaffirm a student's sense of identity and ultimately a students chances for "success" in society.

In essence, perhaps our initial discussion revealed an important question relevant to our discussion about a critical literacy stance: How do we, as teachers, learn to become more experienced so that we might learn to step outside of ourselves and our own identities to allow multiple identities in? Perhaps this entails the commitment to be continually vigilant concerning what conditions truly support literacy, particularly for children of poverty or for those who have been labeled "at-risk". These are of course ideological considerations and cannot be dealt with in short order. However, through beginning with our own teaching practices, and acting locally, we believed that we might move from our local position to more global issues relevant in literacy education today.

In order to make this connection, it may be helpful to look briefly at how literacy has been historically constructed. The following definitions may serve to illustrate that literacy is storied according to changing economies, cultures, institutions and possible worlds we inhabit.

- A literate person is a person who can, with understanding, both read and write a short, simple statement on his everyday life (Unesco, 1951).

- Functional literacy is the ability to engage effectively in all those reading activities normally expected of a literate adult in his community (Hunter & Harman, 1979).
- [Literacy is] using print and written information to function in society, to achieve one's goals, and to develop one's knowledge and potential (Southam Literacy, 1987).

As teachers/educators of literacy then, is it not incumbent upon us to consider our role(s) in shaping the 'construct' of what it is that literacy embodies? Is it to ask, "Who is deemed to be a 'literate' individual, and by whom", particularly in the times in which we live; in this pluralistic milieu of the twenty-first century? If so, then it would seem that we must choose our definitions well. Let us return to the quotation from Chambers, cited in the prologue, to add another dimension to the discussion:

> To inhabit the multiplicity of cultural borders, historical temporalities and hybrid identities calls for a state of knowledge, an ethics of the intellect, an aperture in politics, able to acknowledge more than itself; a state of knowledge that is prepared to suffer modification and interrogation by what it neither possesses nor can claim as its own…and permits us to lend our ears to what is unsaid in the discourses we employ (Chambers, 1996, 50).

What Chambers refers to as a "state of knowledge" reveals a growing critical awareness of the need to acknowledge multiple identities within any enclosed system, educational systems not excepted. The Chambers quotation is perhaps particularly important when considering a critical literacy stance because it embodies the key elements of identity and context when considering a state of knowledge capable of "lending our ears to what is unsaid in the discourses [or teaching practices] we employ". In our particular school research context, the research team felt that the rich cultural diversity of the children and parents in their school community is not always defined favourably by policy-makers. While on the surface, multiculturalism is touted to be beneficial to student learning; there may be issues still hiding in the light. A quotation from one of the team members may best express this:

> Suzanne: With talking about what you think and see with students, particularly impoverished students like those in our multicultural school, they're often written off for various reasons.

As another team member expressed it:

> Dianne: Our children are incredibly capable but there is somehow a mismatch between the school's version of intelligence and what is occurring at home.

And:

> Karyn: I've had students in Special Education who are very intelligent in terms of the way they use higher order thinking or critical thinking, but it is situational. Perhaps the key is to make critical thinking more dispositional than situational, thereby developing critical learning capacities that are derived from critical literacy.

The powerful research of Shirley Brice Heath (1983), highlights the discord that Suzanne, Dianne and Karyn express regarding the politics of power inherent in the difference between literacy practices at home and literacy practices at school. Her *Ways with words* (1983) documents the different language and literacy practices of two communities in the rural Carolinas. This seminal piece of research delves into the critical role that power plays in society, our educational systems, and within literacy education as it gives us a close view of what happens when the worldview of those with privileged positions are the dominant reality. Through our own research discussion, it became clear that the identity of "minority" students' is congruent with cultural differences. There is a need to be sensitive and to not judge these students as having deficits, but rather to enable them to also enjoy the privileges of the larger society (Delpit, 1995). Perhaps this begs the question, "How can teachers begin to question policies, practices and procedures in order to ensure that choice and freedom, and concomitantly, social justice, liberty and democracy are preserved in our educational institutions and hence, in the larger society"? Clearly, the answer to this question depends on deeper fundamental beliefs about the purposes of learning and the role teacher/researchers play. These are endemic to the contemporary socio-political power systems that have formed them, in alignment with their own ideals and goals. The research team wanted to dig deeper and try to draw attention to some underlying patterns of dominant approaches to curriculum theory and practice in literacy education both locally and internationally. Simply put, putting critical literacy into practice takes thought and hard work and the full time teacher is the one charged with the responsibility of being, accountable, effective and efficient. This made us more cognizant of the fact that although the idea of "teacher as researcher" may be desirable, teachers also need the time and the support of administration if they, too, are to have the power to question more deeply, to become critical agents of change. Shutz (2000) places this thought in context:

> ...what we are led to believe about ourselves, what we learn about how we are supposed to act, the ways we are taught to frame "problems" and even the tools of reason that we use to solve these problems, do not simply represent neutral skills but are in fact ways of forming us into particular kinds of subjects. 'Power' in this vision does not merely suppress or restrict but actually produces actions and desires (216).

If critical literacy is to promote democracy, social justice and equity in schools, then what circumstances need to arise in schools for an increase in democracy and shared power? Recognition of the need to challenge the balance of power in the classroom is perhaps the first step towards acknowledging the pivotal role of critical literacy in facilitating change. In our critical literacy action research project, as teachers/researchers uncomfortable with pedagogical strategies which relegate children to the role of passive recipients rather than invested participants in the process of their own learning, we struggled to explore what constitutes a critically literate classroom environment where such declarative acts of freedom and choice do not have to be subverted, but are encouraged to take place. We began to wonder.

3. "W" REPRESENTS THE ACTION RESEARCH PLAN: WHAT THE RESEARCH TEAM IS SEEKING TO KNOW

Jamilla, the grade three teacher on the project, was keen to examine the provincial language arts curriculum, specifically with an eye towards understanding how critical literacy is mentioned, understood or in some way factored into the document. We began by looking at specific and global expectations within sections of the grade three-literacy curriculum (Ontario Language Curriculum, 1997). As the following examples suggest the language curriculum document seemed to consist of mainly decontextualized skills. It was also in fact difficult to find the language that was directly relevant to our critical literacy practices. The section under reasoning and 'critical' thinking was particularly problematic because, not only were the skills decontextualized, the term "critical" had been co-opted and misapplied. The term "critical" no longer meant critical in any sense of the word. Following is an example from the grade three Language Arts curriculum that was recently in use:

Overall Expectations - Grade 3 Reading. By the end of Grade 3, students will:

- read a variety of fiction and non-fiction materials (e.g., chapter books, children's reference books) for different purposes;
- read independently, using a variety of reading strategies;
- express clear responses to written materials, relating the ideas in them to their own knowledge and experience and to ideas in other materials that they have read;
- select material that they need from a variety of sources;
- understand the vocabulary and language structures appropriate for this grade level;
- use conventions of written materials to help them understand and use the materials.

Expectations in Specific Areas. By the end of Grade 3, students will:

Reasoning and Critical Thinking:	Knowledge of Language Structures:
<ul><li>identify and restate the main idea in a piece of writing, and cite supporting details;</li><li>identify and describe some elements of stories (e.g., plot, central idea, characters, setting);</li><li>distinguish between fact and fiction;</li><li>begin to make inferences while reading;</li><li>use familiar vocabulary and the context to determine the meaning of a passage containing unfamiliar words;</li><li>begin to develop their own opinions by considering some ideas from various written materials;</li></ul>	<ul><li>use their knowledge of word order in oral and written language to determine the meaning of sentences;</li></ul> **Vocabulary Building:** <ul><li>use a variety of strategies to determine the meaning of unfamiliar words (e.g., use the context, break the word into syllables or other recognizable units, use a dictionary, use phonics);</li></ul> **Use of Conventions:** <ul><li>use punctuation to help them understand what they read (e.g., exclamation mark, quotation marks);</li></ul>

Understanding of Form and Style: • identify and describe different forms of writing (e.g., poems, stories, plays); • use their knowledge of the organization and characteristics of different forms of writing as a guide before and during reading (e.g., chapters in an adventure story often end with cliff-hangers; menus usually list the items of food on the left and the price of each item on the right);	• identify various conventions of formal texts and use them to find information (e.g., table of contents, chapter titles, headings, index, glossary, charts, graphs).

In spite of the "stage" approach to literacy, in practical terms the research team struggled with how the literacy curriculum might be a useful guide for our students, particularly when we all shared the belief that the students are capable language learners and we wanted to honor this in our teaching practices. Perhaps the key to using curricular documents is to first be cognizant of the language used to structure these documents; that is to become more literate in our own understanding of these documents. What research does the document rest on? What belief structures are inherent in the teaching practices espoused within this document? How is language learning understood? For example, is it anchored in development stage theory? Cultural studies theory? Ultimately, what are the purposes of literacy and who gets to define these purposes? And why? Moreover, team members in the study often commented on the tension between the need for teaching explicit skill instruction *and* critical literacy practices:

> Jamilla: "What kinds of things do you do when you come to a word you don't know?" and it took me about twenty minutes to get them to say something other than "sounding out".... So I just have to look at the problem more deeply because they don't look at it as the big picture. Decoding and comprehension go together.... But they think, "If I have a problem with reading, it's because I don't know what *that* word says. It's about *that* word or these *lists* of words that I have to know."... This is the piece that we need to help them understand - the whole and I'm having a problem with this part here by just letting them be aware of the things they need to do to get to the next level, instead of keeping it a secret that only the teacher knows

> Dianne: It makes sense to wrap the strategies they need to know around it, such as decoding, and to understand *their* thinking processes. We'd have to have an open dialogue with them whether it be direct skill instruction or crit. lit.

It can be imagined, in reading this text, some readers might think that this is all well and fine but what about teaching reading and writing skills? Of course this is a valid concern particularly given that so many students continue to fail in school despite the concerted efforts of educators to make it not so. Rather than fuel the 'either/or' debate over whether the central purposes of literacy education should focus on strategic reading or reading to make sense of life, perhaps a literacy model that incorporates both sides of the debate is useful. Freebody and Luke (1990) add to this discussion through their conceptualization of literate practices as involving four roles – code-breaker, meaning-maker, text user and text analyst. Being a code breaker involves understanding the sound symbol relationship and the alphabetic principles. Being text participant or "meaning-maker" calls upon the reader to draw inferences, using background knowledge to fill out unexplicated aspects of the text. Being a text user means knowing how to use a variety of texts for a variety of purposes in real life situations — For example, reading instructions on a soup can versus writing a friendly letter versus reading instructions on how to put a piece of complex equipment together. Being a text analyst means applying critical discourse analysis and asking questions about absences in texts, how gendered cultural storylines work across texts, who texts are written for, who benefits from a particular storyline and how might it have been written differently.

If we return to the previous teaching event involving Jamilla's concern regarding the teaching of explicit skills *and* critical literacy practices, the role of meaning-maker and text analyst were the literacy practices that were deliberately invoked. Although the role of code breaker was used earlier in the day through such literacy practices as the morning message and making words, some students spontaneously modeled the role of text-user.

Although all four roles appear to be important in conceptualizing literacy practice, it is important to be aware that literacy practices are mediated through social institutions and power relations and for these reasons alone we need to consider that identity and language practices go hand in hand. Perhaps with open dialogue, critical literacy may be capable of reducing inequalities in power in order to allow all stakeholders, including students, a voice. Issues of equity and equality have, at their core, the consideration of power and privilege. If all students were equally funded and had equal amounts of intellectual, social, cultural (Bourdieu, 1977), educational and physical capital, we would have not only equality, but equity as well. Sadly, this is not the case and hence the need to began locally with local curricula. In schools, as in the real world, inequality and inequity are maintained through the power and privilege of some while others become more and more marginalized.

Bearing this in mind, the first of a series of fifteen minute mini-lessons with the students were also based on the "K-W-L" strategy. This was accomplished by specifically tying critical literacy into the curriculum guidelines by accessing students' prior knowledge of what their experiences of critical literacy were like. This lesson dealt with "Looking at the Big Picture" through a brainstorming session with the children in a large group. Examples of priming questions were, "Why do people need to learn to read"? and "Does everyone [around the world] have the same chance to learn to read"? Responses were recorded on a wall chart.

Another theme was developed around "How to chose a book for reading". Again brainstorming was used to identify strategies for selecting an appropriate book for independent reading. These strategies were recorded on another chart. A third theme dealt with decoding strategies, discussed earlier, through the priming question of "What do you do when you come to a word you don't know?" Strategies were recorded on an additional chart so that the students would begin to articulate more strategies than just "sounding out." This follows up on similar work already happening in the classroom.

Another fifteen-minute mini-lesson set the routines for "Sharing and Celebrating" by recording different thinking strategies, as we work with students on an ongoing basis, on a chart called "Strategies for Sharing Our Thinking." Miller (2002) calls this "Making Tracks of Our Thinking." The priming question for meta-cognitive thinking was "What does thinking about reading look like, sound like and feel like?" It was revealing to see the students' thinking as we learned together throughout the project.

For example, Mohammed suggested that the "teacher reminds us that we can use anything in our life" in order to learn. He goes on to note that TV has helped him make connections to literature and he went on to talk about how Muslims are now "the bad guys" in the "big" story because of 9/11. Mohammed sees this with his own eyes and makes connections to the world he knows (Delpit, 1995). As a new immigrant to Canada and a Muslim, Mohammed's comment revealed his own feeling of insecurity on a global level, but also showed how safe he felt in being able to reveal his feelings on the local level, within his classroom. It may be useful to note that Mohammed's grade three teacher in the project acknowledges that many of her students watch a lot of television. However, she attempts to help them be more critical or discerning in their choices of programs to watch and how to critique systems of domination. In other words, Jamilla recognizes that television is the foremost source of information available to many children living in poverty and otherwise, and is working towards the development of agency in these students.

A dilemma encountered by both teachers and instructors interested in the promotion of critical literacy in teacher education programs is perhaps how to keep the dialogue hopeful when one begins to question what is taken as "the truth". This may necessitate a curriculum for learning that allows for students to understand not only the message that is presented, but also to make connections with their own lives and lived experiences (Cooper and White, 2004). The following poem is an example of a spontaneous piece of writing from Erina, a grade three student in the research project. Entitled "A Poem about Hope", this poem is dedicated to her teachers.

A Poem about Hope

Don't look in the
stocking's or under the
tree. The thing that we're
looking for is something
we can't see. You can't
feel it or tuch it but
it will tuch you it
move's with you grow's
with you. It will always
follow you. It's deeper then
snow stronger then ice.
The gift that we resev
is the gift of hope.

- Erina (8 years of age)

The aim of critical literacy is to not only question one's own assumptions, but to examine issues of power. Differentials in power tend to involve inequities and it is the purpose of critical pedagogy to question policies, processes and practices that perpetuate these power differentials. In Chapter Three of this volume, Inglis and Willinsky highlight some troubling questions they encountered when introducing democratic structures in order to promote student voice:

> ... Such questions quickly led us to other, more troubling questions over what *democracy* can possibly mean for high school students, as they feel the weight of compulsory attendance, almost no choice among classes and teachers, parental pressure to achieve, and their own vaguely focused sense of schooling as a necessary credential to get through life. What does democracy hold for the teacher facing a need to make sure some students stay in line, while moving all students toward increased achievement scores? The students are in school as the result of a democratic process. What they study is similarly determined. Their parents may have exercised some choice in the selection of the school. The students have certain democratic rights within the school, and these rights have been tested many times in the courts, largely in the area of freedom of expression, from fashion to student newspapers. But these are rights exercised largely apart from the curriculum and the work of the critical educator (Inglis and Willinsky, this volume).

In hindsight, in our study, examining underlying assumptions of the literacy curriculum was not a bad place to begin, yet Inglis and Willinsky remind us of the importance of revisiting current thinking about democracy in order to consider what constitutes democracy in action. At the heart of our actions and in those teachable moments rests the need for continuous critical reflection.

The "W" in our reflection strategy is useful only in as much as it provides the framework to continually ask those difficult questions so fundamental to Critical literacy and a democratic education for all students. This we found takes humility and desire or perhaps, as Erina suggests, hope which is deeper than snow or ice

4. "L" REPRESENTS CRITICAL LITERACY: WHAT THE RESEARCH TEAM LEARNED

> Schools exist to promote learning in all their inhabitants. Whether we are teachers, principals, professors, or parents, our primary responsibility is to promote learning in others and in ourselves." (Barth, 2002, p. 9)

The exploratory research story recounted above suggests a need to continue to challenge the taken-for-granted assumptions embedded in existing orthodoxies that comprise research and teaching practice, through re-framing questions to examine not only what has been offered but also what has been missing. As Delpit (1998) points out the key may be to understand the variety of meanings available for any human interaction, and not to assume that the voice of majority speaks for all.

Through this lens, if students do not gain from mandated curriculum or policies relating to the development of critical literacy, directly or over the long term, these curricular policies may not be useful educational policies. It is incumbent upon all educators to be able and willing to develop, identify and implement curricular policies that are inclusive, for the benefit of all students. Educators in particular must acknowledge the force of these patterns and see their implications for shaping and constraining choices available to educational policies, practices and procedures while resisting the attendant consumer corporatist rhetoric (Burbules and Torres, 2000) relating to employment literacy rhetoric. Teacher educators may also work towards these goals of critical literacy development as well, resulting in a sort of spiral curriculum of literacy development where school improvement may occur through a "bottom-up" utilizing action research programs such as the one presented in this article. As one of the members of our exploratory critical action research project notes:

> When I think about asking questions and inferring, all of those strategies that have been defined as what critical readers do with text is quite important, too. But you can apply those strategies to anything you need to learn.

Along with the process of critical literacy comes the ability to transfer information and knowledge to other disciplines and frameworks in order to develop one's capacity and potential for critical learning and ultimately for a kind of critical leadership. Perhaps this is congruent with Delpit's framework regarding the "culture of power" (Delpit, 1995, 24). Foremost is the idea that critical literacy can assist not only in developing the capacity for esteem and agency but can also assist in the understanding and reduction of power differentials in the interests of promoting positive social change.

Teachers can benefit their students by becoming more enlightened about the ways in which their own self-understandings prevent them from being properly or appropriately aware of social and political mechanisms operating to distort or limit the "proper conduct" of education in society (Carr and Kemmis, 1989, 32). Clearly this entails that teachers not only need to be reflective and critical users of research knowledge, but need to establish self-critical communities of teacher-researchers, establishing their own critical and self-critical research traditions (Carr and Kemmis, 1989).

A consequence of the reality of the dynamic and complex life we lead today has lead many researchers in the field of literacy education to focus on new literacy practices (Luke, 2000; Lanshear and Knobel, 2003). Many educators around the world are incorporating new concepts such as multimodality, multiliteracies and multiple identities to frame their language teaching. Such new and rich thought beckons educators to consider the dynamics of context, identity and literacy practices particularly in this new millennium of rapid change.

While there is still a battle raging within the field of literacy over the central goals of literacy education (For a more complete discussion, see Short, 1999), struggling literacy students are at the heart of much of what we do as literacy educators and this struggle is manifested in the following questions: What conditions truly support literacy learning in the pluralistic milieu of the twenty-first century? How do literacy practices used in educational settings serve to affirm or disaffirm a student's own sense of identity? Why consider identity and language teaching in the same breath?

Such questions serve to flag the notion that outside pressures, a globalized society notwithstanding, are being brought to bear on curricula and programs provided by Canadian schools, and potentially, in schools world-wide. At issue is the problem of "recognizing the pattern", to develop a critical awareness in order to understand what is truly important in our schools and to develop standards around such critical ideas as what it is we are doing, why we are doing it and who the major benefactors of these transactions are. There is, therefore, a need for a pedagogy capable of recognizing such patterns and asking questions about innate standards, about what is important to schooling and about how external forces such as globalization serve to pattern schooling after pre-determined images.

We believe the pattern of encroaching forces and private agendae in our schools necessitates a concentrated effort towards developing a critical literacy; one that considers the voice of students and teachers above the voice of industry or the central board office. What is needed is the establishment of communities of critical action-researchers committed to working with individuals and groups outside the immediate learning communities. At the system levels, advisors, organizers and curriculum developers must devolve the responsibility for learning about programs and associated policies relating to teachers and others in the field. There is a need for the learning organization to support and protect its professional work. If a central aim of education can become the critical transmission, interpretation and development of the cultural traditions of our society, there is the need for a form of research that focuses its energies and resources on the policies, processes and practices by which this aim is pursued (Carr and Kemmis, 1989). These voices, in order to be heard must respect the notion of a democratic education not just for some citizens but for all citizens. Hopeful trends are beginning to emerge. Changes, and dare we say improvements, are being made in individual classrooms and schools as the chapters in this book might suggest.

ENDNOTES

[1] The authors of this paper would like to acknowledge Dianne Riehl, Jamilla Arindell, Cindy Bird, Suzanne Thomson and the grade three students at "Sir Simon George" elementary school for their assistance with this project.

REFERENCES

Barth, R.S. (2002). The culture builder. *Educational Leadership,* 59(8), 6-12.
Bourdieu, P. (1977). *Outline of a theory of practice.* Translated by R. Nice. Cambridge; New York: Cambridge University Press.
Burbules, N. and Torres, C. A. (2000). Globalization and education: An introduction. In N. Burbules and C. A. Torres (Eds.) *Globalization and education: Critical perspectives.* New York: Routlege.
Carr, W. and Kemmis, S. (1989). *Becoming critical: Education, knowledge and action research.* London and Philadelphia: The Falmer Press.
Chambers, I. (1996). *The post-colonial question: common skies, divided horizons.* London: Routledge.
Comber, B., Thomson, P. & Wells, M. (2001). Critical literacy finds a place: Writing and social action in a low-income Australian grade two/three classroom. *Elementary School Journal* 101(4), 451-464.
Delpit, L. (1995). *Other people's children: Cultural conflict in the classroom.* New York: New Press.
Delpit, L. (1998). The silenced dialogue: Power and pedagogy in education of other people's children. *Harvard Educational Review,* 58(3), 280-298.
Freebody, P. & Luke, A. (1990). "Literacies" programs: Debates and demands in cultural context. *Prospect: The Journal of Adult Migrant Education Programs,* 5(30), 7-16.

Heath, S. B. (1983). *Ways with words: Language, Life and Work in Communities and Classrooms.* Cambridge: Cambridge University Press.
Hunter, C. S. and Harmon, D. (1979). *Adult illiteracy in the United States*: A Report to the Ford Foundation. New York: McGraw-Hill.
Lankshear, C. and Knobel, M. (2003). *New literacies: Changing knowledge and classroom learning.* Buckingham and Philadelphia, PA: Open University Press.
Luke, A. (2000). Critical literacy in Australia. *Journal of Adolescent and Adult literacy,* (43), 448-461.
Miller, D. (2002). *Reading with meaning: Teaching comprehension in the primary grades.* Portland, Maine: Stenhouse.
Mills, G. E. (2000). *Action research: A guide for the teacher researcher.* New Jersey: Merrill, Prentice Hall.
Ontario Curriculum Grades 1-8, Language. (1997). Ontario: Ministry of Education and Training.
Short, K. (1999).). The search for "balance" in a literature-rich curriculum. *Theory into Practice* 38(3). 130-137.
Shutz, A. (2000). Teaching freedom? Postmodern perspectives. *Review of Educational Research.* 70(2), 215-251.
Southam Literacy, (1987). In P. Calamai. *Broken words: Why five million Canadians are illiterate.* Southam Press: Toronto.
Thompkins, G. E. (1998). *50 Literacy strategies: Step by step.* New Jersey: Merrill, Prentice Hall.
UNESCO, (1951). A definition of fundamental education.

CAROLE EDELSKY AND MEREDITH CHERLAND

A CRITICAL ISSUE IN CRITICAL LITERACY:

The "Popularity Effect"[1]

Abstract. Partly through the efforts of practitioners (present contributors included) to present critical literacy widely and favorably, and thus by implication to promote it, critical literacy is attracting increasing interest, becoming a familiar fixture on the educational scene. Favorable attention— popularity—is often accompanied by popularization, which may include trivializing, co-opting, and misnaming. In this chapter, we focus on the latter: giving the name "critical literacy" to practices we believe do not warrant that name. We offer six descriptions of "critical literacy" in action, and present our arguments for why each does or does not warrant that label. Our arguments are simultaneously definitional and political, linked to a particular lens (critical emancipatory). We also discuss how educators might view our descriptions through two other lenses (liberal humanist and poststructuralist).

1. INTRODUCTION

Critical literacy has become popular enough in North America to appear as a topic at the annual meetings of mainstream professional organizations alongside sessions on techniques for teaching vocabulary. "Critical literacy," a term that once signified teaching with conscious radical intent, a quest for broad democratic participation for social transformation, and a critique of the systems of dominance that produce injustice (Lankshear and McLaren, 1993), used to characterize the pedagogical practice of only a few. After all, since education is an arm of the state, and since the state is not usually disposed to transforming itself or the class(es) it serves, a pedagogy intent on transformation would not be expected to be a widespread phenomenon. But lately, we have been hearing the term "critical literacy" used widely and favorably to characterize the practice of a large number of teachers. This concerns us. We have met many fine teachers who tell us that they do critical literacy in their classrooms. But, while we admire many things about their teaching practices, we do not think that what they do should be called "critical literacy". For us, it simply isn't.

We think critical literacy instruction has certain defining features: It includes the critique of social systems of dominance, injustice, and privilege, and it calls for systemic change. We think that critical literacy instruction worthy of the name is offered by those teachers who have a predilection for noting systemic privilege, and who engage their students in using literacy to work against those systems of injustice. Others think so too (see Altwerger and Saavedra, 1999, for example). Definitions are political (Willinsky, 1994), and we are declaring our politics through this one.

K. Cooper and R. White (eds.), The Practical Critical Education, 17–33.

Why do we want to distinguish between critical literacy instruction and literacy instruction that claims to be critical, or is thought to be critical, but in our view is not? Because we believe that when a term like "critical literacy" is overextended, and is used in connection with ways of teaching that do *not* involve a critique of systems of injustice, then something is obscured. The alternate vision of education for genuine participatory democracy that "critical literacy" has pointed to (Edelsky, 1994) is lost.

We think that "critical literacy" has become a buzzword. Buzzwords are current, popular terms or slogans that lack precise meaning. Their currency, their glamour if you will, has allowed them to attain the kind of popularity that encourages instant categorization, rather than the examination of the substance of an underlying idea. The buzzword's original meaning and the ideas that were of such importance in the first place are glossed over. People then borrow the buzzword without really understanding or buying into the idea that created the term in the first place. As it becomes used more generally, the original idea is lost or trivialized. One of the first things to go is any radical, ideology-shifting content.

We have had some experience with buzzwords. "Whole language" became such a phenomenon (Edelsky, 1987). At first, it was the designation chosen by some reflective teachers who had read work by Kenneth Goodman (1967) and began to observe their students' learning through the lens of language learning, standing back to note students' hypotheses about written language. These teachers began studying the assumptions underlying their own practice, aiming for student-centeredness (e.g., student choice, student-teacher negotiation of curriculum), and meeting with like-minded others to support their professional, theoretical shifts. Their energy, camaraderie, and enthusiasm attracted attention; in a world of professional burnout, whole language sparkled. Soon, publishers grabbed the label to boost sales, marketing such oxymoronic materials as "whole language workbooks." With a one-weekend workshop behind them, entire schools (dragging along veteran teachers who saw no reason to examine or even acknowledge their own theoretical assumptions, let alone change them) declared themselves "whole language" to show parents and the community at large that they were on the cutting edge. The net effect was that in the larger professional community and also among the public, "whole language" came to be an empty term, signifying just about any educational practice. Achieving buzzword status meant there were no widely accepted semantic borders around what was and was not intended by "whole language." That absence of boundaries, along with insufficient political strategizing on the part of whole language activists, left both the buzzword and the committed whole language movement vulnerable to isolation and manipulation (Altwerger & Saavedra, 1999). With an intensified rightwing assault on public education, "whole language"— once a buzzword with a positive valence—became a negative one, an epithet, still semantically empty but now demonized.

We are concerned that "critical literacy" not suffer the same fate. We believe it has already become a buzzword that glosses over its original meaning. Lankshear and McLaren (1993) recognized over a decade ago that the words *critical* and *literacy* could mean different things for different educators with different worldviews. It is clear to us that they still do. Later we will analyze some of those worldviews and their implications for literacy instruction. But now, in order to highlight the distinction between what we see as critical and non-critical literacy instruction, we offer descriptions of several classrooms.

2. A DISCLAIMER

Each set of practices and each of these classrooms, like an historical novel, is both fictionalized and based on fact. The examples come from observational notes and videotapes of teachers who, over the past twenty years, have awed us with the brilliance of their work and who have given generously to the professional development of other teachers. All of them are extraordinary teachers of literacy. In our view, however, all of them are not teachers of critical literacy, even though some claim to be. That claim and our disagreement against the backdrop of, on the one hand, our long-standing admiration for them; on the other hand, the current "trendiness" of critical literacy (one of our points in this chapter) and therefore the possible shame of being designated non-critical and thus not "in"; and on yet a third hand, the present context of a published description by us, not them, of aspects of their work, led us to a decision we have never made before. Instead of our usual approach (representing the work of actual teachers and students), this time we decided to fictionalize descriptions (inventing teachers' names, disguising the source of the examples, and changing details) in order to prevent personalized discussions about who is and who is not critical and to keep the focus on our point: what distinguishes critical literacy instruction from its non-critical version.

3. THE EXAMPLES

We believe all six examples below show gorgeous teaching. All are democratic in that they show children having a say about significant aspects of the curriculum and having some freedom concerning at least some of their work time. In each, students are positioned as rational, intelligent beings capable of making good choices, and the details of their lives worthy of educational recognition. Each teacher helps children learn to care about themselves, each other, and the classroom collectivity. In each, students are provided with rich literacy materials—real books, classroom libraries, projects to read and write about. Each creates opportunities for children's work to have audiences other than the teacher. Each teaches literacy building on what students already know. But only the last two examples include critique of systems of privilege and domination as part of their curriculum.

The first example portrays a teacher attending to students' in- and out-of-school lives as a central focus for literacy instruction.

3.1 "I've Got Just the Book for You"

> The building is new. The children are almost all blondes. The teacher is White. The teacher's car is valued at less than half of any parent's car parked in the parking lot. Typical details for a school in a new, middle to upper-middle class suburb. The only immediately observable exception to the norm is that the teacher is a middle-aged man.

Rick Randall's second grade classroom has no windows, but he has placed lamps strategically so that light divides the space and signals curricular structures. Diffuse light from a table lamp in a darkened room means circle time (for serious discussions); spotlights are for "author on stage." Rick's room is crowded: easels with poems; quotes from children posted on tagboard above the bulletin boards; a loft for climbing, huddling, and escaping; a terrarium for the hermit crab; a cage with gerbils and another with a rabbit; intriguing questions children have asked hanging from the ceiling. And books. Books everywhere. In bookcases. In the corners of the loft. In baskets by the rocking chair. Books by favorite authors stacked on students' desks. Rick Randall loves books, loves poetry, loves ideas. And he gives those as "gifts." A child's parents are divorcing? Rick leads him to a poem that speaks to devastating life changes. A child saw an oddly shaped cloud while walking to school? Rick offers a book that celebrates such phenomena. Most often, the book or poem is a piece of children's literature, but sometimes the perfect lines are from Thoreau's *Walden* or from a piece written by a former student.

Rick's literacy instruction is woven throughout the day. There are no assigned texts, no workbooks, no practice exercises. Literacy instruction leans heavily on writing— writing "seeds" for possible development into published pieces, sharing writing (his own and the students') with the class and giving polished writing to parents and grandparents as gifts, finding writers and writings that "speak" to individuals at particular times. Writing is treated as thinking. For example, after a horrifying event appeared in the news, Rick told two students he had tried unsuccessfully to find a poem that matched his feelings; that now he had "so much going on inside" he didn't know what to write. He urged them to do what he was going to do: "think in your notebooks, get the ideas and feelings and memories out; as they keep coming, keep on thinking them into your notebook." Literacy skills (spelling, handwriting, punctuation) are highlighted often as children take turns teaching editing mini-lessons with an overhead projector and periodically as students look over their previous notebooks and methodically chart their progress (e.g., "On what date did I begin to capitalize proper names?") In addition to his frequent offers throughout the day of the perfect book, story, or poem, Rick connects phrases in students' writing and in their talk to well-loved books, repeating the children's phrases, almost crooning them, adding "Ah, like *Stellaluna*" (Cannon, 1993).

Rick puts a spotlight on children's talk—their artful phrases and metaphors, their powerful words, writing them down, explicitly praising their talk ("You come in with such great words." "I love that metaphor"). In fact, in this classroom, talk is a topic—not just phrasing but tone and topics and how these reflect values of respect, choice, and concern for others. Children do not raise their hands to speak as they "talk into the circle"—not addressing their contributions to Rick, but to their peers—because if they are "really listening," they know when they can take a turn.

"Really listening" is part of an overriding value: "take the time to pay attention to the little things." "The little things"—anything from attention to words to a hint of a classmate's discomfort—include objects and creatures in puddles after a rainstorm. While students from other classes are splashing in the puddles on the playground, Rick's students crouch by the side, observing closely, noting with wonder this piece of the natural world.

The second example also highlights children's lives, but in this portrayal, the teacher occasionally links life events to "current events" that obviously concern systems of privilege, such as racism. However, that link does not then become a topic of study guided by critical questions.

3.2 "We Start with Stories"

The lights are off and the music is on. Today it is Ravel's "Bolero"—as the fifth graders file in. They go directly to the rug, sit down, and wait for their teacher to sit down with them and give the familiar direction, "Take a deep breath. Let it out slowly. We're ready to start the day." Elaine Ramirez has been teaching in this barrio school for 15 years. The granddaughter of immigrants from Mexico, her limitations in Spanish have never permitted her to teach bilingually. But she can understand enough so that she has felt comfortable encouraging students to use Spanish themselves when they desire. Despite the fact that her district is beginning to shrink its bilingual program, she continues to do as she has always done; i.e., encourage students to use Spanish to aid understanding or to fit their purposes in writing, and she sprinkles Spanish words or phrases into her talk to create a greater intimacy in the classroom.

Over the years, stories have come to occupy an increasingly central role in this classroom. Ms. Ramirez frames the morning news as stories, and in so doing, helps students see that stories have themes ("*Who* has a story about friendship?" about loss? about giving? about the unexpected?). She calls attention to aspects of stories in the daily background music (mood, perhaps, or setting; sometimes a build-up of tension and release, as in a plot, or characterization when the music is part of an opera). And, crucially, she makes students' own stories (i.e., the stuff of their lives) the center of her writing program. She emphasizes the need for minorities to write their own stories rather than be written about—and often misrepresented—by others. Elaine allots ample time each day for students to tell each other memories ("a time I felt different," "a time I was glad to get home"), demonstrating the educational value she places on students' lives outside of school, helping them connect with each other ("oh, that happened to you too!"), and warming them up for writing.

The writing program is organized around genres: poetry, memoir, picture books, mysteries, high fantasy, book reviews. For the picture book study, for instance, students and teacher pored over hundreds of picture books, identifying features of style, and both students and teacher tried their hand at producing features that appealed to them. For each genre studied, students develop, through multiple revisions and peer and teacher conferences, one polished piece that goes into an anthology distributed to the immediate community at the quick stop market near the school.

Writing instruction is also intimately tied to the other main structure for literacy instruction: reading clubs. During whole class read-alouds (and the ensuing discussions), Elaine presents reading as conjuring up a world constructed by the author—entering that world and empathizing with it or rejecting it. That view of reading is to be carried into reading clubs. In these clubs, self-chosen groups of students choose one book to read, determine their own pacing through the book, and hold their own discussions each day. Meanwhile, Elaine Ramirez works with individuals who need help developing a repertoire of reading strategies, but even more important, who need to stop tolerating nonsense in their interactions with print. Elaine also sits in on one reading club meeting each day, providing club members with "notes" afterwards (suggestions for improving their performances, similar to the notes a director gives to actors). Reading club books and books from read-aloud time figure prominently in Elaine's writing conferences ("What you're doing is like what Judy Blume does." "This phrase at the beginning sounds like Gary Soto; you might check his leads and see how he brings readers in quickly.") Even more significant for literacy instruction in this fifth grade is Elaine Ramirez' main teaching tool: making each student's contribution sound smart, finding the sensibleness in the connections between what the student has just said and the intended instructional story.

In the example below, fairness—and justice—takes center stage. But the focus is either on what are considered unique interpersonal interactions or on empathizing with characters who might be considered members of a category (e.g., homeless people, physically challenged people). The systems of privilege that are implicated in the category are not interrogated.

3.3 "Is This Fair?"

> Finally, the tears come. Usually bubbly Brianne has been out of sorts since lunch—keeping to herself, silent. Lucille Goins goes over, kneels, gets almost nose-to-nose to ask what the tears are about. Between sobbing hiccups Brianne manages, "I don't call *them* names. I play with both of *them*." Lucille hugs Brianne, smoothing her hair, rocking her, "I know it hurts, Baby," and after awhile, "Are you ready to go talk to Kaisha and Sari?" With an assent, teacher and student approach Kaisha and Sari, with Lucille paving the way ("Brianne wants to tell you something.") Brianne states her complaint. Ms. Goins asks the other two girls if they heard what was just said. After several turns among the three—with Lucille Goins mediating each turn—the girls seem on their way to a subdued reconciliation.

> Lucille Goins takes children's conflicts seriously. Even in this seemingly idyllic space—a new school built partly into the ground as an environmentally friendly model, situated in a new development of "starter homes" in this small city full of parks; in this third grade classroom with its well-designed wooden furniture, upholstered couch, big pillows on the floor, a bank of computers, an ample classroom library, a puppet stage and a raised platform for a stage—tensions abound. An African American woman who grew up in a working class segregated neighborhood, and who now teaches this racially and ethnically mixed group of children, Lucille knows about tensions. She knows how worlds can bump up against each other through the "vehicles" of small bodies, leaving feelings raw; and how the "brute fact" of 25 people in one room for almost seven hours each day creates a site for complications. Thus, she has made caring about feelings and fairness, resolving conflicts, and creating a close-knit community a major strand of everyone's work in this classroom.

> Drama is integral to instruction in general in this classroom and to literacy instruction in particular. "Repeat role playing" (different trios of students taking turns enacting the same situation several times in succession in order to play out different possible resolutions) is used to help students with complicated interpersonal struggles. Especially apt or witty dialogue from role-plays and innovative solutions to conflicts become part of charts posted on the walls. Students write and then perform puppet shows for the kindergarten each Friday. As a revising strategy, a student may ask others to dramatize sections of her writing to help her make her writing more believable. And the raised platform stage is a favorite site for acting out scenes from literature Lucille Goins reads aloud each day.

> This literature most often concerns social issues or themes of (in)justice: homelessness, class-based tension, gangs, racism, immigration, sexism, heterosexism, environmental degradation, culture clash. Considerable time is allotted for discussion after the reading, with Lucille encouraging students to think about how the situation depicted in a book might look to different people. These books are frequently the ones students act out on the raised platform, the ones they choose during DEAR time (Drop Everything And Read), the ones they read with a friend in Buddy Reading, the ones chosen for literature study. Sometimes, they spark investigations (e.g., into homelessness). In addition to the questions students raise (e.g., How many people are without homes in our city? Do they have jobs? How do they get dressed for work?), for

these investigations—as well as for the class discussions about the literature—Lucille Goins keeps two overarching questions at the forefront: Is it fair? How do people feel? For her, the two are connected; caring about unfairness and developing empathy for various perspectives are fundamental in this classroom.

The following provides an instance of a project that actually transforms a small part of a community (one home). The project might have included a study of neighborhood housing, investigating both individual and bureaucratic, sources of and responses to blight in different neighborhoods. But it did not.

3.4 "A Makeover"

Against the wall are the school supplies—scrapers, hammers, putty knives, nails and screws, screwdrivers, pliers, metal measuring tapes, levels, shovels, trowels, paint and brushes. On the wall is a list of tasks. "Scrape paint," "prime," "paint," and "measure windows for new glass," have been checked off. "Dig beds" and "enrich soil" have not. Clearly, these are not ordinary activities for middle school. But they are necessary given that Mr. Bloome's sixth grade is fixing up a house across the street. How did this class come to take on such a project?

When Art Bloome starting teaching sixth grade in this school that serves mostly African American and Latino students, 95 percent of whom qualified then for the free or reduced lunch program, the pattern was already worn off the vinyl flooring and one corner of the ceiling was already stained from leaking water. Ten years later, the vinyl is more worn; the stain has been joined by others. Nevertheless, into that shabby shell Art has built a well-stocked library, He also removed the door to the teacher's coat closet and installed cast-off recording equipment (microphones, tape-decks, sound mixers). He put in a considerable stock of hats for role-plays and just plain playing (fedoras, a ten gallon felt, berets, baseball caps, sunbonnets, cocktail hats from the 1940s)—a concrete manifestation of one of his metaphorical goals for students; i.e., that they have a chance to try on new and varied roles.

Over the years, Art has involved students in complex projects that made explicit attention to learning an essential layer. For example, in pairing his sixth graders with kindergartners for twice weekly meetings, he set their task as not just reading to the younger ones but as studying how young children become literate. The additional layer, loaded with meta-language about learning, language, and literacy, is spotlighted in the debriefing sessions following these meetings at which Art and the students discuss their observations about kindergartners' hypotheses about written language.

For some time, Art has been interested in authentic work—work done primarily for some reason other then getting a grade, often for some audience outside the classroom. The kindergarten literacy project grew out of that interest. So did developing a weekly five minute radio show that included neighborhood news and community history, investigated and scripted by his students, recorded in the closet without doors, and broadcast over the public address system to the entire school. Recently, his concerns about authenticity were overlaid with something else: his urge to teach his students that they can make a recognized difference.

Which brings us to the house renovation project. Art Bloome proposed it to the students "almost cold." That is, his only effort at groundwork was to get the consent of Mrs. Sanchez, the neighbor living near the school, to have the outside of her house repaired by his students, and to clear with the principal the possibility of taking students off campus for several hours each week until the job was finished. Art was excited about the project. Earlier in the year, for a study of the neighborhood that had spilled over into some of their radio broadcasts, the students had made maps of the blocks around the school, noting particularly blighted spots and interviewing long-time residents about their memories of those spots. Had they changed? Had they always been in poor condition? Here was a chance, Art thought, for the students to make a significant difference in the life of one woman and also the neighborhood. But the students were skeptical. Where would they get paint (or anything else), and who would pay for it? How could they fix the window they already knew was broken? Or a hanging screen door? How could they even begin?

And that, indeed, is where they began. Art and his students listed the questions and reservations, each of which suggested things to do. (Question: Who will pay for the paint? Task: Approach nearby building supply stores, explaining the purpose and requesting donations of supplies. Question: How can they paint a wall or fix a window if they don't know how? Task: Contact local experts such as hardware store workers, skilled parents and neighbors for help.) Each task, of course, required preliminary tasks (e.g., drafting, revising, and editing letters to building suppliers; planning and practicing what to say on the phone to handy neighbors). The letters to neighborhood businesses were effective. Students received donations, as evidenced by what is now stacked against the wall: supplies (primer, paint, window panes, nails, soil mix, plants, and so on); loans of tools; and offers for instructing and supervising the actual work. Today, the soil in the beds will be tilled and enriched with compost. Tomorrow is planting day. Mrs. Sanchez has chosen marigolds.

In contrast with the previous four examples, the next two present instances of critical literacy instruction. These classrooms too provide children with richly provisioned environments (art materials, well-stocked classroom libraries, science equipment, electronic technology) and opportunities to have a significant voice in determining educational choices regarding curricular topics, daily schedules, and work partners. Like the teachers featured above, these next two also position students through talk and texts as competent learners whose homes and communities provide education-worthy resources. As do the prior teachers, those portrayed below work mightily to create caring classroom communities. And like all teachers who, in helping children learn to read the word also promote, wittingly or not, a reading of the world, these two teachers offer a frame for the latter reading. But unlike the teachers above, their frame is systemic privilege. In the two classrooms presented below, teachers devise curriculum so that students can attend to such systems as corporate privilege and privilege attached to heterosexuality, maleness, whiteness, and wealth. The first example has students addressing issues such as the subjective—and "interested"—nature of presentations of history, connections between individual and institutionalized inequities, and "structures" for resistance.

3.5 "Freedom Fighters"

Kellie Owen is known in her district as a "creative teacher." A quick look into her classroom seems to justify her reputation. The room is stocked with visual art materials (jars of paint, big brushes, easels, clay packed in plastic bags and stored in covered cans, pinhole cameras lined up along the counter, charcoal, colored pencils, a tiny space reserved against a draped cloth for a still life or a live model). But Kellie resists that "creative" label with its connotations of an individual's in-the-head abilities. Instead she credits a long-time teacher friend for helping her see the academic potential of art materials: colored pencils allow fine-lined copying—and noticing and learning—of botanical details of flowers and anatomical details in photographs of wild animals;

symbolism can be discussed by noting that qualities of charcoal lines (a sweeping swoosh, thick short lines, interrupted faint lines) convey different messages; drawing from a model can highlight the meaning of proportion. The same friend tipped her off to the stress-relieving value of wedging clay (repetitively throwing it onto a slab to beat out air bubbles that otherwise would cause a pot to break when fired in a kiln).

Kellie gives most of the credit for her unorthodox teaching, however, to like-minded colleagues who meet weekly to think with each other about equity and social justice. It is this group that helps her keep her eye on the justice-promoting potential of her practice. Not that all or even most of her teaching is explicitly tied to political themes. Two years ago she initiated a once monthly Neighborhood Teachers project. Family members and people from the community volunteer to teach what they do well to a small group of fourth grade students. Students elect which "course" they will "take" from such options as crocheting, knitting, making paper flowers, woodworking, building models, cooking, storytelling, yoga, tai chi, and repairing dolls. Kellie could use Neighborhood Teachers as a starting point for a study of gendered roles or for a study of the differential status of different knowledges (the prestige of neighbors' funds of knowledge [Moll, Amanti, Neff and Gonzales, 1992] as compared with "basic skills" as compared with "specials" such as music and physical education). But she doesn't. Neighborhood Teachers, instruction about reading strategies, setting up a still life, and many more practices in this classroom are enjoyed, taught, and learned from without foregrounding a critical edge. But some of her curricular activity does incorporate that edge. And it is as "creative" as the artwork.

Take the study of the genre of biography. Kellie reads biographies to the students, and students do "biography study" using text sets. That is, in small groups, each student picks one from a set of related texts (e.g., biographies of Native Americans, biographies of Helen Keller, biographies of women, biographies of former slaves), reads that book, discusses it with the others in the group who have read the other books in that text set. Their discussion includes addressing questions about style pertaining to the book they chose (What part of the historical figure's life did the author use for the beginning? The ending? How did the author create a sense of tension at particular parts of the book?). It also includes a discussion of genre questions pertaining to the entire text set (What makes a biography different from an autobiography? From a novel?) The students try their hand at writing a biography of someone close to them, adhering to the features of the genre they have identified, and they design a book cover for that biography explaining how the colors, shapes, and lines of the design reflect aspects of that person's life.

A solid study of a genre. What makes this different—and critical—are the subjects of the biographies, the further class discussions, and a related subsequent project about resistance. The biographies that Kellie reads aloud and that comprise the text sets do not feature George Washington but rather John Brown. Not Dolly Madison but Dolores Huerta. In other words, people who have struggled for justice. The discussions not only center on the characteristics of biographies as a genre but of how a life story is represented depending on the interests being served. Kellie starts these discussions by referring to author's stylistic choices (e.g., starting a life story with an event from adulthood and then flashing back to early childhood). She then moves to other choices authors make, emphasizing the human hand in the writing rather than a mythical, neutral, mechanical writing down of "facts." She asks students to consider how the author of the biography they selected portrayed that historical figure (as a deliberate strategist? as an "accidental" hero?) and how the author represented that figure's role in history (as the work of an individual acting alone? as the work of someone who is part of a movement?) (This question is especially fruitful for those in the group whose text set features Rosa Parks; biographies range from depicting her as a tired old woman who finally said "that's enough" to a woman who had helped an organized group plan and carry out significant civil disobedience.)

These discussions lead to more work, stretching out over several days, on what Kellie Owen calls "structures of resistance". Kellie begins listing people in students' families who have worked to resist the status quo—to improve the local or larger community. She lists Rocco's mother who led a petition drive to get better playground equipment, Yolanda's uncle who went out on strike. The students begin to contribute. Frank's grandmother writes letters to the editor. Latanya's sister goes to anti-war demonstrations. Kellie asks students to include the figures from the biographies they have read. As the list gets longer, Kellie asks the class to begin developing categories for kinds of resistance (e.g., contributing money or goods, attending a peaceful demonstration, using violence, participating in civil disobedience), contexts for resisting (e.g., acting alone, acting as part of a physically present group, acting as part of a disparate movement), starting positions (e.g., from positions of privilege, from positions of subordination) and targets of resistance or injustices (e.g., calling a classmate a faggot, lynching, corporate dumping of toxic chemicals, inequities perpetrated by individuals, inequities institutionalized in policies and practices of banks, courts, schools, and so on). Kellie then asks students to talk with each other about which forms of resistance seem more effective and which injustices they see themselves resisting.

Throughout the rest of the school year, students refer to these discussions and these categories as they occasionally try on the role of "freedom fighter" to see how it fits.

In our final example, the teacher takes a critical approach to messages in cartoons and to the interests these serve.

3.6 "More to Think About"

Mollie White is a newcomer. It was only six years ago that she came to this school in a densely populated urban area. Many of her students' families, however, are rarities in an intensely mobile society. They are descendants of people who moved into this neighborhood in the early and middle twentieth century—into these same two-family flats and urban bungalows where her students now live. The neighborhood school, Mollie's K-8 school, was built over a century ago. Her students' grandparents, even some great-grandparents, immigrants from Europe, sat in these same bolted-down desks in Mollie's classroom, daydreamed out the tall double-sash windows now protected by wire grates, hung coats on hooks in the coat closet running behind the length of the back wall.

Mollie has made significant additions to this eighth grade classroom. Recognizing that her students still teeter between childhood and teenage-hood, Mollie stocked a corner with pillows (more adult-like than stuffed toys) for her students to cuddle when she reads aloud to them each day. She built a unique classroom library of multiple copies of novels to be read by her students and their parents and other family members for "family book discussions" held one evening each month. She has furnished spaces for small groups to work together on projects and other spaces as "don't bother me" zones for students who want solitude to read and write, and she designed stations with earphones for transcribing tape recordings.

The audiotapes are part of an on-going project Mollie initiated in her second year of teaching at this school: a community oral history. In the first year of that project, a part of her 2 1/2 hour language arts/social studies block was devoted to reading oral histories, setting up and preparing for interviews with older, long-time community members, seeking out men and women of different ethnicities and from various social networks with different statuses in this community. In that first year, students interviewed, transcribed, and analyzed the transcripts to find out what daily life was like for these different individuals fifty, sixty, even seventy years ago. They also passed the written report on to the next year's students. These, and subsequent eighth graders, read what had been documented, looking for gaps in the analyses in order to do follow-up interviews with the same or additional long-time community members, and to write the annual sequel (or massive revision) to the oral history project. Two years ago, Mollie's students began working with a professor at a local college who has special expertise in oral history to help them sharpen their focus as they interview and analyze.

Each year the oral history project has been shared with the public. That first year, the students created a readers' theatre to dramatize their results. One year, two parent-musicians helped students put on a musical presentation. An illustrated fifteen foot-long time line put up in the hall facing the school entrance was last-year's offering. This year, the morning and the afternoon classes are collaborating on an annotated book of photographs, and, in the process, learning how to restore old photos.

In analyzing the life stories elicited by the oral history interviews, students occasionally comment on gender-based constraints made obvious by the passage of time (e.g., Mrs. DiLorenzo's regrets about not being permitted to learn how to drive because only men drove cars) or anti-immigrant slurs such as "dirty Wop," "dumb Polack." Mollie guides students in thinking about these in relation to persistence and change (then vs. now), and connects them to social studies topics (twentieth century U.S. history, the labor movement, industrialization and corporatization). But she does not use the comments to launch an extended critical study. After all, the oral history project and family book nights (another curricular site for such potent comments that could, but do not, initiate a study) all show clear respect and affection for students' families. These projects have played a major role in forging warm bonds between school and home. Mollie does not want critical literacy to effect a temperature change—from warm to hot or, maybe worse, to freezing cold.

Recently, Molly has begun to question whether critical literacy should or even if it can "force" a "moral conversion." An essay she read by Annette Patterson (1997) weighs heavily on her. Mollie knows now she wants to take pains to distinguish constructing from adopting or converting (e.g., learning to construct an anti-sexist reading of a short story without being *required* to "convert" to such a reading). But she is struggling with this distinction. She worries that students would "see through her," would know that underneath that distinction she is trying to make is actually a desire for them to adopt her anti-sexist views. And even if she could establish that fine line she would like to draw, she is nevertheless quite certain that an inquiry that would implicate students' families' ways or life stories would backfire. Therefore, she decided to steer clear of *explicit* connections to families and instead highlight systemic inequities in fantasy worlds, specifically, in a unit about how hierarchies are taught through cartoons.

The unit is one she borrowed from Linda Christensen (2000). It follows the original in outline and goals (to teach students how to critique inequities and how to act to reduce them). Mollie begins with reading aloud to students from Ariel Dorfman's (1983) *The Empire's Old Clothes: What the Lone Ranger, Babar, and Other Innocent Heroes Do to Our Minds.* Each day, she reads a few paragraphs, and then gives students copies so they can cite passages as they respond in a dialogue journal (a format that urges them to argue and converse with Dorfman). From there, the class moves on to viewing old cartoons with their more blatant stereotypical portrayals. With each cartoon they watch, students "chart stereotypes" (Christensen, 2000, pp. 50-51) of women, men, people of color, and poor people, "filling in the charts in response to questions such as who is the hero? Who plays the buffoon? Who plays the servant? What is the body type of each character? What does each character want out of life? What jobs do women do who are not the main character? Who has money, possessions, and power? Who wants it?" Under Mollie's prodding, students also search for seeming contradictions and complications (fatness attached to the buffoon and also to the powerful king, women's roles that limit options and that also offer seeming protection). Meanwhile, the recurring thematic questions for discussion and writing are: What do children learn about women (men, people of color, poor people) from how they are portrayed in this film? Hierarchies in more recent cartoons are more subtle but the experience of critiquing the older films helps.

As the chart fills in, students note patterns; they begin to see not only a "bad deal" for a single cartoon character but a pattern of inequity. The patterns are described, but Mollie refrains from labeling them as racist, sexist, and so on. She suspects that students would perceive these labels as personal affronts. By contrast, substantive descriptions engage students. As the discussions continue, they branch out from being solely about the texts and subtexts of the cartoons. Now, they also touch on production and distribution by corporate media and the connections between the content of the cartoons and the corporate drive for profit and for promoting a market mentality. An assignment late in the unit is to create a project (e.g., write a letter, a plan, a petition) that both critiques and also pushes for change. The critique, an argument backed up by evidence from the cartoons, can focus on one cartoon or on a portrayal of one group represented in the cartoons. The audience is a person or group with the power to change a practice (e.g., a librarian, a video storeowner, an advertiser, peer-consumers). In a modification of Christensen's unit, students have the option of whether or not to mail the letter (distribute the flyer, pass around the petition), whether, that is, to appropriate as their own the anti-racist (anti-sexist, anti-classist) critique they learn to construct.

This option reflects Mollie's desire to refrain from seeking "converts"; but she is till struggling with this notion. After all, can students really learn to "perform" anti-racist readings without "converting" to the values and caring that go with these readings? On the other hand, she knows that significant progress has occurred through legislating behavior (not attitudes). And she also assures herself (for the moment) that she is not asking students to learn rhetoric - to mouth a "line." Instead, she is teaching them to use a tool—argument plus evidence—in relation to systemic privilege. Maybe, she thinks, she is on the right track.

4. THREE WAYS TO SEE CRITICAL LITERACY

All six of the excellent teachers described above know that schooling is never neutral. They know that schooling educates children in the shared meanings of a cultural group, and that schooling can also take children beyond those shared meanings (Cherland, 1994). They know that schooling can empower children to reinterpret the world, and to act upon it. On these grounds alone, many would say that all six of these teachers are teachers of critical literacy. But we see important differences among them. In our view, the first four teachers are not teaching critical literacy, and the last two are, because only the last two teachers are including a critique of systems of dominance, privilege and power.

What is the harm in labeling all six as stories of critical literacy? What's wrong with the kind of popularity that sees all six as critical literacy? We will answer by returning to the idea that the words *critical* and *literacy* mean different things for different educators with different worldviews (Lankshear and McLaren, 1993). We will discuss three different ways of viewing the world, each of which has different ways of defining self, justice, power, and transformation. The different worldviews are not just different, however. Two of them, those at work in the popularizing (and the de-radicalizing) of critical literacy, remove the potential for promoting systematic change. And that, in our perspective, is the harm. We will present these three worldviews (a liberal humanist view, a poststructuralist view, and our critical emancipatory view of the world) one by one, and see how educators with each worldview might look at our six teacher stories. What would they see?

Those who subscribe to a **liberal humanist** view of the world—and this would be most of us—would see exemplary and inspiring teachers. Liberal humanism is, after all, the dominant paradigm within which we all still live three hundred years after the Enlightenment, and it is still really difficult to think outside it (St. Pierre, 2000). Liberal humanism views the human self as rational, unified, coherent, and individual. In this worldview, power resides in individuals, and is something that individual people can and do possess. For that reason, when a liberal humanist educator considers our stories, she would see teachers working for justice—or certainly for a better world, one that children have reinterpreted and acted upon—by changing the individual child's mind. Assuming that we have injustice because some individuals are unfair, liberal humanist educators see sense in working to get every individual to act fairly, so that injustice will end, and justice will be achieved. Believing that power resides in individuals, and that power is something individuals can possess, the liberal humanist educator sees reading and writing as personally "empowering" tools which give the individual access to power and allow his "voice" to be heard. The liberal humanist educator approves of teaching literature to help people empathize with others, so that they come to understand why good people don't want to abuse power. She calls it "critical literacy" when a teacher works for justice by empowering individuals, and motivating them to be fair. She would be filled with admiration for the work of all these teachers, and believe they were all doing critical literacy work, but she would be especially impressed with the work of Lucille Goins. It is Ms. Goins especially who helps children play act, talk through, and write out their struggles with each other while keeping fairness in mind and empathy at heart.

Educators who subscribe to a postmodern view of the world, and who work with **poststructuralist** theories of identity formation, would see something different in our stories. Because they see language and discourse as the site of struggle over meanings that are never fixed and stable, they view the human self as something that is produced in interaction with the cultural discourses that surround it. The "self", in their view, is constantly changing and in flux, as people "take up" and perform the subject positions available to them. These educators see the world itself as socially constructed, and constantly changing. Some of these educators (who must find their desire to act for justice in something other than poststructuralist theorizing) *do* take action for a better world. They see hope for justice in the poststructural view that the world is continually reconstructed through discourse and in language (St. Pierre, 2000). In this view, teachers can work for justice by enabling new subject positions that their students can then take up and perform.

Some educators (only a few) who speak of doing "critical literacy" are making use of Foucault's (1980) theories of the nature of power. In Foucault's view, power is not a commodity that one can possess. It is created through discourse. It can be positive, and productive. Foucault proposes that wealth and authority and dominance are the *effects* of power. In this view, power is a productive network that runs through the entire social body, a network carried in ideas and discourses that human subjects internalize, so that people come to discipline and control and direct themselves to act as "normal". They ensure their survival within the social body by internalizing and living by the discourses that produce markers of whiteness and privilege, for example, and also produce the materiality of oppression as people act upon them. Power produces pleasure, as well as misery, and many forms of knowledge. Every person becomes a conduit of power.

Foucault does not speak of transformation, but we have spoken with educators who, subscribing to poststructural theories of identity formation, believe that transformation might occur through the creation of new subject positions that children can take up and operate within. The idea is that human subjects, produced as powerful through new discourses, can reconstruct the meanings of the world. These educators tell us that "critical literacy" happens when teachers focus on producing these new subjectivities and therefore new futures, and so enable oppressed peoples to "write their worlds", and to move beyond negative critique.

We expect that these educators would look at our teacher stories and understand all of them as attempts to enable new subject positions, to allow for new subjectivities to be constructed and performed, and for society to be transformed at the local level. But we expect they would be most impressed by Art Bloome's makeover project. Educators with a poststructuralist worldview might see repairing the neighbor's house as going furthest toward allowing children to re-produce themselves as capable people with positive agency, who can dream of different futures and act upon the world to produce them.

Still other educators would share our view that the last two teacher stories are the only examples of critical literacy. They, like us, would subscribe to a more **critical, emancipatory** view of the world. They would not agree with liberal humanist educators or with some poststructuralist educators that the human self (or subject) is where the action is, where the world could be reconstructed. In the critical emancipatory view, people are born into social categories (race, gender, class, others), and some are marginalized and oppressed while others are privileged. The categories intersect, and so it becomes difficult for people to understand what is happening to them and why, but power relationships are key. The self needs to be conscious of the way systems (often economic systems) operate to create the unjust world we inhabit.

Some people are privileged by their social categories, and by the intersections of those categories, and other people are oppressed. The world is structured unevenly, and does not provide a level playing field. Systems of privilege produce inequities, and so we must work for justice by working to change systems of dominance and privilege. To do that, we must first recognize them. We then work for justice by vorking to redistribute resources and power more evenly. We try to lessen the power systems of dominance (e.g., the corporate media in which six mega-corporations rol news and entertainment around the globe today [Steger, 2003]). We work ps by teaching school) to get power into the hands of those who have been subordinated and marginalized. We try to help them claim it. We desire fundamental change that will take power and resources away from some and redistribute these to others. We work to change systems.

Critical emancipatory educators believe that local action and agency will have only short-term effects, and that transformation and change will not be permanent if systems do not change. Following Freire (1973), believing that the first step toward changing systems is to understand what they are, critical emancipatory educators begin by working locally, but then they work globally, to take on the larger world. Critical literacy instruction is about taking on the larger world, by understanding systems of injustice, and then arming individuals to challenge those systems of privilege and power. In this view (our view) only Kellie Owen (who teaches resistance to systems) and Mollie White (who critiques systems of domination) are teachers of critical literacy.

5. THE EFFECTS OF POPULARITY

How, then, is each of these worldviews connected to what we have said about the de-radicalizing "effects of popularity"? What is popular appeals to the *populus*, and suits the dominant paradigm. The liberal humanist (dominant) paradigm de-radicalizes critical literacy by bringing its own views of the world to bear on the phenomenon. It ignores aspects of critical literacy that do not fit with its own views of the self, of power, and of social change. The radical content of critical literacy (a critique of systems of dominance which says that the individual acting alone does not necessarily have the power to act upon the world) does not fit very well with a view that looks to the individual to save the world. When liberal humanist educators, wanting individual teachers to shine, to be seen as up-to-date and *au courant,* label those they admire as teachers of *critical literacy*, they appropriate the term for their own purposes and they make the radical content invisible. As the individual is valorized and the label is popularized, critical literacy is trivialized and means less than it should.

On the other hand, poststructuralist educators, most of whom are academics, living in academic worlds that also valorize individual efforts, may also ignore the critique of systems that critical literacy requires. The individualism of the academy encourages scholars to "maximally differentiate" their own ideas from those which have come before (Gore, 1993), and certainly from those ideas which have become popular. During the last five years we have encountered several educators with poststructuralist views who argue that critique looks only to the past, and who suggest that we must look in other directions to create new futures. Again, educators bring their own views of the world to bear on *critical literacy*, altering the radical content that would critique systems. This time, as Teresa Ebert (1991) has pointed out, they argue that there *are* no systems, that concepts like *patriarchy* and *racism* are totalizing narratives and therefore, *ipso facto*, inadequate. They argue that we have to go beyond critique. Again, the radical content that is behind the popular phenomenon is abandoned, or made invisible.

6. CONCLUSION

We know that there are some people who work to reconcile two different views of the world and several different views of critical literacy. They call for *both* a poststructuralist emphasis on working locally and at the level of subjectivity construction, *and* a Marxist critique of systems (Luke, 2002). Yes, both together are very strong, but we insist that critique of systems must be present, if the work is to be critical literacy, and if it is to have more than temporary effect. Working on the self, whether from a liberal humanist perspective or a poststructuralist perspective, will not change systems of dominance and privilege for long. Popularizing the words *critical literacy* amounts to an appropriation of the term that guts it of its radical content, that trivializes its meanings. We want to resist that appropriation and reclaim the term. We have speculated about *how* the popularizing and the de-radicalizing happens. We will close by wondering why.

What do the buzzwords "critical literacy" convey that many literacy teachers would want to claim? What is so glamorous about the label "critical literacy"? Perhaps it is a liberal humanist valorization of the individual, an admiration that many people feel for brilliant teacher heroes who engage their students fully in working for a better world; who create curriculum which in turn creates hope; who are current and radical and outspoken and well-informed. What thoughtful educator would *not* admire the six teachers in our stories? There *is* something heroic, and womanly, and *individualistic* about fighting for justice with the children in tow. Whatever it is that makes teachers want to claim the label, many who are indeed teacher heroes in a variety of ways have claimed it (or used it to label others). But not all of these teach with conscious radical intent, or with purposeful critique of systems of dominance in mind. It is that intent and that critique that makes teaching *critical*.

ENDNOTE

[1] We thank Carol Schick for her helpful comments on an earlier draft of this chapter.

REFERENCES

Altwerger, B. & Saavedra, E.R. (1999). Forward. In C. Edelsky (ed.). *Making justice our project: Teachers working toward critical whole language practice* (pp. vii-xii). Urbana, IL: NCTE.
Cannon, J. (1993). *Stellaluna.* New York: Harcourt.
Cherland, M. (1994). *Private practices: Girls reading fiction and constructing identity.* London: Taylor and Francis.
Christiansen, L. (2000). *Reading, writing, and rising up: Teaching about social justice and the power of the written word.* Milwaukee, WI: Rethinking Schools.
Dorfman, A. (1983). *The empire's old clothes: What the Lone Ranger, Babar, and other innocent heroes do to our minds.* New York: Pantheon.
ert, T. (1991). Postmodernism's infinite variety. *The Women's Review of Books* 8(4).
sky, C. (1987). *Buzzwords.* Paper presented at the annual meeting of the International Reading ssociation, Anaheim, California.
C. (1994). Education for democracy. *Language Arts,* 71, 252-257.
M. (1980). *Power/knowledge* (C. Gordon, Ed., C. Gordon, L. Marshall, J. Mepham, K. Soper, New York: Pantheon Books.

Freire, P. (1973). *Pedagogy of the oppressed.* New York: Seabury Press.

Goodman, K. (1967). Reading: A psycholinguistic guessing game. *Journal of the Reading Specialist*, 6, 126-135.

Gore, J. (1993). *The struggle for pedagogies: Critical and feminist discourses as regimes of truth.* New York: Routledge.

Lankshear, C. & McLaren, P. (Eds.). (1993). *Critical literacy: Politics, praxis and the postmodern.* Albany, NY: SUNY Press.

Luke, A. (2002). Beyond science and ideology critique: Development in critical discourse analysis. *Annual Review of Applied Linguistics*, 22, 96-110.

Moll, L., Amanti, C., Neff, D., & Gonzales, N. (1992). Funds of knowledge for teaching: Using a qualitative approach to connect homes and classrooms. *Theory Into Practice* 31(2), 132-141.

Patterson, A. (1997). Setting limits to English. In S. Muspratt, A. Luke, & P. Freebody (eds.), *Constructing critical literacies: Teaching and learning textual practice* (pp. 335-352). Cresskill, NJ: Hampton Press.

St. Pierre, E. A. (2000). Poststructural feminism in education: An overview. *Qualitative Studies in Education*, 13(5), 477-515.

Steger, M. B. (2003). *Globalization: A very short introduction.* Oxford, UK: Oxford University Press.

Willinsky, J. (1994). *Empire of words: The reign of the OED.* Princeton, NJ: Princeton University Press.

PATRICK INGLIS AND JOHN WILLINSKY

SOUP KITCHEN DEMOCRACY:

Practical, critical lessons in theory

Abstract. The chapter uses a class field trip, working in a downtown soup kitchen, to explore what can be done to increase the educational value and service of such important experiences for students and teachers. By drawing on four theories of democracy – constitutional, procedural, deliberative and rhetorical – the chapter constructs a very practical twelve-step program for democratic inquiry, skill development and community service. This highly schematic approach toward exercising and practicing democratic rights, on behalf of oneself and others, is intended to demonstrate to students a broad range of practical, critical activities which can be undertaken to address the soup kitchens of democracy.

1. INTRODUCTION

In the fall of 2000, Patrick Inglis's grade 10 English class of 27 students visited a soup kitchen to prepare and serve lunch to a group of homeless men living in Vancouver's Downtown Eastside, as it is widely known. The trip was organized in conjunction with a study of Harper Lee's *To Kill a Mockingbird* (1960), as well as a number of writing workshop activities and discussions used to enhance the students' understanding of the novel. Mini-lessons held at the beginning of class were based on the ideas presented by workshop advocates on genre studies (Atwell, 1998; Bomer, 1995; Calkins, 1994) and used examples from Lee's book to teach students plot development, the use of dialogue and specificity in story-telling. In order to combine what they were learning in the writing workshop with the conversations on the themes of race, poverty and class in *To Kill a Mockingbird*, students wrote fictional accounts of what it might be like to live in the shoes of a homeless person. Lessons in empathy, of course, are not easily learned by writing and sharing such stories; Patrick felt something more might be gained if the classroom writing was arranged alongside performing community service at the soup kitchen. In addition to the stories written before the trip, students wrote poetry expressing their reaction to the visit in the weeks following it.

The students certainly grew in their awareness of the issues of race, poverty and class as a result of reading *To Kill a Mockingbird* and in visiting the soup kitchen, and the use of the writing workshop approach was helpful to this end. In the weeks leading up to the visit, the writing workshop provided students with the opportunity in both time and space to speculate on the experiences lived by homeless people and to articulate their apprehensions about the soup kitchen visit to come. Once at the soup kitchen, the men were accessible, sharing their personal stories and inquiring about the ones the students had to tell about their own lives. Playing cards and

35

K. Cooper and R. White (eds.), The Practical Critical Education, 35–49.

sharing in conversation with the men at the soup kitchen helped students to see that the homeless were not so different from them. In their poetry, written following the trip, it was not uncommon for them to suggest that the men were "normal." In their writing, the students were adamant that the men deserved respect; all of this in spite of what is typically given in the media and reinforced in the popular stereotypes familiar to them. The experience at the soup kitchen challenged students' assumptions about the homeless and relieved their worries. It was obvious that the experience at the soup kitchen changed the way students thought about the homeless and made them appreciate their own quality of life, which was significantly different than what they had seen and experienced in Vancouver's Downtown Eastside.

But these new understandings also gave way to a romanticization of the homeless, which made it easy for the students to write about the men and their experience of serving them food without considering how things might be different and what they may do to contribute to necessary change in the way society treats its homeless. In the end, it was not enough to ask students to write imaginative narratives about living poor and destitute on the streets prior to our trip to the soup kitchen; nor was it enough to have them write poetry reminiscing about the time spent there upon a return to the classroom. As important as this writing was to each student, there is room here to pause and think about what this writing could have meant had it been directed in quite different ways, for example, if it had been used to challenge our responsibilities in respect to these men and other homeless people. The question to ask is how the trip may have better achieved its aims if the workshop activities used to guide it were given a focus toward what brought about poverty and what, if anything more, should a community be doing about it, even on a small scale, to effect democratic change. That no significant change came about in this sense and, in part, because of what was borrowed from workshop advocates, suggests not a failure but a missed opportunity in democratic learning.

To be fair, workshop advocates never suggest teachers take their students to soup kitchens, or really anywhere else for that matter. But in reading the writing workshop literature there is the implicit promise made that writing drawn from personal experiences, be they realized in the classroom, at home, or in the community, can develop in students a greater appreciation for those experiences (Atwell, 1998; Bomer, 1995; Calkins 1994; Graves, 1983; Rief, 1992; Romano, 1987). There is also an assumption that experiences written about in the workshop classroom and retold in writing conferences alongside other writers, can provide a foundation for education in citizenship and democracy (Atwell, 1998; Bomer, 1995; Calkins, 1994; Smith, 1995). Inspired by workshop advocates, it was easy to think that the use of a workshop approach would compel the students to probe further into the larger social and political issues presented to them in *To Kill a Mockingbird* and again at the soup kitchen. But the use of the workshop approach to direct the in-class reading and, more specifically, the soup kitchen experience fell short in realizing these objectives. The writing was always personal, which was not such a bad thing but for the fact that it was never discussed in any critical way that would have led to more meaningful writing and more democratic efforts at talk, decision-making and action than was had at the time of the study-unit. Essentially, in hindsight, it was wrong to think that a writing workshop, at least in its current conception, could make for more than personal edification in student conversations and writing, even when these conversations and this writing were inspired by the good deeds performed at the soup kitchen that day.

2. DEMOCRACY REVISITED

We have come to look back on the field trip in order to make more sense of what can be done to increase the educational value of what was clearly an important experience for students and teacher. We have decided to focus on the question of how the students could learn more about, and do more about, a democracy of soup kitchens. What does democracy have to do with soup kitchens? And what can soup kitchens teach us about democracy? Such questions quickly led us to other, more troubling questions over what *democracy* can possibly mean for high school students, as they feel the weight of compulsory attendance, almost no choice among classes and teachers, parental pressure to achieve and their own vaguely focused sense of schooling as a necessary credential to get through life. What does democracy hold for the teacher facing a need to make sure some students stay in line, while moving all students toward increased achievement scores? The students are in school as the result of a democratic process. What they study is similarly determined. Their parents may have exercised some choice in the selection of the school. The students have certain democratic rights within the school and these rights have been tested many times in the courts, largely in the area of freedom of expression, from fashion to student newspapers. But these are rights exercised largely apart from the curriculum and the work of the critical educator.

Given democracy's peculiar position, always at the periphery of the classroom, we wanted to set out what could begin to constitute a strikingly schematic approach to introducing democratic structures to students that would equip them to learn more about, and do more about, the soup kitchens of democracy. What sources of compassion and intuition, what skills and habits of the mind, what resources and technologies do they need to call upon in furthering democracy in such settings? How can we do better with these good intentions, especially in the spirit of democracy's great philosopher and educator, John Dewey, who would have us work against "an undesirable split between the experience gained in more direct associations and what is acquired in school" (1916, 9)? In the final page of *Democracy and Education*, Dewey writes that "all education which develops power to share effectively in social life is moral" (1916, 360). That sharing, in ways that advanced the experience of democratic hope, labor and frustration, simply had to figure more prominently in our thinking about the field trip. It had to provide a way of structuring what the students were to do with this experience, in helping them to see that "a democracy is more than a form of government; it is primarily a mode of associated living, of cojoint communicated experience" (1916, 87). But it is also, we began to understand, in looking at current thinking about democracy, a matter of learning to appeal to constitutional principles, scrutinize the fairness of procedures, engage in reciprocal deliberations and orchestrate coherent campaigns. It is just as much, as well, a matter of learning how to act effectively on the world. This ability is the very thing, according to Aaron Schutz (2001), that John Dewey's Laboratory

School did not do, leading Dewey to doubt the school's prospects of fostering democracy.

Certainly, much lip service has been paid to creating democratic classrooms and curriculums, not least of all through the writing workshop, with Inglis (2003) providing a systematic critique of the shortcomings and possibilities there. Here, however, we want to stay focused on a single curriculum event, the visit to a soup kitchen following on the reading of Harper Lee's novel, and work out how that experience of a particularly democratic quality could possibly take place in a very practical sense as well as a political sense.[1]

Our plan was to turn to current thinking about democracy, that is, to begin with this great political ideal in theory and then draw from that work both critical and practical measures that promised to increase students' engagement with democracy and soup kitchens. Democratic theory is, of course, a vast and unruly field of discourse, with each thinker organizing and emphasizing one aspect or another of democracy, whether it be democracy's particular quality of liberty (Macpherson, 1973), popular sovereignty (Dahl, 1956), deliberation (Elster, 1998), justice (Shapiro, 1999), rational communication (Habermas, 1998), or even indeterminacy (Lefort, 1988) and paradox (Mouffe, 2000).

As we sought a relatively comprehensive approach to structuring students' engagement with democratic theory, without engaging the challenging diversity of terms and standpoints that makes current debate, we were persuaded to take Amy Gutmann and David Thompson's (1996) tidy grouping of democratic theory into three schools. As Gutmann and Thompson would have it, some political philosophers prefer to think about democracies as *constitutionally* determined; others give more importance to democracies' *procedural* aspects. More recently, scholars in this area have been drawn to developing democracy's *deliberative* potential, which is the focus for Gutmann and Thompson. To these three prevailing orientations to democratic theory, we have added a fourth, concerned with democracy's *rhetorical* force. This rhetorical approach holds that what is critical is how people are persuaded or dissuaded from acting on constitutional, procedural, or deliberative matters. It recognizes the increasing democratic pervasiveness of interest groups, lobbies and public relation campaigns.

Now we have, in other contexts, been strong advocates of a deliberative approach to democracy, finding its emphasis on the exchange of ideas particularly congruent with the educational goals of democracy (Inglis, 2003; Willinsky, 2002). Yet coming out of the students' field trip to the east end of Vancouver, we can also see considerable value in helping students to see how each of these four theoretical orientations – constitutional, procedural, deliberative and rhetorical – can contribute to a democratic response to the soup kitchen. We were also struck by how closely connected these four orientations toward democracy are, the one feeding into the other, even as each of them provided a valuable starting point. That is, the democratic quality of certain processes and procedures (associated with, say, the daily life of a soup kitchen patron) can be advanced by careful deliberations, which are informed by constitutional principles, while persuasive campaigning can sway those deliberations, result in changed processes and, even in rare cases, alter constitutional principles.

We will go on to show how each of these approaches figures in the modern democratic state and, as such, should form part of the student's education. We will also illustrate, using the visit to the soup kitchens as the teachable moment, having students engage these four approaches to, or theories of, democracy. Only in this way, we believe, will students gain a feel for responding in a democratically responsible way to a democracy of soup kitchens as just one place for such work to be carried forth. But before we ask you to imagine how a class of students and a teacher, who set out on such a well-intentioned field trip, could turn the experience into a crossroads that greatly expands their democratic education, let us briefly introduce each of the four theoretical approaches to democracy. We have gently massaged each of these theories for (our) educational purposes, which we take as entirely *fair use* when it comes to practicing theory.

Constitutional theories of democracy focus on the principles and values which are enshrined in democratic states and which support, move beyond, need to be reconciled with, and act as a check on, the basic democratic tenet of majority rule. While these values are often eloquently expressed in written constitutions, they need to be constantly re-interpreted, balanced and applied, while being open to challenge at each of those points. As Gutmann and Thompson point out, "the search for substantive values that can resolve moral disagreements" can also go on beyond the scope of the original constitution, just as the constitution itself can be changed through an elaborate procedure (1996, 34). Still, from an educational perspective, the values that can be said to clearly constitute a democratic state provide an important starting point in thinking about what people can expect from the state and world they live in; in judging how well existing structures and processes honor people's rights; in focusing deliberations on how this democracy can be better realized; and in grounding campaigns for needed reforms.

Procedural theories of democracy emphasize the need for fair and legitimate processes for making political decisions and protecting people's rights. They begin with the fundamental fairness of popular rule, but do not limit themselves to that principle (Dahl, 1956). That is, they seek to protect "permanent minorities" from discrimination by majorities and seek ways and means to ensure that the rights of all are not subject to undue tyranny on the basis of numbers alone. Given our interest in having students explore modern democratic life, we want them to focus on the relevant and practical processes and programs that relate to the rights of the minority (and minorities) involved in soup kitchens. How are the rights of the poor and homeless recognized, negotiated, or overlooked; how are their interests, and those who work on their behalf, represented? We want students and teachers to examine the democratic quality of the processes available to them, through social welfare, basic education, employment agencies, food banks, soup kitchens and the courts. What recourse do people have, what limits do they face – we want to ask with students – what hope lies within this focus on democratic processes? How can people be assisted in taking advantage of their procedural rights and how can the procedures themselves be improved?

Deliberative theories of democracy hold to the value of people getting together to give an account of their position, to listen to others' accounts and to work toward a common understanding and plan, even in the face of significant moral disagreement, as Gutmann and Thompson (1996) work out in their analysis of the deliberative contribution. When it comes to managing the "economy of moral disagreement" which they recognize as "a permanent condition of democratic politics" (3, 9), they speak of a need for reciprocity, not only in the sort of mutual respect deliberators need to show each other, but in appealing to reasons "that are shared or could come to be shared by our fellow citizens" (14). Here is the need for a civic space, a public sphere that Habermas celebrates for its possibilities of a democratic exchange. Within such a space, Gutmann and Thompson hold to the importance of making this public reasoning available and accountable; this again strikes us as a helpful educational principle to introduce to students of democracy in asking them to deliberate and to gather others to deliberate on the soup kitchens of democracy. It also raises the challenge of setting up successful sites of deliberation, whether in person or through Internet technologies, as this, too, will provide its own learning experience in democracy.[2]

Rhetorical theories of democracy, as we are postulating it here, are obviously not about a nation of empty talk swept by overblown turns of phrase. We use *rhetoric* to refer to a necessary art of persuasion, central to the democratic call to articulate, promote and campaign for what you believe to be right (Cmiel, 1990). Such theories speak to the need for making people aware of issues, by convincing them, first of all, to hear one another out. It can entail the rhetorical willingness of interest groups, citizens' coalitions and well-heeled lobbyists (Berry, 2000; Kollman, 1998). But rhetoric can also lead, on rare but critical occasions, to a change of mind on the scale of the civil rights movement. The democratic play of ideas calls for concerted efforts to assemble information and precedents, reasons and rhetoric, to ensure that this thinking and work is not dismissed without the case for it even being noticed. This rhetorical theory distinguishes itself from deliberation in its promotion of one's ideas, in a widespread and focused way. Deliberation is about exchange and sharing. Students need to see that, without actively promoting constitutional reflections, procedural critiques and reciprocal deliberations, this democratic work may yet come to naught without even a hearing. One may be ignored or out-voted. But democracy may yet have its way only after being heard, which is a critical function of the great space that democracy creates for the art of persuasion.

Our practical pedagogical approach to this handful of democratic theories is to ask what they mean for the educational field trip of social concern. What can a class of high school students do, in learning about and engaging in, what it takes to make democracies stand and deliver on their promise? Now obviously, there will be many ways for students to experience these constitutional, procedural, deliberative and rhetorical aspects of democracy. But in the very name of practicality, we have created a far-too-schematic step-by-step program, consisting of a sample of three activities for each theoretical perspective, which students could undertake in relation to a school field trip to the soup kitchens of democracy (Table 2.1).

Now, of course, this table full of activities is already to suggest more than can possibly be accomplished with a single field trip, or perhaps in a single term, given the curricular responsibilities that teachers face today. Yet the practical and critical educator need not despair, at least not just yet. We have focused these four theories of democracy on a singular event to afford a coherent, if compressed, instance of teaching to democracy, given the limitations of a book chapter. So while we go on to

---

Table 2.1 Student Activities Derived from Four Democratic Theories

---

For the appreciable benefit of those who partake of, work in and organize the soup kitchens of democracy, and as the direct result of a field trip to one such kitchen, the students and teacher will...

A. Constitutional
    1. Determine relevant constitutional principles, rights and court cases.
    2. Check against available procedures, services, etc. (see B1).
    3. Prepare constitutional brief for deliberative and rhetorical purposes.

B. Procedural
    1. Ascertain relevant procedures, services and opportunities.
    2. Assist people in managing those procedures, services, etc.
    3. Consult with those involved on ways to improve procedures, etc.

C. Deliberative
    1. Formulate relevant, critical questions in need of deliberation.
    2. Assemble background and context (from A-B and outside sources).
    3. Set up infrastructure (actual/virtual) and invite participation in deliberation.

Rhetorical
    1. Target principles, procedures and/or services for reform (see A2, B3, C3).
    2. Develop informative materials and devise campaign strategies (see A-C).
    3. Lobby and promote through public and political channels (including C3).

---

provide a brief guide to how this step-by-step program would work with the soup kitchen field trip, we do believe that a democratic education worthy of the name can still be had if students have an opportunity over the course of a year or a few years, ideally, to touch on democratically motivated activities such as these. Through a series of illustrative field trips and collaborations with the community, the students could bring a certain focus to the democratic experience making it more real, we would hope, than reality television.

3. IN PRACTICE

In his book on education, *Aristocracy of Everyone* (1992) Benjamin Barber writes: "Democracy is not a natural form of association; it is an extraordinary and rare contrivance of cultivated imagination" (5). As such, it is taught and, when learned, requires constant attention in the way of critical, engaged and responsible participation in the public sphere. Realistically, children will learn democracy, as well as many other things not democratic, in the home or in the community. The school, however, is "the only place where, as a collective, self-conscious public pursuing common goods, we try to shape our children to live in a democratic world" (ibid., 14-15). As teachers serious about democracy, we must seek out moments when our students' thinking about an issue, their hearing out of others' positions and their careful working out of their own informed position can contribute to decision-making processes and effective change, whether in schools, communities, or globally. It cannot be given to chance that students may learn democracy on their own or as the distant and secondary by-product of learning any other number of things in school.

It falls to practical, critical educators to work with students around those critical democratic incidents by providing structure and guidance. Like those fabled teachable moments, radically democratic moments can be uncovered by those who make it their pedagogical practice to look for them. There are, of course, moments everyday in the language arts or humanities classroom that are less ideally democratic, not only in the teaching of a written convention or learning the specifics of an unfamiliar genre, but in getting everyone into their seat. It is not practical, short of returning to A.S. Neil's Summerhill free school, to think that the classroom will ever be all democracy all the time. The proposals that follow only suggest to teachers what might be done in using our best ideas about democracy as guides for students learning how to support forms of democratic action.

Although we have placed constitutional theory first in Table 2.1, as if to suggest that it is the best starting point in thinking about democracy, it is really a foundation that should be returned to, once the more immediate project is underway, as suggested by the activities we have drawn from the *procedural theories* of democracy (Table 2.1, B) which touch more directly on the lives of soup kitchen patrons. We envision students learning more about the grassroots organizations and non-profit agencies that serve the Downtown Eastside and the sort of procedural activities organizations and agencies themselves are involved in facilitating. If teachers are interested in preparing students for democratic citizenship, and we hope all teachers would be so inclined, acquiring firsthand knowledge into the way in which a democratic society responds to its inherent inequities is essential. These non-profit groups are situated at the centre of this work on exposing such inequities and, more importantly, doing something about them.

Students could begin by looking into the various programs in education, rehabilitation, health care, housing and food offered by these organizations and agencies. In the process, they could assess the support and justification behind promoting the programs and develop reports on the effectiveness and efficiency of them. What are the problems these programs are designed to fix or mitigate? What data or tools are currently used to determine the severity of the problems? How does an organization or agency measure the success of a program? How are specific programs connected to other programs? Depending on what they find, some or all of the students could present their ideas or suggestions for modifying existing programs or perhaps making an argument for a new alternative program, that is, if it is the case that they find some programs problematic or not as helpful as they are meant to be. In making these conclusions and preparing their reports they would need to acquaint themselves with the proponents and detractors of these programs, which would invariably mean talking to the people within the community itself and the people directly involved with the daily operations of these non-profit groups. To avoid overwhelming the students, we suggest that the class work with one of the many non-profit agencies in the area, The Downtown Eastside Women's Centre, Covenant House Vancouver and the Downtown South Residents Rights Association all being good places to start. It is our idea that students would not only learn about these non-profit organizations and agencies and the programs they advocate, but also work directly with them in their mission to help the underprivileged help themselves. Students could assume apprenticeships and assist these organizations in finding food, clothing and safe housing, and locating and filling out important forms such as those related to jobs, voter registration and financial services.

Another avenue of research or study is to investigate the politics and processes of the electoral system. The first opportunity for representation in any democracy is the vote, so it might be good for students to assess the local, provincial and national voting procedures to figure out how such procedures affect the homeless. They could study why some vote and others do not and what role voting behaviour plays, either way, in determining the life of a community. The students could study the relationship between voter participation within a given community and the standard of living of that community, including its general maintenance and upkeep. An analysis of voter registration and participation in Vancouver's Downtown Eastside would shed some light on the nature of life in the community and the possibility for growth and development. It would also be interesting, and perhaps more telling, for students to learn what happens after the vote is cast and whether it is even the case that voting matters that much at all, especially for the homeless whose situation oftentimes remains the same regardless of which party is elected. Even as politicians make poverty and homelessness key issues in almost every election it is not uncommon that the conditions of oppression and dehumanization that produce poverty and homelessness and the concomitant problems of mental disease and drug and alcohol addiction continue. Students could match promises made to the poor and homeless during an election campaign with the types of commitments fulfilled in the wake of it. One area worth considering is the taxes paid and tax dollars spent in a community like the Downtown Eastside compared to that paid and spent in other, wealthier parts of the city, province and even country. In the end, students could focus on where money is spent and who decides upon its allocation. The results of such a study might baffle students and teacher alike. But far from making students pessimistic about the voting process and therefore less likely to participate in elections when they are of age, we think that this study into electoral politics and its effects upon the underprivileged would encourage students to see the value in holding politicians accountable to the people they are meant to serve.

Once the students have become involved in the soup kitchens and other advocacy groups and agencies and understand how each is situated in a larger social pattern, they could undertake work related to *constitutional theories* of democracy (Table 2.1, A). In the first place, it would be helpful for students to get a feel for the rights and privileges that are afforded people in democracies. Understanding the present day constitutions of Western democracies and the history of these documents would be helpful to that end. They could consider the struggle to achieve the constitutional promise of democracy, especially in light of those occupying the soup kitchens of democracy. They could also mine the International Declaration of Human Rights and Freedoms for its relevant clauses in considering the democratic conditions at issue.

While a study of human rights – as constitutive of democratic theory – is warranted in the case of assessing poverty and homelessness and necessary as a platform for advocating change, we think that teachers can and should go further with their students than this type of activity alone would allow. To go beyond simply naming human rights would mean to consider why recognition of human rights on paper and voiced in political speeches does not always translate into actual recognition for individuals and groups, particularly in the case of minorities. In order to see this discrepancy, we suggest that students assess the legitimacy of national and international standards for human rights, specifically, the rights to freedom, education, housing and healthcare, alongside real incidents of human rights abuses that hinder the personal growth and development of the people who visit the soup kitchens of Vancouver's Downtown Eastside.

This is no doubt a tough task made all the more difficult because not all students, if any, will have been exposed to poverty and homelessness on the scale of what might be found in the Downtown Eastside. It is important for the themes of study to arise from the students' own observations. What students see, perhaps best aided by discussion with the men at the soup kitchen, can be narrowed down to three or four critical incidents. One incident might be the lack of safe and affordable housing on the Downtown Eastside made apparent by people sleeping under benches or in back alleys, another the sight of prostitutes lining the street corners, and yet one more the relative unseemliness of the physical environment littered with trash and walls strewn with graffiti. There are more, many more, but this would be enough to start in on why rights are reserved for some—the educated, the wealthy, etc.—but not for others, namely, the men sleeping under benches, the women selling their bodies on street corners and the people living in an environment most of us would find unfit for animals. How is it that we determine some people more worthy of the title "human being" than others? At what point, under what conditions, do we strip people of their human rights?

Now, it should be made clear with this constitutional focus, as with the other activities inspired by these four democratic theories, we do not suppose that every student will interpret these democratic rights and responsibilities in a similar manner. In fact, we would expect the political divides of the larger society to be recreated in the classroom and would want to foster a spirit of interest and respect for these differences in interpretations and in values. There may well be students who support libertarian, conservative, liberal, or socialist interpretations of democracy's constitutional promise. Encouraging dissent within the framework of the democratic classroom would give students a chance to sort out these issues, but it would also teach them the valuable lesson that the democratic state of the classroom and the world in general is measured by the degree of dissent that is allowed in social and public spaces. The differences might appear, in the case of the United States, with the opening line, in terms of what is entailed "in order to form a more perfect Union, establish Justice, insure domestic Tranquility, provide for the common defence, promote the general Welfare, and secure the Blessings of Liberty to ourselves and our Posterity." In Canada, questions may arise around the Canadian Charter of Rights and Freedom: "Everyone has the right to life, liberty and security of the person and the right not to be deprived thereof except in accordance with the principles of fundamental justice."

Which is only to say that even a selective reading of constitutional documents is bound to give rise to its own critical democratic moment of hearing how students bring a set of values to bear on their reading, and helping them to see how the courts and others have managed, over time, to change their minds about what such statements mean. It could lead, in the practical context of the field trip, to students making the constitutional case for workfare programs, a reduction in government services, or a greater reliance on community volunteerism and self-help. This is not our own orientation on these issues, as will continue to be made clear by the examples that follow, but we take it as an educational service and democratic responsibility to assist in the articulation of these various positions and to encourage the students to address these differences in values as inherent qualities of the democratic landscape.

Equipped with an understanding of, as well as possibly statements or briefs on, the constitutive rights of those living in a context of poverty and homelessness, the students would then be in a position to work on what comes of *deliberative theories* of democracy (Table 2.1, C). We find that deliberative talk encourages people to develop new perspectives while leaving open the possibility for reformulating old ones. Teachers need to steer students away from just leveling criticism at the people and events that will confront them in the Downtown Eastside. Criticism itself is not altogether productive or generative. Neither is it conducive to citizenship. Instead, teachers, students and other people interested in this work should be encouraged to weigh carefully multiple and diverging perspectives against their own tightly held interests so that they may develop a broader understanding for the complexity involved with life in the Downtown Eastside. We see deliberation as a clarification of many interests that provides a platform for people to discover commonalities and to explore and establish mutuality. The necessary critique of action and ideas guided by democratic talk and, with careful and timely intervention on the part of others, notably the teacher, can help students to see the world as others might see it, which is, of course, a step towards citizenship.

Again, we do not mean for this sharing and exchange to be idealistic and harmonious, as it is so rarely the case that collaborative discussions do not entail some sort of conflict and never the case that social interaction can avoid it, be it manifested in overt behaviours, aggressive or otherwise, or in more subversive forms like attempts made at avoiding others. In truth, talk engaged in social spaces, especially those within the classroom or at a soup kitchen, is never free of conflict for the simple reason that it is an undeniable and irrepressible product of social interaction. But even as conflict is an always pervasive and persistent factor in human interaction, this does not mean to say that it is immutable to the effects of deliberative democracy. While talk as we understand it is not meant to incite conflict, it certainly does not shy away from it. Instead, talk within a framework of deliberative democracy provides a way to work through and transform conflict, making it a resource rather than an impediment to citizenship.

An excellent way to nurture deliberative skills and the attributes of good citizenship would be for students to organize and lead public hearings. The site for these public hearings might be the school, a community centre in the Downtown Eastside, or elsewhere in the city that houses a suitable venue. The hearing or deliberation would be focused upon practical topics related to poverty and homelessness, including, but not limited to, topics of race, gender, class and religion. In coordinating these hearings students could invite the men and women of the Downtown Eastside as well as the people working with the nonprofit and volunteer advocacy groups to present their perspectives on the given topics and themes. Faculty from local universities and colleges, as well as local political representatives could also be invited.

Students might work with members from each of these parties to strike an agenda. Students would prepare their own statements or, as might be the case, poetry and fiction readings, musical and dramatic presentations and whatever else would invite and support critical exchanges between participants. One particular topic students might examine, for example, may include where we get our assumptions about the homeless from, which would lead, perhaps, into discussions about the influence of the home, the community and the media in our construction of the identities and behaviours students associate with the homeless. Students would use their writing to further sort out their thinking on the issue at hand and marshal the resources for an informed argument that can contribute productively to an ongoing conversation about possibilities for change. After the hearings, students would be responsible for charting the progress made and planning subsequent hearings. If the hearings come at the end of the year, the students could meet with another grade of students to share with them the experience and prepare this next group for continuing the work started by them.

The deliberative activities surrounding the public hearings we have suggested would lead up to a series of culminating activities in which the students take on the *rhetorical theories* of democracy (Table 2.1, D), as they seek to persuade relevant parties of the need for small and perhaps large reforms, based on what has come out of their previous work with democratic theories A-C. Now is the time for the students to think about going political with what they know, a time for thinking about campaigning and lobbying. It is a time for creating convincing materials and meeting with the media, officials and policymakers. The press release becomes the critical genre to master. Websites and emails are linked in reaching key people with a key message. Securing results and getting a hearing become measures of democratic effectiveness of any given strategy, any single story or multimedia presentation. The rhetorical activities we have in mind entail more than asking students to write, say, editorials to the local newspaper so they can voice their opinion on an event while remaining removed from the situation they are commenting on. The students need to see how democracy is an open, and sometimes not so open, competition for the ear, eye and mind of the public, in which they consider the full range of methods, from Madison Avenue marketing gimmicks, through Martin Luther King Jr.'s speeches, to the Internet campaigns of the Zapatista movement in Chiapas.

The focus of the students' work needs to focus on a practical but manageable problem that affects these Eastside neighborhoods. Where is the promise of democracy breaking down at the level of housing, food, health, security, voice, hope? Students, along with a small collection of advocates for the homeless and some of the homeless men themselves, could initiate a number of projects designed to improve theirs and others' knowledge about a particular "action-able" item in Vancouver's Downtown Eastside. Students could also use their writing to start up, implement or support a neighborhood safe-walk program, a local literacy project, or possibly reconstitute a public space for the construction of a park or playground. They could gather background information about related programs elsewhere or gather local information by interviewing community members that could be used to inform the process. These projects may involve further work with local media and see students drafting service announcements; the crafting of dramatic scripts with help from local-area actors which would cast students and others in the community in plays performed at a community center or park in the Downtown Eastside or, if that is not possible, within the area the school is situated in; or a collaboration on a series of murals designed to showcase the interplay of language, text and visual art in suggesting positive representations of communities defined by differences in race, gender, class and religion, while being mindful of the conflict and tension these differences reflect in the community itself.

In any case and whatever the project, it is important to work *with* and alongside the people whom the students are intending to serve and to understand that these community service projects are never just a matter performing acts of charity *for* them. Successful projects in "service learning" and democracy, such as Meta Mendel-Reyes (1998) at Swarthmore, have been focused on developing a range of skills that serve equally well in academic and activist settings, that serve both student and those who would be served (also see Hepburn, 1997). Charity, while important, is not altogether a legitimating condition of citizenship and may, in some cases, forestall citizenship. "The language of charity," remarks Barber, " drives a wedge between self-interest and altruism, leading students to believe that service is a matter of sacrificing private interests to moral value" (1992, 249). In contrast, continues Barber, "The language of citizenship suggests that self-interests are always embedded in communities of action and that in serving neighbors one also serves oneself" (ibid.). Rhetorical activities and projects for action and community service would side with fostering citizenship rather than selfless altruism and would reflect the shared interests and principles of not only the people their projects are meant to serve but also their interests as well, as might be demonstrated, for example, on standardized tests, in job applications and college applications.

In each case here, our intent is not to teach *democracy*, in any one aspect, form or theory. Our intent is treat these ideas about democracy as a means of focusing the practical, critical and, above all, educational work needed for democratic states to live up to their own standards. We want to encourage people to become students of those democratic forms and strategies, by putting those forms and strategies to the test, to see just how it is they are able to move the world, beginning with the soup kitchens of democracy. Each of the four theoretical approaches – constitutional, procedural, deliberative and rhetorical – is already at work in modern democracies just waiting to be caught in the act or called up for active service. Each can be neatly applied by students, as we have tried to show, in fostering democratic responses to the soup kitchen. And while we have still to put this theory about democratic theory to the most practical of tests, what has surprised and encouraged us, in the course of this reflection on Patrick Inglis's field trip, is how well a certain eclecticism would seem to work across these four orientations, as the twelve steps set out here take on a cumulative and complementary force.

It makes perfect sense that something as full and rich with contested and contingent meanings, and as often troubled and discouraging, as *democracy* should be capable of supporting a wide variety of theories and practices. It falls to practical, critical educators to push against all of the possibilities, to put theories to work, to see what comes of what we think we know. We are not in search of the one best theory of democracy. That is neither practical nor critical. Rather we are intent on exhausting the possibilities and prospects of the current range of theories in pursuit of those democratic moments in which the world appears to have become a better place. It is not that we imagine that we are without prejudices and theories. Those we do favor are part, after all, of the originating impulse behind the soup kitchens of democracy. For that reason alone, there can be no finer place to begin to share and develop with students an understanding of this form of governing by the people and for the people.

ENDNOTES

[1] This chapter represents a second working of the soup–kitchen visit, and draws on the initial version in Inglis (2003). It illustrates, in this way, how much it takes to work through what is needed, beyond the initial impetus to visit the soup kitchen, to see what can be done to sharpen the democratic and educational experience.

[2] See, for example, the online Public Knowledge Policy Forum established by the Public Knowledge Project at the University of British Columbia (http://pkp.ubc.ca), as analyzed by Klinger (2001).

REFERENCES

Atwell, N. (1998). *In the middle: New understandings about writing, reading, and learning.* Portsmouth, NH: Heinemann.
Barber, B. (1992). *Aristocracy of everyone.* New York: Oxford University Press.
Berry, Jeffrey M. (2000). *The new liberalism: The rising power of citizen groups.* Washington: Brookings Institution Press.

Bomer, R. (1995). *Time for meaning: Crafting literate lives in middle and high school.* Portsmouth, NH: Heinemann.

Calkins, L. (1994). *The art of teaching writing.* Portsmouth, NH: Heinemann.

Cmiel, Kenneth. (1990). *Democratic eloquence: The fight over popular speech in nineteenth-century America.* New York: William Morrow and Company.

Dahl, R. (1956). *A preface to democratic theory.* Chicago: University of Chicago Press.

Dewey, J. (1916). *Democracy and education.* New York: Macmillan.

Elster, J. (Ed.), (1998). *Deliberative democracy.* Cambridge: Cambridge University Press.

Graves, D. (1983). *Writing: Teachers and children at work.* Portsmouth, NH: Heinemann.

Gutmann, A. & Thompson, D. (1996). *Democracy and disagreement.* Cambridge, MA: Harvard University Press.

Habermas, J. (1998). *The inclusion of the other: Studies in political theory.* Cambridge, MA: MIT Press.

Hepburn. M. A. (1997). Service learning in civic education: A concept with long sturdy roots. *Theory into Practice,* 36(3), 136-142.

Inglis, P. (2003). *Keeping promises: Strong democracy for a new writing workshop classroom.* Unpublished master's thesis, University of British Columbia, Vancouver, British Columbia.

Klinger, S. 2001. *"Are they talking yet?":* Online discourse as political action in an education policy forum. PhD dissertation, University of British Columbia.

Kollman, Ken. (1998). *Outside lobbying: Public opinion, interest group strategies.* Princeton, NJ: Princeton University Press.

Lee, H. (1960). *To kill a mockingbird.* New York: Warner Books.

Lefort, C. (1988). *Democracy and political theory* (trans. David Macey). Minneapolis: University of Minnesota Press.

Macpherson, C. B. (1973). *Democratic theory: Essays in retrieval.* New York: Oxford University Press.

Mendel-Reyes, M. (1998). A pedagogy for citizenship: Service learning and democratic education. *New Directions for Teaching and Learning,* 73, 31-38.

Mouffe, C. (2000). *The democratic paradox.* London: Verso.

Rief, L. (1992). *Seeking diversity: Language arts with adolescents.* Portsmouth, NH: Heinemann.

Romano, T. (1987). *Clearing the way: Working with teenage writers.* Portsmouth, NH: Heinemann.

Schutz, A. (2001). John Dewey's conundrum: Can democratic schools empower? *Teachers College Record,* 103(2), 267-302.

Shapiro, I. (1999). *Democratic justice.* New Haven: Yale University Press.

Smith, B. (1995). Learning democratic dispositions in the writing workshop. *Indiana English,* 18(2), 5-9.

Willinsky, J. (2002). Education and democracy: The missing link may be ours. *Harvard Educational Review,* 72(3), 367-392.

BARBARA COMBER

CRITICAL LITERACY EDUCATORS AT WORK:

Examining dispositions, discursive resources and repertoires of practice

Abstract. Teaching democratically in increasingly undemocratic and globalizing times is seriously challenging work. What are the ethical commitments, professional knowledges and pedagogical repertoires that fuel teachers' practices? In this chapter I consider the dispositions, discursive resources and practices of teachers who take a critical literacy standpoint. I discuss different approaches to critical language awareness, analysis and action through studies of practical critical educators at work in literacy classrooms through drawing variously on my own observations, their writings and other professional artifacts. I argue that a key move in fostering critical literacy in educational institutions is democratizing research and knowledge producing practices.

1. ACQUIRING A 'CRITICAL HABITUS'

This chapter begins with a brief autobiographical introduction and historical notes because I believe that as educators we are continually in the process of revision – our selves, our curriculum, and our pedagogies. Teachers, I argue, do not simply adopt a theoretical or political position and adhere to it in the messiness of educational institutions and changing times.

I started teaching in the mid-seventies when *language across the curriculum, action research* and *negotiating the curriculum* were elements of a familiar educational discourse in my home state of South Australia. A key player in this radical and progressive approach to education, and to literacy education in particular, was Garth Boomer[1] (Boomer, 1982; Boomer et al., 1992; Green, 1999). In the seventies, eighties, and nineties, he explored key elements of being a practical critical educator – language (language across the curriculum), teachers and knowledge (action research), and students' positioning (negotiating the curriculum). He wrote of the art and science of 'pragmatic-radical teaching' and teachers' work as curriculum designers. As a young teacher of English and History I entered the profession with great optimism about the potential of schooling to make a positive difference to marginalized and disadvantaged students, although I was aware of the impact of class on school achievement (Connell, Ashenden, Kessler & Dowsett, 1982). Being 'radical', as we understood it at that time, was almost the norm amongst my cohort of newly appointed high school English teachers on our first appointments in schools located in regional and low socio-economic areas. I was one of many young graduates whose own university education had been supported by federal government scholarships, and was firmly convinced of the inherent empowering potential of education and, in particular, literacy education. A radical

51

K. Cooper and R. White (eds.), The Practical Critical Education, 51–65.
© 2007 *Springer.*

approach to literacy education was part of my local educational heritage – an early and enduring layer of my professional habitus (Bourdieu, 1977), as was a belief in the significance of teacher knowledge and research.

The need for a democratic education was not disputed and many of us believed we knew what it was and how to deliver it. At that time we did not interrogate our assumptions about what constituted empowerment, democracy, or literacy. We 'simply' needed to learn how to 'translate' these laudable goals into classroom practice. That was our job – to invent ways of applying 'the theory' in everyday life in classrooms. Yet Boomer also understood that teachers do much more than translate other people's theories into practice, that teachers' work involves intellectual exploration of, and with, theory:

> Teachers have been theorizing their practice ever since there have been teachers. Most teachers are not gropers. They cannot afford to grope, faced with classes that must be taught. With more or less deliberation they have to punt on what is best and modify 'on the run', according to the consequences of their actions. They work with theory to plan and predict. They create fiction about possible classroom worlds and then see if these can be created. Of course, the theory may be submerged, but it is there. Without it, teachers could not act. (Boomer, 1999, 3)

This theme – teachers' theoretical work – I revisit later in the chapter when I consider teachers' discursive resources and repertoires of practice. However, to return to my narrative, by the nineties Boomer was questioning, along with many others, the concept of empowerment (see also Ellsworth, 1992; Gore, 1993), that is, whether teachers could 'empower' marginalized students. Yet at the same time he was arguing even more strongly for 'global literacy' (Boomer, 1999), for 'critical literacy' – reading the world – and leading, by now as a senior bureaucrat, moves towards explicit teaching, clear assessment criteria, and a serious examination of what was being accomplished, particularly in the "disadvantaged schools" (Boomer, 1999). He was arguing for overt attainment levels and a serious curriculum, driven by intellectual goals that went beyond building students' self esteem. 'Global literacy' (the capacity to read the world), according to Boomer, involved the "capacity to *make* and *do*, capacity to *interact* socially, and capacity to *imagine*" (Boomer, 1999, 118).

At the same time as Boomer outlined his concerns with the limiting emphasis on 'self-esteem' at the expense of intellectual rigor, a number of critical and feminist studies of the enacted curriculum in English/ literacy classrooms indicated that progressive pedagogies (including process approaches to writing, literature-based reading programs, and so on), which had espoused empowerment for marginalized students, were continuing to position certain groups of children at a disadvantage (Baker & Freebody, 1989; Baker & Luke, 1991; Christie, 1990; Gilbert, 1990). These critiques made it clear that what we had taken as instances of democratic literacy education and in children's best interests, in their enacted forms, sometimes continued to consign some groups of students, particularly ESL, Indigenous, poor and marginalized students to limited and limiting, rather than powerful and empowering, literacies. Despite the best intentions of committed educators, the differential educational effects of normative schooling practices (whatever the rhetoric of their theoretical protagonists) on different groups of children continued to haunt the field of literacy education. Something was undercutting the potential of these pedagogies in high poverty locations – the limits of pedagogy to overcome the effects of poverty, teachers' expectations, neo-conservative policies, institutionalized racism? Writing pedagogies intending to 'give children voice' in certain conditions positioned certain children as harassers and others as targets – powerful literacies yes, but not in the interests of all. I will not rehearse the critiques of progressive pedagogies here (see Comber, 1994, 2003). However it is important to understand that the cumulative building of critical literacies grew, at least in part, out of a critique of certain aspects of enacted progressive pedagogies. Also important, is that what counts as 'critical' has been and continues to be subject to intense debate at a local level as well as in the wider international scholarly community. What constitutes critical literacy and/or democratic education needs to be negotiated in particular places at particular times and to be informed by our personal and professional histories.

As well as being informed by feminist and critical studies of progressive pedagogies in action, critical literacy in Australia, as a feature of curriculum, has also drawn upon critical discourse analysis (Fairclough, 1992a, 1992b; Janks, 1993; Luke, 2000), poststructuralist feminist analysis (Mellor, Patterson & O'Neill, 1991), and new ways of theorizing literacy (Freebody & Luke, 1990; Green, 1988). Each of these developments has brought with it associated repertoires of practices and ways of thinking about 'literacy' itself. Since the early nineties, Norman Fairclough's approach to critical discourse analysis (as a research methodology) has been taken up pedagogically in school and tertiary classrooms (e.g., Fairclough, 1992a; Janks & Ivanic, 1992; Wallace, 1992). Hilary Janks, working with South African secondary school students and teachers, developed six workbooks – the *Critical Language Awareness* Series (Janks, 1993) – which demonstrated clearly how critical discourse analysis could be approached with ESL students in school. These texts introduced young people and their teachers to concepts such as language and power, identity and positioning. The workbooks developed and modelled a pedagogy for applying critical discourse analysis in classrooms. Similarly the Chalkface Press materials developed in Western Australia by Annette Patterson, Bronwyn Mellor and Marnie O'Neill (e.g., Mellor, Patterson & O'Neill, 1991) showed English teachers how to apply feminist poststructuralist theories to the texts they were studying, asking questions about absences in texts, how gendered cultural storylines work across texts, who texts were written for and how they might have been written differently (Mellor & Patterson, 2001).

Literacy then, was seen as complicated and as more than a measurable skill. Green (1988) had developed his 3-D model of literacy which incorporated its operational, cultural, and critical dimensions. Freebody and Luke (1990) had conceptualized literate practice as involving four roles – code-breaker, meaning-maker, text user, and text analyst. In both models the critical ideological dimension was incorporated as part of the conceptualizing of literacy.

However, my goal is not to provide a full history of how literacy education, in particular critical literacy, has evolved. Rather, my objective is to paint a broad picture of the discursive scene in literacy education in Australia especially with respect to teachers approaching critical literacy and democratic education. I am interested in both the theoretical and practical resources available to teachers to take up in their curriculum design, that key part of teachers' work as Boomer understood it. In other words, teachers assemble pedagogical repertoires, shape professional standpoints, and take up discursive resources from a myriad of possible educational options. Becoming – and staying – a practical critical educator is a complex project which is accomplished across a career.

Since the nineties some would argue it has become more difficult to be overtly 'critical', to frontload one's social justice agenda in curriculum initiatives, and to politicize the language classroom, due to a burgeoning conservative backlash (Gutierrez, Asato, Santos & Gotanda, 2002; Luke, 2003a, 2003b) evident in the proliferation of standardized testing, the insistence on 'scientific research', the demonization of certain refugee groups, and the unrelenting blaming of the poor for their poverty and for their children's lower educational levels of attainment. The extent to which different nation states are 'closing down', or 'opening up', in terms of progressive and critical educational agendas, is worthy of extensive examination. And the picture may be very different in Singapore, the US, Australia, and the UK. It may even vary within countries with different provincial regimes and bureaucracies supporting opposing and hybrid policies. Within these conditions and policy constraints and potentials, teachers assess what they might do with particular groups of children in the name of critical literacy and democracy.

What constitutes a 'critical educator' is contingent in part on the place and time. How practical critical educators assemble dispositions, discursive repertoires, and pedagogical practices requires further examination. Part of my goal as a critical literacy educator is to collect, analyze, and publish the contextualized narratives and theorized accounts of committed teachers (e.g., see Comber, Thomson & Wells, 2001; Comber & Nixon, 1999; Nixon & Comber, 2005). Further I note that it is typically, in elementary schools at least, women teachers doing this work. Often, too, women educators do large amounts of the teacher training. Hence increasingly, though not exclusively, I document the work of women who are critical practical educators working with and on theory, often 'on the run', as Boomer notes, as they go about the messiness of everyday life in classrooms.

2. CRITICAL LITERACY: ELEMENTARY SCHOOL TEACHERS AS CRITICAL PEDAGOGUES

Since the eighties I have worked on an organic project – namely, documenting the work of primary school educators working in high poverty contexts who make a difference (Connell et al., 1982; Connell, 1993). My goal is to tell counter-hegemonic 'good news' stories of public schooling for poor and diverse communities, without bracketing out the complexity of teachers' work or children's lives. More recently I have worked to co-author/edit accounts of critical literacies negotiated in particular places with particular students and teachers (Comber & Simpson, 2001). Following Boomer et al's (1992, 33) point that "curriculum... can only be described and fully comprehended in retrospect", I have conceived of a project of analyzing and describing the work of practical critical educators with richly illustrated narratives (and also in some case film documentaries) in the interests of other educators learning from their theorized practice (Comber, 1987, 2003; Comber, Cormack & O'Brien, 2001; Comber & Nixon, 1999; Comber & Simpson, 2001; Comber, Thomson & Wells, 2001; see also Edelsky, 1999).

For over a decade now I have been actively seeking out and documenting the pedagogical practices of teachers taking a critical approach to literacy. Here I provide a brief profile of just three teachers, each of whom, I believe has contributed in significant ways as a practical critical educator (see also Searle, 1998; Vasquez, 2003 for teacher self-portrayals). I have chosen to focus on the work of these teachers in particular because their work is documented in more detail elsewhere and readers may wish to explore that further. The teachers are Helen Grant, Marg Wells and Jennifer O'Brien. In describing their work here my aim is not to make them heroines or give them the stamp of best practice, but rather to begin to examine what's involved practically in being a critical educator and particularly in the context of early and elementary education. I am interested in what sustains these teachers, as both critical and practical, and how they resist wider pressures on teachers to engage in 'consumer-like behaviour' (Luke, 2003a). Of these three educators, two are classroom teachers at the time of writing and one has retired. I 'know' these teachers through talking with them, through reading about their work, through examining the artifacts of their everyday classroom practices, and direct observation in their classrooms. In each case I provide a brief profile outlining their professional dispositions, discursive resources, and pedagogical practices.

Helen Grant teaches English as a Second Language (ESL) to grades one through seven. In this role she works in classrooms with teachers and also withdraws small groups of children who have recently arrived in Australia, often refugees, for intensive English language work. She has been teaching for over twenty years. Her over-riding dispositions, evident in all her teaching, are her respect for cultural and linguistic diversity, her passion for the arts and media, her high expectations of children and her demonstrable pleasure in teaching. Across her career she has actively sought opportunities for professional learning and has become knowledgeable about a functional approach to grammar (Halliday, 1978) in the context of ESL teaching, media studies, critical language awareness (Janks, 1993), and critical literacy (Comber, 1993; Luke, 2000) to name just a few areas of her expertise. This, when combined with her strong personal commitments to multiculturalism, world music, travel, and the arts, can be seen as a strong set of resources for a critical literacy educator. Grant has recently begun to write about her work, in particular the ways she incorporates children's knowledge of popular culture and home languages and cultures into the business of acquiring school literacies (Grant, 1999; Luke, Comber & Grant, 2003; Walsh & Grant, 2003). Yet her most significant contribution to her educational peers and her preferred way of making a difference is her work as a teacher-filmmaker where with her students she explores ways of representing culture, identity, language, and power.

In the past few years Grant has co-produced films with her elementary students with titles such as: *Aussie Slang, Waves of Culture, About Being Me, Cooking Afghani Style* (Nixon & Comber, 2005). Grant's approach is to tackle complex ideas using the collective linguistic and cultural resources of the group and to produce films that represent what the students are able to communicate at this point. She takes a position of cultural worker making language, identity, culture, and everyday life the object of classroom study (Freire, 1998; Luke, Comber & Grant, 2003).

Each of the films listed above are concerned with the young people's language, cultures, and identities, albeit in different ways. In *Cooking Afghani Style,* Grant sought to re-position the Afghani children as experts. This was part of her broader agenda of contesting the demonization of people from Afghanistan and from the Middle East which was overtly occurring in the media at that time. Together they studied a range of the numerous cooking/life style televisions programs that were currently showing to investigate how the genre worked. Here we can see her knowledge of systemic functional linguistics having an impact as she begins the unit by deconstructing multiple models of similar texts with the children. Her choice of the film medium is interesting too. She could have put together a recipe book. Yet her own passion for film as a medium, along with her knowledge that television, videos, and movies were common cultural material amongst her culturally diverse class, led her to opt for the short film, reconstituted here as both a pedagogic and cultural text.

Grant's knowledge of the language of systemic functional linguistics, of media studies and film-making, and about teaching English as a second language meant that she was able to assemble a rich pedagogical repertoire to successfully negotiate making films as an extended curriculum sequence. In the process she explored complex issues of representation with the children as they decided what could be said and by whom, what could be shown and how best to portray it. They addressed questions about which languages, music, artifacts to include in making the film, and in which contexts within or outside the school they might shoot the footage. This approach positions all the children as contributors; they draw on their cultural resources both from their homelands and family ethnicities as well as their knowledge of global and local popular and media culture.

How Grant realizes these ambitious goals in practice is more than can be fully explained here, but she does have explicit criteria for assessment which she makes clear to students at the outset. For example in another film project with recently arrived refugee children, *About being me,* her goals were:

- The young people's stories would be created and told by them.
- Students choose their own images and consider how they were represented.
- Students consider their own and their families' safety in what could be shown and told.
- Every aspect of the film – visual images, spoken and written text, music, transitions, balance of all of these – would be positive and uplifting to counter-act the negativity of the media.
- Respect for cultural practices was to be ensured by having the Bilingual School Services Officer and parents check it.
- Aesthetics would be taken into consideration in the production for example, when choosing location (Luke, Comber & Grant, 2003, 28).

In discussion with the students they agreed that the film should also show them:

- Speaking in their first language.
- Talking about their experiences (both positive and negative).
- Working against demonized representations of 'boat people', Middle-Eastern people in particular (Luke, Comber & Grant, 2003, 28-29).

These are complex matters to be tackling with elementary aged children. As the work of this film and others progressed beyond the original storyboarding and filming, which Grant explicitly taught the children to do, a range of dilemmas arose in the context of crafting the final artifacts. For instance: Would children read English sub-titles? Was it safe to show photographs of families on temporary protection visas? What was actually being said in the songs chosen by the children in their first languages? When such questions are discussed in a shared context of co-producing a text, children's investments in talking about appropriateness, audience, and issues of censorship, become more than academic. When the film was finished and suitably launched Grant worked with students to make it the object of critical scrutiny, reviewing it through questions such as:

- Who's telling this story? How were you portrayed? Did you get the important aspects of your culture in the film?
- What parts of the story remain untold?
- Is there a common story?
- How many different stories were there amongst this group of children?
- What could be selected in the next film?

The lesson here is that all texts are open to question and that as producers of cultural artifacts young people need to be aware of their decision-making and its effects.

Grant's semi-professional interests in world music, travel, culture and film have become part of her professional habitus along with her knowledge of systemic functional linguistics and critical literacy. Over time she designs, assembles and crafts everyday pedagogic resources for mediating such knowledges in curriculum contexts with her students.

Marg Wells has also taught for over twenty years and mostly in the first years of school. Wells has a strong interest in working with children in their neighborhood and since 1996 has been located in a poor suburban area which is located amidst a large-scale urban renewal project. Wells lives in the nearby area. Like Grant, Wells welcomes children's home and peer resources into the classroom through a permeable curriculum (Dyson, 1993) and children are encouraged to read, write, draw and talk about the pleasures and projects in which they have strong personal investments, whether that be Mario Brothers, Bart Simpson, or riding their bikes. Like Grant, Wells is a traveler and actively works on accumulating her own knowledge of places, peoples, and cultures. She has been involved in a number of education department and school-based research projects. Across a range of projects and everyday classroom life Wells designs a problem-based curriculum which positions young children as researchers of their community. Her strong disposition is to make children's experiences of growing up and going to school in a particular locality the object of study. Wells' inquiry disposition leads her to explore the taken-for-granted, to find out where and how positive action might be taken. Her theoretical resources which she explicitly named in a concept map of a unit entitled *Literacy and power*, included teaching for resistance, critical literacy, literacy across the curriculum, student voice and attending to children's home literacies.

Over the past decade Wells has continued to work with children's interests in designing her literacy curriculum, including popular culture, fantasy, sport, computer games, and so on. Here I focus on her approach to the neighborhood as the object of study because it represents another approach to critical literacy that goes beyond critical language awareness and towards re-positioning children as active researchers of everyday life, and as people who can participate as active critical citizens whilst still at school. However I mention her work with popular culture and the like because I do not wish to suggest that her curriculum provides an unrelenting focus on the material realities of everyday life in a poor community. Indeed she moves between worlds of pleasure, play, and the 'local' and the 'global' in designing her curriculum.

I turn now briefly to her approach to studying the neighborhood (see also Comber, Thomson & Wells, 2001). Within a unit designed around place and identity, within the wider context of the urban redevelopment project, known as Westwood, Wells engaged the children in activities such as the following:

2.1 Action in relation to the redevelopment of their suburb

- Meetings with the developers to find out about specific plans and timeline.
- Acting as research assistants to the developers about a proposed park. Children investigated indigenous vegetation, animals and birds.
- Developing a specific proposal for the planned wetlands

2.2. Exploring the neighborhood

- Mapping the class's houses in relation to the school.
- Mapping the routes to school.
- Responding to surveys about the good and bad aspects of the neighborhood.
- Neighborhood walks.
- Producing a wall map of the area.

2.3. Focussing on houses

- Photographing their own houses and other buildings of interest (e.g., partly demolished houses).
- Drawing their own houses.

- Using the computer to design their dream home.
- Using the computer to rebuild or redecorate their own or a half-demolished house.

2.4. Thinking about 'my place' in the future

- Discussing and writing about their possible futures

2.5. Considering points of view

- Producing a picture book focussing on perspective and objects in places. (Comber, Thomson & Wells, 2002).

Wells' curriculum design is too complex to fully elaborate here, however a quick review of the above outline signals her attention to action, futures, multi-media and research beyond the school – all key components of a practical critical educator's repertoire in these times, yet also situated in the everyday life-worlds of her students. Here, I want to foreground two teacher-initiated activities, built around surveys, which are indicative of the way Wells repositions her students to take an analytical, yet optimistic, approach to everyday life. These surveys were entitled *Our house* and *My neighborhood*. (Later she also invited the students to project into the future and imagine themselves and their lives five years and ten years on in terms of where and how they might be living.) In using each of the surveys as initiating and framing devices, she worked with the children to analyze the here-and-now, and simultaneously she worked with them to re-imagine and re-design possible futures and dwellings. The 'Our House' survey invited students to talk and write about what they liked and didn't like about the house they were currently living in, their preferred places within the house and the activities associated with that, and what they would like to change or improve about their house. Given that the children were witnessing the area change around them, as empty houses were boarded up or demolished and new houses were being constructed, these were pertinent questions to consider.

Wells followed the initial discussion about the children's houses with a survey of the neighborhood which included three main questions with some sub-prompts, as follows:

1. *Where is it safe in your neighborhood? What do you like to do there?*
2. *Are there places in your neighborhood that you think are unsafe?*
3. *Where are the places in your neighborhood that you are allowed to go?*
   - on your own
   - only with your family
   - with a friend (or friends)
   - never
   - only in daylight

There was considerable space on this survey for the children to write their comments, but what was equally important was the discussion that followed where children noted points of difference and commonality. Depending on the particular part of the neighborhood where children lived there were different challenges to consider. Children wrote of burglaries, traffic, angry people, unsafe streets and pockets of land. They wrote of their favourite Vietnamese restaurants and shopping centres. As a class they decided they needed to know more about the neighborhood, the urban renewal and redevelopment sites, and where each other lived. They went on three different excursions where they walked the neighborhood with their teachers, including visiting student houses located within a reasonable distance to the school. As they walked the local area, Wells noticed that the child whose house they were approaching would appear at her side proudly pointing out aspects of their garden, the surrounds and so on. Sometimes parents, grandparents and siblings would appear at the front of the house to greet the class. Wells noted later how these excursions into the neighborhood improved her relationships and communications with individual children and their families. The children photographed their own houses and other places of interest to post on a class wall-map and in some case to 'rebuild' digitally later using various software programs. At the same time the children noted things that could be improved such as sidewalks, lighting, and removal of rubbish. Wells worked with the children to think about how to convey this information to the developers and they became involved in making a documentary about how the Westwood project might affect them and the area.

During the period that they walked and investigated the neighborhood, they also wrote and illustrated an alphabet book for primary students in Pretoria, South Africa, to tell them about their lives and where they lived, entitled *A is for Arndale*. In the book each student chose an aspect of their lives and locality to foreground, such as the local shopping centre, the video store, the movie theatre, the local bike track, the netball court, eating at McDonalds, busy roads and so on. The book is aesthetically quite beautiful with each page of writing complemented by a full colour painting replicating elements of the style of Elaine Russell, an Aboriginal artist, who had produced a book about the places where she grew up, entitled *A is for Aunty* (Russell, 2000). In this, and indeed all the representational work Wells has the children engage in, the children are positioned as knowledgeable and perceptive observers of their local environment. Their critical analysis (for example, of the conditions of local streets and pavement, the dangers of deserted houses) works alongside their appreciation and enjoyment of aspects of popular culture (Movieland, McDonalds, TV) and other local attractions (the bike track, the reserve). My point here is that their critical engagement with the neighborhood doesn't leave them bleak and cynical. On the contrary these children are becoming increasingly persuasive communicators in a range of media and modes with local and global audiences.

In order to make the neighborhood an object of study, Wells has needed to make two significant moves as an educator: firstly, she has needed to undertake her own research about the council, housing trust and private developers and how they were working in an articulated way on the Westwood redevelopment project, secondly, she has needed to make overt contacts with these bodies. In other words she has made the urban renewal project her business and embarked on a project of building her own knowledge base and networks. In this way we can see that Wells cumulatively builds her resources as a 'pragmatic radical' teacher, in Boomer's terms, in order to do the intellectual and sociological work she needs in the classroom.

Jennifer O'Brien was an experienced teacher-researcher who recently retired from classroom teaching and curriculum writing. She published many papers on critical literacy, as well as co-authoring a book for teachers and being a mentor in a teacher-researcher network (O'Brien, 1994a, 1994b; O'Brien & Hole, 1995). Importantly, she was for a number of years a teacher-librarian. Her detailed attention to texts was perhaps already a part of her professional disposition before she encountered and worked with feminist post-structural theory and critical discourse analysis.

O'Brien conducted a number of related studies over a period of several years, investigating how early childhood teachers might negotiate a critical literacy curriculum with young children. Working directly with feminist and poststructuralist theories about the construction of gender, the critiques of socially critical researchers of school literacies and theories of social justice, she sought to disrupt her pedagogical practices and to re-build them differently. In the opening chapter of her Masters thesis, entitled 'Theory/Research/Practice Nexus', she wrote:

> In this chapter I review the critically-based literature, linking theory, research and pedagogical change which inspired me to introduce a critical discourse analysis into my junior primary classroom; at the same time I discuss how the poststructuralist prediction of multiplicity, confusion, contradiction and possibility impacted on my research and pedagogical positions. (O'Brien, 1994c, p.1)

Making use of feminist, critical discourse analytic, and poststructuralist theories in her everyday classroom practices, O'Brien changed the questions she asked about texts to indicate the constructedness of texts and the gendered representations in texts designed for children and for wider use in the community. Influenced by cultural studies, O'Brien also changed the kinds of texts she used in the classroom and began to incorporate everyday texts such as the junk mail put out by department stores and the spin-off materials associated with television programs and movies which children read at home. Informed by educational research that suggested that teachers controlled most of the talk around texts and thereby ensured their own authorized readings, she changed the rules and the everyday practices around who could speak about the texts and when. This meant that children were able to comment uninvited as O'Brien read to them. As well, O'Brien avoided asking all the questions and evaluating each of the children's comments. She also changed the associated writing and drawing she asked children to do in order for children to write and draw from the position of text analysts.

> I aimed to raise with my students questions about the versions of the social world, particularly the inequities in gender relations, constructed in and by their classroom texts. I decided to problematize the authority relations between teacher and students which resulted in the teacher's textual reading being preferred to that of her students. (O'Brien, 1994c, p.4)

As she made these changes, she deliberately took up the insights of theorists and researchers and simultaneously she researched the effects of her changed practices from a critical feminist standpoint. She considered, for example, the different responses of boys and girls to the new literacies she was making available. These complex changes to practice were the result of considerable intellectual work with a repertoire of theories assembled in professional development provided by the education of girls unit, graduate studies in language and literacy, attendance at national and local conferences, and O'Brien's own extensive self-directed reading in feminism and cultural studies.

3. ASSEMBLING AND RE-INVENTING THE CRITICAL TEACHER ACROSS A PROFESSIONAL LIFE-SPAN

Brian Street (2001) has written recently of the extent to which different communities 'take hold' of literacy and make use of it in their daily lives. Literacy theorists have encouraged us to think of literacy as acquiring specific repertoires of practice over time (Luke & Freebody, 1999). Here I have argued for a similar approach to thinking about teachers' work in designing curriculum and negotiating pedagogies in everyday classroom life. If we think of teachers as 'taking hold' of theories of social justice, democracy, multi-literacies, and also as acquiring pedagogical repertoires, then 'teacher education' and 'professional development' need to be constituted accordingly.

The complex nature of the critical literacy work of these teachers is more than I can hope to portray here. However, I have begun to explore, in the relationships between teachers' dispositions, their grappling with theory and their curriculum design and classroom pedagogies. As O'Brien explained in her dissertation:

> I take a position as critical practitioner/researcher/student, looking back at the issues raised for me in feminist poststructuralist theory, feminist poststructuralist pedagogy. I reflect on how the action I took in my classroom was interwoven with my continued reading in my area of interest. At the same time I point to gaps I uncovered in theory and practice and show how I drew on a theory/practices nexus to investigate some of these gaps. (O'Brien, 1994c, p.1)

As an experienced teacher O'Brien assembled and worked on an ensemble of theories that she made use of in her everyday classroom life and which re-made O'Brien in terms of professional identity. As a researcher she documented and analyzed her theories in action in a specific location at a particular time. In one sense, O'Brien, along with Grant and Wells, addressed not only theorized practice, but also practiced theory; that is, in their everyday work they negotiate ways of bringing to life theoretical material with children, and, in so doing design and enact curriculum and pedagogy. The practical critical educator is simultaneously and multiply positioned as a worker, a thinker, a researcher and more. How different teachers put this together has a lot to do with their own identities and dispositions, both their primary discourses and their personal and professionally acquired funds of knowledge. Locally, I contend, and sometimes more widely, the work of such teachers has catalytic effects on changing practice through teacher publications and professional development events. However the academic community has been slow to acknowledge that critical practical knowledge developed in school-based practice might make valuable theoretical contributions to the field (Zeichner & Noffke, 2001).

There is a dearth of research which explicitly documents and analyzes what occurs when teachers work with theories of justice informing/driving their everyday practice, and even less which is conducted and authored by teachers (Fecho & Allen, 2003). I am not suggesting that simply working with such theories guarantees empowering results (Ellsworth, 1992; Weiler, 1991). Rather, I am interested in the possibilities of teachers researching the effects of their theorized practices over time, where those theories of practice attend to social difference, where indeed the very habitus of the teacher changes over time. Such research might directly inform/change educational theorizing.

Critical literacy educators, such as Boomer, Green, Janks, and Luke, mediate, co-construct and re-invent educational discourses that permeate policy, programs, and curriculum. Through professional development events, university programs, policy interventions, and publications, teachers, either directly or indirectly, access the resources they make available to school-based educators. Teaching communities and individual educators either 'take hold' (Street, 2001) of critical literacy in their working lives or not. In this chapter I have explored how three teachers who have taken hold of critical literacy, have taken it up and, 'on the run' in Boomer's words, put it with other aspects of their personal and professional identities in order to do particular kinds of work with particular groups of children.

Whether we think of these teachers in terms of Boomer's 'critical-pragmatic intellectual', Freire's 'cultural worker' or Luke's 'cosmopolitan teacher', what is clear is that these are not fearful teachers; they are not afraid of theory, policy or their students. Each worked in high poverty, highly cultural diverse communities. They embrace the complexity of material reality, changing cultural practices, changing student populations and changing literacies in order to re-invent curriculum designs, which take them and their students to the edge of their capacities. They are sustained by like-minded fellow teacher researchers, school leaders and university-based educators who make the time for serious intellectual play amongst the busy-ness of educational institutions. Boomer imagined some time ago now how this might work:

> The new intellectualism would be strongly earthed in the local, but informed by astute and rigorous scrutiny of the world at large (Boomer, 1999, 124).

ENDNOTE

[1] While Garth Boomer left a significant body of published work in his own right before his untimely death in 1993, recently Australian curriculum and literacy education scholar, Bill Green, has edited a selection of his important papers in a volume entitled Designs on Learning: Essays on Curriculum and Teaching by Garth Boomer (1999), published by the Australian Curriculum Studies Association. I have drawn on this significant volume in preparing this chapter, rather than earlier versions in local journals, which may be more difficult for readers to access

REFERENCES

Baker, C., & Freebody, P. (1989). *Children's first schoolbooks: Introductions to the culture of literacy.* London: Blackwell.

Baker, C., & Luke, A. (Eds.). (1991). *Towards a critical sociology of reading pedagogy.* Philadelphia: John Benjamins Publishing.

Boomer, G. (1982). *Negotiating the curriculum.* Sydney: Ashton Scholastic.

Boomer, G. (1999). Pragmatic-Radical teaching and the disadvantaged schools program. In B. Green (ed.), *Designs on learning: Essays on curriculum and teaching by Garth Boomer.* Canberra: Australian Curriculum Studies Association.

Boomer, G., Lester, N., Onore, C., & Cook, J. (Eds.). (1992). *Negotiating the curriculum: Educating for the Twenty First Century.* London: The Falmer Press.

Bourdieu, P. (1977). *Outline of a theory of practice.* (R. Nice, Trans.). Cambridge: Cambridge University Press.

Christie, F. (1990). The morning news genre. *Language and Education,* 4 (3), 161-179.

Comber, B. (1987). Celebrating and analysing successful teaching. *Language Arts,* 64(2), 182-195.

Comber, B. (1993). Classroom explorations in critical literacy. *The Australian Journal of Language and Literacy.* 16(1), 73-83.

Comber, B. (1994). Critical literacy: An introduction to Australian debates and perspectives. *Journal of Curriculum Studies,* 26(6), 655-668.

Comber, B. (2003). Critical literacy: What does it look like in the early years? In N. Hall, J. Larson, & J. Marsh (eds.), *Handbook of Research in Early Childhood Literacy* (355-368). United Kingdom: Sage/Paul Chapman.

Comber, B., Cormack, P., & O'Brien, J. (2001). Schooling disruptions: The case of critical literacy. In C. Dudley-Marling & C. Edelsky (eds.), *Where did all the promise go? Case histories of progressive language policies and practices* (83-104). Urbana, Illinois: National Council of Teachers of English.

Comber, B., & Nixon, H. (1999). Literacy education as a site for social justice: What do our practices do? In C. Edelsky (ed.), *Making justice our project: Critical Whole Language Teachers talk about their work* (316-351). Urbana, Illinois: National Council of Teachers of English.

Comber, B., & Simpson, A. (Eds.). (2001). *Negotiating critical literacies in classrooms.* Mahwah, New Jersey & London: Lawrence Erlbaum.

Comber, B., Thomson, P. (with Wells, M.). (2002). *Critical literacy, social action and children's representations of "place".* Paper presented at the American Educational Research Association Annual Meeting, April 1-5, 2002. New Orleans, Louisiana.

Comber, B., Thomson, P. (with Wells, M.). (2001). Critical literacy finds a "place": Writing and social action in a neighborhood school. *Elementary School Journal,* 101 (4): 451-464.

Connell, R. W. (1993). *Schools and social justice, Our schools/our selves.* Toronto: Education Foundation.

Connell, R.W., Ashendon, D.J., Kessler, S., & Dowsett, G. W. (1982). *Making the difference: schools, families and social division.* Sydney: Allen & Unwin.

Dyson, A. (1993). *Social worlds of children learning to write in an urban primary school.* New York: Teachers College Press.

Edelsky, C. (Ed.). (1999). *Making justice our project: Critical whole language teachers talk about their work.* Urbana, Illinois: National Council of Teachers of English.

Ellsworth, E. (1992). Why doesn't this feel empowering? Working through the repressive myths of critical pedagogy. In C. Luke & J. Gore (eds.), *Feminisms and critical pedagogy* (90-119). New York: Routledge.

Fairclough, N. (1992a). (ed.), *Critical language awareness.* London: Longman.

Fairclough, N. (1992b). *Discourse and social change.* Cambridge: Polity Press.

Fecho, B., & Allen, J. (2003). Teacher inquiry into literacy, social justice, and power. In J. Flood, D. Lapp, J. Jensen, & J. Squire (eds.), *The handbook of research on teaching the English language arts* (2nd ed., 232-246). Mahwah, NJ: Lawrence Erlbaum.

Freire, P. (1998). *Teachers as cultural workers: Letters to those who dare to teach* (D. Macedo, D. Koike & A. Oliveira, Trans.). Colorado: Westview Press.

Freebody, P., & Luke, A. (1990). "Literacies" programs: Debates and demands in cultural context. *Prospect: the Journal of Adult Migrant Education Programs,* 5(30), 7-16.

Gilbert, P. (1990). Authorizing disadvantage: Authorship and creativity in the language classroom. In F. Christie (ed.), *Literacy for a changing world* (54-78). Hawthorn: Australian Council of Educational Research.

Gore, J. (1993). *The struggle for pedagogies: Critical and feminist discourses as regimes of truth.* New York: Routledge.

Grant, H. (1999). Topdogs and underdogs. *Practically Primary*, 4(3), 40-42.

Green, B. (1988). Subject-specific literacy and school learning: A focus on writing. *Australian Journal of Education,* 32(2), 156-179.

Green, B. (Ed.). (1999). *Designs on learning: Essays on curriculum and teaching by Garth Boomer.* Canberra: Australian Curriculum Studies Association.

Gutiérrez, K., Asato, J., Santos, M., & Gotanda, N. (2002). Backlash pedagogy: Language and culture and the politics of reform. *The Review of Education, Pedagogy, and Cultural Studies*, 24 (4), 335-351.

Halliday, M. (1978). *Language as social semiotic: The social interpretation of language and meaning.* London: Edward Arnold.

Janks, H. (Ed.). (1993). *Critical language awareness series.* Johannesburg: Witwatersrand University Press and Hodder & Stoughton Educational.

Janks, H., & Ivanic, R. (1992). Critical language awareness and emancipatory discourse. In N. Fairclough (ed.), *Critical language awareness* (305-331). London & New York: Longman.

Luke, A. (2000). Critical literacy in Australia: A matter of context and standpoint, *Journal of Adolescent and Adult Literacy*, 43(5), 448-461.

Luke, A. (2003a). Teaching after the market: From commodity to cosmopolitanism. In P. Thomson & A. Reid (eds.), *Rethinking public education: Towards a public curriculum* (139-155). Flaxton, Queensland: Post Pressed.

Luke, A. (2003b). Making literacy policy and practice with a difference. *Australian Journal of Language and Literacy*, 26(3), 58-82.

Luke, A., Comber, B., & Grant, H. (2003). Critical literacies and cultural studies. In G. Bull & M. Anstey, (eds.), *The Literacy Lexicon.* (2nd ed., 15-35). Melbourne: Prentice-Hall.

Luke, A., & Freebody, P. (1999). *Further notes on the four resources model.* Reading Online. Retrieved May 29, 2002, from http://readingonline.org/research/lukefreebody.html.

Mellor, B., & Patterson, A. (2001). Teaching readings? In B. Comber & A. Simpson (eds.), *Negotiating critical literacies in classrooms* (119-134). Mahwah, New Jersey & London: Lawrence Erlbaum.

Mellor, B., Patterson, A., & O'Neill, M. (1991). *Reading fictions.* Western Australia: Chalkface Press.

Nixon, H., & Comber, B. (2005). Behind the scenes: Making movies in early years classrooms. In J. Marsh (ed.), *Popular culture, media and digital literacies in early childhood.* London: Routledge/Falmer.

O'Brien, J. (1994a). Critical literacy in an early childhood classroom: A progress report. *The Australian Journal of Language and Literacy,* 17(1), 36-44.

O'Brien, J. (1994b). Show mum you love her: Taking a new look at junk mail. *Reading,* 28(1), 43-6.

O'Brien, J. (1994c). *'It's written in our head': The possibilities and contradictions of a feminist poststructuralist discourse in a junior primary classroom.* Unpublished Masters of Education Thesis. Adelaide, Australia: University of South Australia.

O'Brien, J., & Hole, T. (1995). *Key literacy planning: Planning and programming for literacy equity.* Carlton, Victoria: Curriculum Corporation.

Russell, E. (2000). *A is for Aunty.* Sydney: ABC Books for the Australian Broadcasting Corporation.

Searle, C. (1998). *None but our words: Critical literacy in the classroom.* Buckingham: Open University Press.

Street, B. (2001). *Literacy and development: Ethnographic perspectives.* London: Routledge.

Vasquez, V. M. (2003). *Negotiating critical literacies with young children.* Mahwah, New Jersey & London: Lawrence Erlbaum Associates.

Wallace, C. (1992). Critical literacy awareness in the EFL classroom. In N. Fairclough (ed.), *Critical language awareness* (59-92). London & New York: Longman.

Walsh, C., & Grant, H. (2003). Teacher research: What's it all about? *Practically Primary,* 8(2), 4-6.

Weiler, K. (1991). Freire and a feminist pedagogy of difference. *Harvard Educational Review.* 61(4), 449-74.

Zeichner, K., & Noffke, S. (2001). Practitioner research. In V. Richardson (ed.), *Handbook of research on teaching* (298-330). Washington, DC: American Educational Research Association.

PART TWO:

CRITICAL LEARNING FOR A DEMOCRATIC EDUCATION

To lay aside the Critical aspect of this volume for a moment, it can be seen that learning is both a process in its own right and a result of becoming literate. It may also be said that leadership is a process as well and that it also depends on learning in order to be most effective. This Critical learning is intricately connected to both Critical literacy and Critical leadership. It is at this point that the Critical nature of literacy, learning and leadership must be examined. To wax existential for a moment, we may consider the question, "For what purpose?" For what purpose do we need to become literate, learned leaders? To engage Albert Camus (1969) for a moment, in *The Myth of Sisyphus,* one's reason for being must be greater than oneself. Hopefully, this in itself provides purpose enough for individuals to become Critically literate learners. The need to become Critical, in the political sense of the word, is an essential aspect in the promotion of human agency. And why is the promotion of human agency so necessary? Again, human agency and agentry is essential to develop Critically literate learners and leaders who will foreground social justice issues in the pursuit of positive social change.

This second section of *The Practical Critical Educator* seeks to connect the individual's 'state of knowledge' to the broader problematics in society. Issues are brought forward, examined and discussed in order to establish, develop and promote the realization that we are learning, functioning and interacting within the larger societal context. Through concrete examples, the contributors continue to promote the concept that every educator, including students, can become and should become agents of positive social change.

Richard A. Brosio begins this section of the book with a riveting account of the progress of Critical theory. Chapter 5 is entitled "Critical theory for school-education and society: Grounded in political economy" In this account, the author addresses various "states of knowledge" that can assist practical Critical educators in achieving transitions from theory to practice. In his work, Brosio notes that Critical theorists seek school and societal outcomes that favor authentic democratic empowerment, social justice, and broad inclusion of our diverse populations. The epistemologies that are developed and clarified in this contribution consider the works of Marx, Gramsci, Dewey, Freire, and others who are convinced that intelligence, competence and a desire to rule ourselves characterize the human condition. Radical inclusion is considered to be necessary for epistemological and moral reasons. The author hastens to note that, while there can be no successful quests for metaphysical and/or religious certainty, in the absence of such we need not be paralyzed by inaction. Brosio goes on to note that secular theories grounded in lived experiences are potent forces that may assist in the construction of superior schools and societies. It is the interrelated nature between social class and "identity" politics that may lead to the successful construction of a more just society and schools that can help to make this a reality.

In Chapter 6 of this volume, "Shared authority in democratic classrooms: Communities-always-in-the-making", Barbara J. Thayer-Bacon offers a perspective that draws on the theme of "shared authority". This concept is developed in conjunction with Thayer-Bacon's study of African American students. Through her work in this chapter, Thayer-Bacon seeks to develop a relational democratic political theory of individuals in relation to their communities, highlighting the transactional relationship that exists between individuals and others while striving to be Critical and anti-racist. This article describes a study of site-based visits to indigenous schools in Africa as well as visits to American school/community settings where this cultural group represents the majority population. This exploration serves as a means of better understanding the ways in which minority students from diverse cultures might be best served in a complex and diverse society such as the United States of America.

William F. Pinar begins his chapter by referring to Foucault, noting the disturbing resemblance among prisons factories, schools, barracks, and hospitals. Pinar, moves this idea, in Chapter 7 in to social institutions and makes transparent some of the linkages between sexuality and racism. In his chapter, "Teaching the queer character of racism", the author explores the notion that all race relations tend to have strong sexual overtones. He provides details about how issues of social class factor into the construction of race and gender. Pinar delves unflinchingly into Critical aspects of racism and the victimization of women and persons of colour. He views race, gender and class oppression as concerted and systematic. His argument is straightforward in asserting that racism is, in some sense, an "affair" between men, and that women are relegated to units of currency. While also noting that this is not the sole reason for racism to exist, Pinar adds that racism is not *only* an affair between men. He says that women have been very much victimized by men, both Black and White. This is not to say that "race" can be reduced to gender, but racism does contain strong sexual overtones. William Pinar conducts his Critical examination of racism, sex and desire through a study of lynching and interracial prison relations. Returning to his opening position, the reader is left to ponder the question that begs to be asked. If such issues abound in prison, can racism in other societal institutions, such as institutions of education, be different? William Pinar concludes by suggesting that teaching tolerance must include a consideration of politics, gender and violence.

The final chapter in this section, Chapter 8, is by David G. Smith. His contribution, entitled "Not rocket science: On the limits of conservative pedagogy" anchors this section by recognizing those "invisible" fences that trammel learning and help to develop and sustain a view that swerves neither to left nor right, but is always focused straight ahead. While this strategy may be useful in some relatively uncomplicated instances, Smith suggests that one may be able to better focus on Critical issues from a more informed point of view. He refers to the concept of the unquestioning perspective as "conservative pedagogy". This article defines conservative pedagogy as any form of teaching and learning constructed through a logic of self-enclosure. Smith draws upon the work of Argentinean philosopher Enrique Dussel, to show how this logic has arisen as the pre-eminent logic of modernity. It is this type of logic that is also connected to contemporary structures of global inequality. The present is also connected to the past history of this way of thinking as David Smith suggests that this pedagogy of conservatism is a typically Western Eurocentric tradition, beginning in the fifteenth century. Smith concludes that it is an impoverished philosophy and its very poverty lies in its own inability or unwillingness to face whatever lies outside the boundaries of its own construction. Pedagogy that seeks to be authentic must understand and confront its own identity.

It is from these chapters that the reader is encouraged to compare their own lived experiences, reflect upon their own histories and draw their own conclusions regarding what it is to be a Critical learner. Let it suffice to be said that Critical learning is much more than the ingesting of information. That is simply data storage. True learning is the rumination, the digestion and the examination, not only of the data, but of the gaps, spaces and interrelationships between and among pieces and systems of knowledge and may even include the scrutiny of the systems of knowledge storage themselves. Critical learning concerns development of wisdom as a result of this process of digestion and reflection. It is this wisdom that is born of the useful application of knowledge: Useful in that it concerns itself with human agency and the promotion of equitable systems of justice for all humans regardless of race; creed; colour; physical, emotional or mental capacity; social status; wealth; health or intellect. In short, Critical learning seeks, as its goal, full and unequivocal inclusion for all people. It is only then that equity and equality will become synonymous.

REFERENCES

Camus, A. (1969/1972). *The myth of Sisyphus, and other essays.* New York: Knopf.

RICHARD A. BROSIO

CRITICAL THEORY FOR SCHOOLING-EDUCATION AND SOCIETY:

Grounded in Political Economy

Abstract. The author addresses various "states of knowledge" that can assist practical critical educators achieve transitions from theory to practice. Critical theorists seek school and societal outcomes that favor bona fide democratic empowerment, social justice and broad inclusion of all our diverse populations. The epistemologies championed herein eschew any quests for certainties. The works of Marx, Gramsci, Dewey, Freire and others who are convinced that intelligence, competence and desire to rule ourselves characterize the human condition are presented to demonstrate liberatory projects that consider radical inclusion necessary for epistemological and moral reasons. In the absence of metaphysical and/or religious certainties we need not be paralyzed by inaction. We can rely on secular theories that are grounded in the experiential concreteness of everyday life in order to construct better – if not best – schools and societies. The interrelatedness between social class and "identity" politics is recognized in reference to the successful construction of a more just society and the schools that can help make this possible.

1. INTRODUCTION

Throughout history people have traveled many paths in order to arrive at the conviction that authentic, de facto, participatory and broadly inclusive democracy was and is the best way to govern them/ourselves. It is warranted to assert that certain philosophical, ultimate beliefs and religious ways of looking at the world and ourselves – as well as systematic versions of these positions – have been comparatively ineffective or effective with regard to providing useful and logical scaffolding for bona fide democracy. This is the case also for schooling-education. Not all world-views are helpful in supporting teaching and learning that enhance more democratic empowerment, social justice, respect for diversity and the possibilities for developing a society within which it is easier and **safer** to act more altruistically – if not "caringly."

During my reflected upon (in a Deweyan sense) experiences as a teacher educator I have interacted with many students who claimed to favor progressive education. Moreover, many of them were seemingly taken with and energized by my "slogan" stated above, namely: education for democracy, social justice, diversity and other possibilities. Many of the students had never been exposed to social foundations of education courses; therefore, most of them were attracted to progressive and democratic education only after having been introduced to them in as systematic a manner as possible, given the paucity of these courses at the undergraduate level. Many students were disposed to "help kids"; moreover, they

71

K. Cooper and R. White (eds.), The Practical Critical Education, 71–93.
© 2007 *Springer.*

were more susceptible to embracing the democratic imperative on schooling-education rather than its incompatible capitalist imperative.

The problems began when we studied philosophies of education within the undergraduate social foundations course. Much attention necessarily had to be given to history and sociology of education – with consideration given to policy studies. These problems were exacerbated in the graduate philosophy of education course. So many of the students who claimed to support progressive democratic education insisted that the politically conservative and uneasily supportive of capitalism position that provided scaffolding for educational essentialism was the best choice. Moreover, they also embraced various forms of revealed and inerrant religious views, idealist and realist philosophies, and other quests for certainty as their philosophical scaffolding. In keeping with my teacher and doctoral mentor's position that the scaffolding for various kinds of curricula and pedagogies must be consistent with the favored outcomes in the classroom, I struggled with my students to think hard and long about what Professor G. Max Wingo had taught me. Obviously, I made clear to the students that what they believed was their right. As long as their essays and term papers were clearly written and within the province of the field and of our particular version of philosophy of education they could earn honor grades. I battled to the end with many comments on their papers – all in the spirit of dialogue, but sticking to my guns. However, the difficulties just described were overcome in many instances and with most students as they began to understand the concepts better. This occurred near semesters' end. The methodology I employed was based on Dewey's idea that teachers and students are in fact co-inquirers into problematic situations. The "complete act of thought" demands that teaching and hoped-for learning have to be based on hypothesis construction and the translation of theory into practice.

Philosophical Scaffolding for the Construction of Critical Democratic Education (*PSCCDE*) is the result of these struggles with my students. This book is built upon Wingo's classic texts: *The Philosophy of American Education* (1965) and the 1974 edition *Philosophies of Education: An Introduction.* I was fortunate to have had Max Wingo read the manuscript of *PSCCDE* before it was published. I used Wingo's texts as the main readings during the first twenty-eight years as a philosophy of education teacher. What follows in this chapter is the result of a career-long project to articulate some of the possible philosophical scaffoldings that effectively support critical theory and pedagogy – and why. Let us begin with Marx, because it is of great importance to understand that the term critical, a term used by many educators, has important roots in his thought.

2. DEMOCRATIC MARXIST THOUGHT

Democratic Marxist thought is best understood as part of the West's secular tradition that places human welfare at the center of philosophy and socioeconomic analyses. It remains a living intellectual form of inquiry that owes much to the Enlightenment as well as critiques of it. Key to this secular, democratic and radical tradition is the belief in human reason as a precursor and spark for action – individual and collective – providing the potential to free us from superstition, ignorance and injustice. This belief and the tradition of which it is a part should be of interest to educators because it serves to connect understanding to action. I have used *PSCCDE* for the main text in the undergraduate cultural foundations of education course since the fall 2000 offering. It has become clear that the students begin to discuss the text and other course materials in the spirit of the forms of inquiry they are studying.

Philosophers of education have been justifiably concerned with teaching and learning in relation to "retention and transfer." After all, many persons who are interested in the human condition and the enhancement of our dignity have come to the conclusion that thinking may not always be for its own sake. Instead of mere contemplation of what allegedly has been already created, with us as mere spectators, progressive and radical democrats have sought to use thinking as a tool for changing the social world – and in the process – ourselves! When these processes have occurred we have "retention and transfer" on a scale much larger than the intramural school that features assignments and tests.

Contrary to popular belief that Marx was a determinist, he insisted that history was "open." He held that human beings make history, although neither under conditions of our making nor just as we like. Marxist thought is embedded in the material conditions of everyday life. Historical materialism is characterized by Marx's dialectical approach in reference to the complex relationships among human thought, action and the material concrete realities within which we live. The dialectic in this case consists of human beings affecting the many facets of our earthly existence and these changes in turn having consequences for us. The key form of our actions is called labour. Philosophically speaking, materialism means that matter-in-motion constitutes the most basic reality. This view opposes philosophical idealism's insistence that ideas per se constitute and/or are responsible for our world. Marx's "new materialism" opposed a cruder version that was dominant at that time which failed to consider the human construction of meanings, ideas and history itself in relation to material conditions. Human beings are productive mentally and materially; moreover, the distinction between the two is not clear-cut. For Marx, that which is external to us consists of the materialization and sensuousness caused, or at least affected, by human labour. When ideas such as these are studied and critiqued, the students and teachers can focus first on their immediate surroundings: classroom, university, city and then broaden their interests to state, national and international human labour examples. Engaging in this process helps students figure out who has had the power to influence policies and why.

Marx understood that volition bumps up against structure. This recognition provides necessary middle ground between those who argue that anyone can pull her/himself by the "bootstraps," as opposed to determinists who believe that environment is everything. Contemporary educators could be well served by comprehending that we can and do help students; however, neither under conditions of our choosing in most cases, nor just as we like. My students at the University of Wisconsin Milwaukee have been very receptive to this concept as it relates to their own experiences. Eric Fromm (1961) thinks that Marx's historical new materialism with its emphasis on the lives of ordinary (honorific connotation) people throughout history, and presently, serves to elevate us all onto the stage of history – where we belong but have been previously excluded. In Milwaukee most teacher education students have little difficulty understanding what exclusion means in terms of class and race.

If Marx's philosophy is to be credible for more than just a few people, they must become aware it claims specifically that the world is knowable to all human beings, especially because we have made so much of it through our labour. Furthermore, it must be understood that we can heighten our awareness of where we are in time and space, allowing us to decide democratically what is to be done about conditions that afflict us. Authentic participatory democracy becomes epistemologically, politically and ethically necessary for those who understand the dire consequences of the failed historical quest for certainty – one based on the erroneous assumption that various elites could and did succeed in knowing about the known in perfect correspondence. Many teacher education students come from working-class and other families that are neither rich nor powerful. Consequently, it is comparatively easy for them to realize their place and stake within this elite-subaltern relationship. Furthermore, students are interested in the argument that in spite of capitalist apologists who claim that there is no alternative to their system, it is warranted to assert that, because it has not come down from the heavens and it is neither inherent to the nature of things nor best for everyone, it can be deconstructed by those of us who think a better system can replace it. During this time of political, economic, social, educational and intellectual reaction, agents seek to convince us that widespread poverty, lack of opportunity and massive student failures are indicative of the natural order of things. Some alleged educational experts, for example, members of the rightist Heritage Foundation in the U.S., have claimed that ghettos, barrios and other places where poverty and exploitation are rampant need not be replaced by better living conditions. They insist instead that if one works hard enough and/or has the "right stuff," then some students will escape from these "inevitable" bad places via high marks on high stakes tests![1]

Educational essentialists, conservatives, reactionaries and even some liberals argue that social-class stratification and a somewhat corresponding "A" through "F" grade scale are fair because there are those who really deserve to be at the bottom of each rank order – and, of course, on the top! Marx and democratic Marxists do not agree. They understand the relationships between school and society. Racism, unemployment, social injustice, school tracking, homophobia, misogyny and so forth can be seen, understood and combated by alert teachers and laypersons. Every society contains its own contradictions and possible negations of that which dominates the majority of its people. Marx argued that class struggle arose from the contradiction between the labour performed by the primary producers and those who benefited unjustly in terms of their profit. We educators can help students and ourselves understand what the contradictions are within our present situations in order to lay bare the unnecessary injustices within work, schooling and other social relations. Critical educators can and do make these ideas "come alive" through their professional practice. The power of these ideas and the opportunity to make them more concrete through examples are apparent to alert students and are discussed within the curriculum and pedagogy that are logically tied to the ideas themselves.

The Marx offered herein belongs to the tradition of subversive educators who seek to call things by their correct names. As Freire has demonstrated, this naming is made possible through the use of incisive theory and related practice – namely, speaking out! These subverters of what they consider to be unjust systems and practices insist that power and privilege that cannot withstand critical interrogation directed at its very foundations do not deserve to stand! This Marx has some very important similarities with Dewey's pragmatism, progressivism and reconstructionism. Marx viewed people as deserving the greatest concern in his philosophy. He constructed also a new unity composed of economics, philosophy and revolution. When one considers the state of affairs in the early twenty-first century it is not irresponsible to ask whether some newer versions of such unity should be considered in order to solve the human crises of our time.

3. AUTHENTIC EDUCATION

Marx did not believe that authentic education could be carried on in societies dominated by capitalism. Certainly not the kind of education he had in mind for the proletariat. Antonio Gramsci, who is two generations younger than Marx, learned, as he struggled within a somewhat different set of conditions, the principal role that education must play in order for workers and other subaltern people to understand themselves better within their working and overall life conditions[2]. Gramsci, like Marx, Dewey and Paulo Freire, grasped that knowing was not just a passive reflection or "getting right with" so-called reality; or the "out there" that was allegedly unaffected by cognition. Instead he argued that knowing could lead to collective liberatory action.[3] I maintain that bona fide criticality must derive from analyses that go far beyond intramural issues, important as they are. In this particular case, students must realize that school reform is dependent on many factors that exist within the larger and historical contexts

Gramsci developed new meanings for the concept of hegemony to help explain that the ruling classes and their agents did not dominate by naked force alone. In fact, the control of subaltern people was grounded in what is presently called manufactured consent. The promoters of the status quo in the Italy of Gramsci's time presented what existed as natural, if not inevitable, and universally beneficial. This propagandistic portrayal was grounded in an implicit claim that the rulers were in the possession, somehow, of the truth - or at least many truths! Of course, the hegemonists enjoyed the liberty to practice their trade because ultimately hegemony was and is backed by armed force. Gramsci believed that hegemony, backed-by state violence, could be contested and overcome. He realized that the institutional school played an important role in exercising hegemony; however, he thought it was possible that intramural teaching and learning could assist students to understand and break free of Plato's and others' caves. This realization that education need not be a part of unjust hegemony is easily understood and sometimes embraced by students who are encouraged to look critically at their school and other experiences. Gramsci tried to make the Italian socialist movement (and especially the Italian Communist Party) into projects for civic education aimed at preparing the working classes to govern themselves.

He understood the still too little recognized fact that all human beings are educable. He asserted that education, as opposed to training, must become a right – an

entitlement – for everyone, not just the rich and powerful Italians. He realized also that there are continuities and similarities between physical and mental labour. The working class youth of his place and time were well acquainted with the discipline of hard labour. As these young persons engaged in the struggle for meaningful education – in some cases in the form of what wealthy Italian youth already enjoyed – they could change the institutions and processes that they gained entrance into, as well as themselves. Gramsci and his comrades believed that engagement in this struggle could result in discrediting the mystification surrounding who could and allegedly could not succeed at academic work. Gramsci's current popularity among those who champion education for more democratic empowerment, social justice, respect for bona fide diversity and a more altruistic – if not "caring" – school and society is based on the realization that his ideas and struggles are relevant today – even in "developed" countries. This point is articulated well in *Gramsci and Education* (Borg et al, 2002). Many teacher education students are attracted to the profession because they "want to help kids." This laudable intention helps some of them to become interested in Gramsci's views on educability.

Gramsci provides support for those of us who contend that everyone has a "culture." Moreover, all of us are "intellectuals" in the sense that we live in various contexts and generate ideas, portrayals, representations and other ways in order to understand how conditions were developed and have become dominant. Furthermore, people who do not benefit from the hegemonic or more directly coercive status quos are capable of figuring out how their conditions could and should be both different and better. Antonio Gramsci started from the perspective of the student and saw the learning process as a movement toward self-realization within the contexts of the social, material and natural worlds. Many other radicals, democrats, progressives and other people of conscience can and do embrace Gramsci's perspective choice. It is my view that our students benefit from studying the tradition of critical theory and practice because they provide precedents upon which they can build. One need not start as though these valuable contributions by our forbears were not available.

He realized that in spite of our commonalities within the human condition there were differences as well. Gramsci anticipated our present understanding of difference and embraced various kinds and levels of intelligence, competencies, aptitudes and interests. He knew that our differences could and should be negotiated and understood in new and humane ways. Not surprisingly, Gramsci insisted that these negotiations must be guided by the necessity of considering the good of all. For him, "democracy ... cannot mean merely that an unskilled worker can become skilled. It must mean that every 'citizen' can 'govern' and that society places him [and her] ... in a general condition [through formal and informal education] to achieve this" (Hoare and Smith, 1971, 40). Every revolution has been preceded by great intellectual and political ferment and actions. Gramsci believed that during his place and time the working class must become conscious of itself and how its real interests were different from its putative "betters" and masters. Workers would learn to become their own masters via thought and struggle. He demonstrated poignantly his realization of education's importance and resulting action by including this on the masthead of the journal called *L'Ordine Nuovo* that he edited: "Instruct yourself because we need our intelligence. Agitate because we shall need our enthusiasm. Organize yourselves because we shall need all of our power." Editor Gramsci's slogan epitomizes his belief that so-called ordinary people can think well, engage in solidaristic collective struggles and hopefully achieve a more just and inclusive society. The Fascist government's "minister of justice" is said to have remarked that it was necessary to jail the best brain in the country so that his ideas would be confined. Gramsci was arrested and jailed even though he was a Member of Parliament at the time. We know also that his "Prison Notebooks" are read today by many who wish to continue the struggle in which he was once engaged. Skillful teachers can help their students make connections with historical precedents. By way of reinforcement, current studies of critical theory and practice are most efficaciously done when initially located within the histories of these ideas and deeds.

He understood that the creation of intellectuals who were "organically" from the working class itself would be very difficult, but possible. W. J. Morgan writes of:

> Gramsci's personal practice was exemplary, resting on his double conviction that theory which could not be translated into terms of fact was useless abstraction, while political action not guided by theory was fruitless and impulsive. His characteristic [teaching] method ... [was] "obstetric" or "Socratic." It envisaged mass education as a process of dialogue rather than a series of rhetorical statements of Party edicts.... A member of a discussion circle for young militants recalled: "Gramsci let us talk ... he never acted like a theoretical know all; he ... was a good listener. .... When he finally said something and summed up the discussion, we usually saw our mistakes and corrected them ourselves.... Gramsci saw education as an essentially critical and collective activity of the working class, judging it by its capacity to create autonomous class organizations and worker intellectuals who would be in an organic relationship with the vanguard Party (Morgan, 2002, 251).

When one considers Critical Theory, it is helpful to realize that it has developed from Marx's dialectical historical materialism and has been further developed by democratic Marxists. One can be "critical" in various ways; however, the specific theory being referred to herein is Marxist. This may sound provocative to some readers, but this is my scholarly thesis. Gramsci believed that democratic Marxism represented the best synthesis of what was most worthwhile in the Western tradition. His project was to develop further the free social person described by Marx – but whose ancestry could be traced back in historical time. He became convinced that a revolution would be needed in order to achieve this goal, namely the abolition of social class divisions that are caused by capitalism. The working class was exploited by capital in many ways. For Gramsci, economics, politics, culture, education and many other social institutions and activities were interdependent and part of a specific historical system or totality. The need to understand things historically and holistically in order to contest and overcome the status quo of his time is central to Gramsci's Critical Theory and education. His work represents a bridge from Marx to the Frankfurt School Critical Theorists. Both he and they had to deal with the failure of the proletariat to make the kind of revolution Marxists had anticipated.

4. ONE-DIMENSIONAL SOCIETIES

Herbert Marcuse, one of the most famous members of the Frankfurt School, wrote an influential book called *One-Dimensional Man* (1964). He maintained the one-dimensional societies that emerged after 1945 in the U.S. and in other so-called Western democracies were quasi-closed systems featuring capitalist hegemony, supported by the various class states. These post-war, capitalist democracies controlled production, distribution and the formulation of desire itself (see Pinar, this volume) in unprecedented ways. The formally democratic, class-stratified, Western countries delivered a multitude of consumer goods to their people; however, they were paradoxically not free. Marcuse argued brilliantly that the choices were confined mostly to what the consumer market had to offer – items to purchase that were developed and produced with ultimate sales, assisted by hidden persuaders, in mind. Moreover, he asserted that the atomizing power of monopoly/consumer capitalism created a commodity-like mass person who is trained to respond favorably to the most effective advertisements. Gratification was to be had mainly by purchasing and using goods, many of which are meretricious in their appeal and usefulness. Neil Postman (1985, 1979) has helped us understand this phenomenon when he claims that advertisement-driven television is the first curriculum in the U.S., whereas the K-12 public schools' curricula are distant seconds! This process has also affected putative democratic politics. Those who favor the democratic imperative on schooling-education over the capitalist one would be well served by taking Marcuse's analysis seriously. The arguments provided by Marcuse and Postman have been of interest to many students with whom I have worked. After all, they live within the aisles and corridors of this hyper-consumer society.

Marcuse called consumer persons in the one-dimensional society "well dressed," but manipulated, people within a non-democratically administered whole. He and his colleagues judged this kind of society irrational as a whole because its vaunted productivity is, in fact, destructive of the possibilities for a new economy that could overcome the unjust capitalist-worker labour contract and instead feature a fair distribution of what was produced. "The acceptance [not without disagreement and opposition by many persons] of this one-dimensional society by the [thus far] vast majority does not make it any less irrational according to Marcuse and his colleagues. The neo-Marxists of the Frankfurt School believed that advanced industrial society in the democratic West is *both* democratic and unfree" (Brosio 1980, 2).

It must be noted that whenever Marcuse and his colleagues posed the question of what is to be done, there was no agreed upon political answer. They did not provide specific plans for action. These Critical Theorists were forced to reconsider whether the use of reason as presented by Western philosophers was still a warranted process with which to help decide what was better, more just and more achievable than the alternatives. It must be emphasized that these Theorists and others featured in this chapter have never claimed omniscience. In fact, the fragility of our knowledge claims is acknowledged by all of them, as well as the present writer. This does not mean that we should disregard the resources of rationality at our disposal. They continued to wrestle with the question of whether secular, historical reason could assist in understanding "reality," in relation to being able to act justly in publicly defensible ways. They asked: how could reason, which became a basis for scientific inquiry, be guided by philosophy – which was still characterized by continuing inquiries into the dependability of reason itself as an epistemic tool and guide for warranted and "more" just action? The Critical Theorists understood the challenge caused by the success of modern science as it explained the world and people in mechanistic and determinist ways. Furthermore, "hard" science was increasingly successful in serving capitalism and the military with powerful products and weapons that threatened to overwhelm the "soft" side of Enlightenment reason – the version that was deemed promising to assist the Marxist democratic project. Marcuse and his Frankfurt colleagues feared that the achievements of the Enlightenment might be leading to the possible victory of totalistic capitalism rather than to liberty, equality and fraternity (hopefully including both genders). These issues must be introduced to those who aspire to become teachers.

Some thinkers were tempted to solve these dichotomies, contradictions and problems through rather abstract philosophy alone. However, Marx had insisted – before the Frankfurt generation – that the solution must be the result of revolutions in ideas *within the material world.* Marx's philosophical conception of historically grounded, human reason was based on his belief that people could achieve solutions through critical theory in synchronicity with mass collective action that could successfully challenge the dangerous, bastardized, "hard" side of Enlightenment reason. The Critical Theorists who came after Marx continued to argue that the best, and most likely only, way out of these contradictions and dichotomies was to consciously and systematically struggle together inclusively and democratically in order to construct rational ways of inquiry that could be trustworthy, albeit imperfect, guides for our epistemological claims and resultant actions. Gramsci would most likely agree had he been able to read the Frankfurt colleagues' work. John Dewey worked on some of the same problems; moreover, his insistence on "warranted assertibility" instead of "truth" claims is quite similar to what democratic Marxists have come to rely on. Paulo Freire can be included in this rough consensus as well. The fragile middle position that some Marxists, Critical Theorists, Dewey and Freire arrived at is located *between* (1) allegedly immutable, universal and transcendental truth claims that were increasingly supported by and/or replaced by misunderstood science – *and* (2) crude relativism, situationalism, or outright cynicism! The Critical Theorists argued that what is "true" and rational are the social forces in history that foster change in the direction of a free and rational community. These inquiries must be made known to teachers so that their practices do not become co-opted into the historical and steady parade characterized by "new' innovations, technical panaceas and camouflaged invitations (really imperatives) to continue the reproductive process of current schooling.

The Frankfurt colleagues argued that knowledge of how things are could not solely enable us to grasp how things might or should become. They struggled with how best to balance knowledge as mere description and as a critical tool. This endeavor has important ramifications for teacher education in terms of theory and practice. For example, should the emphasis be almost entirely on "how to" methodological approaches, mastering official knowledge, reducing problems of achievement or lack of to various psychological disorders and lack of ambition, or should we emphasize more systematically our abilities to critique current realities (including the political, socioeconomic conditions as they have consequences for schooling-education) based on criteria that goes well beyond the givens? Most teachers are in support of inquiry; however, Critical Theory includes asking whether or not the focus of inquiry is about the most profound, systematic and causal forces that must be named, understood and then acted upon. This question is central to the chapter before you.

During these times of turbulence and the melting of all that seemed solid into air, the public schools in democratic countries that also feature capitalist political economies are in the grip of a legitimacy crisis. The role of the school in response to the capitalist imperative, namely to produce willing, competent and uncritical workers, has been rocked by the turbulent "creative destruction" caused by the global economy under neoliberal control. Many students who play by the rules do not get jobs that provide a living wage. The school's response to the democratic imperative, specifically to educate students to become informed and critical citizens – accompanied by rights within the job sites themselves – has been forced on the defensive as a result of the rightist onslaught on bona fide democratic realities and gains caused by past eruptions of democracy.[4] In the face of this crisis how can theoretically empowered teachers convince their students, parents, heterogeneous publics and critics that what they (we) think and do is better (not best) practice compared to other kinds of educational philosophies, resulting curricula and pedagogies? Interested and responsible students and teachers can learn to place their more immediate problems and concerns into contexts like the ones offered above.

Marcuse did not give into despair as some have alleged. He looked to certain cracks in the one-dimensional society and encouraged us to look into aesthetic imagination as well as actual production in order to get beyond the administered capitalist consumer society and its logically complementary politics. Charles Reitz has written:

> Marcuse's aesthetic and social-philosophical links to educational issues are indissoluble. Marcuse stresses the educational value of the arts because of the qualitative difference he finds between the multidimensional kind of knowledge thought to be produced by the aesthetic imagination and the unidimensional kind of knowledge attributed to what he describes as the controlled and repressive rationalities of achievement, performance, and domination (Reitz, 2000, 9-10).

Marcuse looked to the outcasts – those who were not included in the shopping malls, police protection and the living wages provided during the post-war "golden age" of capitalism – for possible agency through which to contest the one-dimensional society. The proletarianization and downward mobility of many who were once inside the system provide opportunities to think beyond this failed current neoliberal experiment during "late" capitalism, as well as act collectively to overcome it. Many professional teachers are already aware of what downward mobility portends for their students and even themselves.

It is not just academic to ascertain if there are places within antidemocratic capitalism's totality where progressive forces can enact strategies and tactics, or if the room to act is increasingly constricted. The foundations of education students with whom I have worked were and are keenly interested in this issue – especially when it is introduced within critical historical contexts. The democratic left has faced this task historically. Are there spaces, where are they, where to begin and who can or should be the most important players in this struggle? Can they be rank ordered, should they be? Carl Boggs helps us to clarify and understand what we face.

> Under the transformed and highly fluid conditions of post-Fordism ... repoliticization demands a rethinking of some familiar dualisms – between the social and political realms, between movements and parties, between community and governance, between local and global. Any effort to ignore or downplay the reality of new social movements and identity politics [in contrast to social class based politics alone] overlooks some unique transformative elements in the post-Fordist context.... Conversely, the glib celebration of "civil society" as an emancipatory realm directed against bureaucratic state power not only sidesteps the issue of corporate colonization but also oversimplifies the nature of both state and civil society insofar as the boundaries that now presumably exist between the two are increasingly blurred.... Only through general popular engagements in the public sphere, leading to democratic transformation of both civil society and the state, can we imagine the kind of political renewal needed to sustain "deep citizenship" and confront major social problems (Boggs, 2000, 255).

Critical educators can help students understand important passages like the one above. Teachers who want to help students should themselves understand what is characteristic of their civil societies. An important question is," Where do the institutional schools fit into the concept and reality of a particular civil society?"

The way rightists and some liberals have used the term/concept – civil society – has played an important role in the reactionary project of the last thirty years in the U.S. and its "democratic" but capitalist allies. It has been argued that civil society is a place between the capitalist economy and the class state. Vaclav Havel celebrated the importance of civil society spaces in the former Soviet "satellite" countries in order to mount liberatory struggles. After the communist systems fell apart, some people in the former East Bloc countries are discovering what radicals in the West have known and even tried to tell their Central and Eastern European friends, namely that the reactionaries such as Reagan and Thatcher were not interested in freedom in their own countries except in terms of putative "free markets." It is quite evident that the U.S. and the other G-8 countries are not supporting bona fide democratic governments in the former communist countries today. John Ehrenberg has written that those who used civil society arguments against communist regimes conflated "economic regulation with political tyranny and their antistatist understanding of civil society blinded them to the dangers of the market. In the end, almost all of their civic forums, citizen groupings ... and social movements were swept away as traditional political structures emerged to apply the iron logic of the market" (Ehrenberg 1999, xv).

We democratic radicals have argued that in the U.S. and other "bourgeois democracies" the power of capitalism and its political and cultural allies have so saturated what is called civil society that it is doubtful this space can be used easily by those who want to fight against colonization of our everyday lives by capitalist logic and realities. This applies to the necessary effort to construct authentically democratic and inclusive ways to decide on public issues and, perhaps most importantly, to build a moral economy that is compatible with "deep" and meaningful, participatory democracy. As things stand today it is problematic at best and farcical at worst to view civil society as a somewhat neutral in (liberal terms) space. Marcuse argued that civil society was closer to a one-dimensional place wherein the forces behind hegemonic control are ready, able and tempted to unleash the gendarmes from their barracks at the first sign of any chance for radical democrats to begin seriously threatening the powers that be. Education that goes beyond training must deal with power in its complexities and places along past and present continuums.

Ehrenberg writes that the Frankfurt School colleagues began to study the development of capitalist dominance over technology, production and distribution. Henri Lefebvre describes this as the colonization of the quotidian by capitalism. I have analyzed this phenomenon in chapter six, "The Consequences of the Capitalist Imperative on Everyday Life," in *A Radical Democratic Critique of Capitalist Education (RDCCE)*. Chapter seven, "Capitalism's Mediated Influence Within School Sites," expands the analysis to the institutional school (Brosio, 1994). These analyses force us to consider carefully how much needs to be, or can be, done by progressives, democrats and their allies within and against societies that are in many ways, paradoxically, "democratic" and yet unfree. Ehrenberg (1999) reminds us that civil society can be justifiably characterized in terms of force, exclusion and great inequalities. If civil society has been conquered by capitalist power, then it is not surprising that rightists and reactionaries in the U.S. and elsewhere have helped sponsor the glorification of their civil society version to use against all who oppose capitalism and favor instead progressive state intervention to stop great transfers of wealth from working people to the very rich. The extension of democracy to economic decision-making is the most important challenge for progressive people who understand that a redistribution of wealth is the sine qua non for success in our attempts to make our schools and the education process more equal, just and relevant for all students.

5. HABERMASIAN THOUGHT

Jurgen Habermas, who is currently the best-known spokesperson of the Frankfurt tradition, believes that there remain many places and processes within our societies where the best of the Enlightenment values – as they have been adjusted by the more radical heirs of the eighteenth century – are still in play. It should not be surprising that educators are attracted to him. Habermas's interest in civil society includes theorizing about discursive public spheres and ideal speech contexts. Although opposed to much of postmodernist thought and a staunch champion of the Enlightenment, Habermas takes spoken and written communication very seriously. He has attempted to understand and promote better discourse within public places that are open to democratic, egalitarian and inclusive participation. A classroom is a public place; therefore, critical educators can develop curriculum and pedagogy that follow logically from the critical theories presented in this chapter. Habermas remains committed as a Critical Theorist to ground reason within the concrete conditions of life, but turns also to and depends on what we human beings can do under ideal – or as close to ideal as possible – conditions with regard to thinking through what is problematic and then hypothesizing how to act effectively in order to clarify and "solve" what was murky and troublesome. Obviously he is aware that these ideal conditions are difficult if not impossible to achieve. Still, constructing models facilitates being able to study problems holistically and profoundly. Habermas's epistemology, like his Marxist forbears, is necessarily radically democratic. His idea of inclusive discourse makes possible the linking of our immediate problems to more systematic analyses that can assist in understanding how what we undergo is linked to forces or causes that may not be recognized at first.

Dewey claimed that good education consists of converting "raw occurrences" – what we undergo – into a "composed tale of meaning," or what he called "experience." Habermas, like Dewey, advocates the democratization of **doing** philosophy, for epistemological and fairness reasons. Educators can and must play important roles in Habermas's project. In accord with the best of liberal progressive education, he advocates non-coercive discourse that allows and insists that we consider other interlocutors as valuable contributors rather than enemies. He believes that agreements are possible, although in class-stratified societies this is highly unlikely because of the great discrepancies in wealth, power and influence. Teachers must be aware of these possibilities and challenges as they develop their practice within the classroom. This challenge has plagued democratic Marxists as well as others who have sought to construct ideal speech contexts, but were blocked by the realities of power that opposed such democratic egalitarianism. What can and should be done about blockages helps us understand some important differences between radicals and liberals.

Habermas, his Frankfurt colleagues, Gramsci and Marx encourage us to examine language and writings critically, in order to find what is hidden or omitted. Good teachers have always done this and can become even better at it. As I have suggested throughout, improvement depends upon greater depth, breadth and the sharpness of critique. Habermas believes that we must keep talking **and acting** in order to make this process better – if not best! The better conditions that Habermas has in mind are related to Marx's views of the world and how capitalism is incompatible with bona fide democracy and the free development of every person. I am not attempting to build restrictive fences and do value allies who are not within the Marxist tradition; however being "critical" can and does mean many things to various people. Critical Theory must be understood as an achievement of Marxist suppositions, interests and intentions. "Criticality" can and has been co-opted by those who direct the hegemony within which we live. In my view there are many critical persons who are very helpful to the radical democratic project I favor. There are similarities and differences – sometimes nuanced but not always – among those of us on the democratic left(s) and this can add to our effectiveness. Having said this, we must keep in mind that Critical Theory is not to be confused with anyone's or everyone's perception of what being critical means. What we analyze, critique and consider possible or worthwhile actions must pose serious challenges to the undemocratic capitalist system and its schools if our work is to be called critical – if not Critical.

Some classroom teachers and their students can and do engage in discourse forms that are favored by Critical Theorists. These practices are based on the traditions of historical communities whose discussants used their collective intelligences to engage in a non-specialized version of the scientific method – a mode of inquiry embraced also by Dewey and some of the most effective progressive educators. Habermas suggests that face-to-face discussants should imagine a third person, namely a "generalized" other, who represents the authentic interests of the larger society. Teachers can practice this with their students. Habermas still believes that various versions of a "common good" can be arrived at through honest and informed talk. It seems self-evident to secularists that inclusive democratic talk and action are the only available means to achieve something beyond individual selfish interests. People who enter into the democratic discussions of Habermas's communication ethic are accountable to others for what they say and do. In fact, we must always be prepared and able to justify, by giving reasons, the beliefs underlying our personal and collective actions. This can and must be taught to our students if we value education for a lifetime of civic responsibility. The democratic imaginary must be made real, in the same way that blueprints are translated into construction - in school and society!

Authentic democratic procedures and discourse ethics championed by Habermas are aimed at making it more possible – and even mandatory – for people to renounce self-interest when confronted by superior arguments. One can understand why Habermas has attacked the postmodernist claim that it is impossible to agree on what words and concepts such as – superior – really mean, in the absence of putatively discredited "transcendental" verification connections. Unfortunately, these democratic procedures that Habermas wants to institutionalize were endangered early on when the bourgeoisie cleared civil society spaces for the emerging capitalist class to articulate mostly its members' fears and desires. Originally organized according to bourgeois concepts of reason, the burgeoning market soon pushed those who opposed its logic and reality to the sidelines. Naked class interest undermined and overwhelmed any believable claims that capitalists spoke for the emerging modern society as a whole. Habermas is aware that increasing commodification has eroded any public sphere's independence, as it becomes an adjunct to the capitalist system itself. According to Ehrenberg's reading of Habermas: "Unable to protect modernity from the commodity form, the public sphere can no longer bring reason to bear on political power" (Ehrenberg, 1999, 221). The great majority of people do not get to help shape public policy; therefore government itself, along with other public institutions, lack the legitimacy required for the general acceptance and subsequent smooth operation within many Western democracies. The legitimacy issue is present when it becomes apparent to students and parents that job preparation for very different slots along the career stratification is occurring instead of education in the broader and deeper sense.

On a cautionary note: my hope for, if not faith in, education that has the potential to help develop critical students, is tempered by worries that the vaunted opportunities in class-dominated democracies for ordinary people to be able to organize collectively in order to achieve better and more just conditions have always been problematic, if not vulnerable and even fragile. Marx believed that class struggle was the best way to combat the injustices of capitalist domination. Obviously the need for education and organized collective action are both necessary; however, I think we must be very careful not to overestimate schooling's (even when it is educative) power to create a "new social order". Ehrenberg supports my cautious concern:

> Habermas wants integration and legitimacy by way of communication instead of domination, but it remains to be seen if the market's structural inequalities can sustain a public sphere from which relations of power ... are purged and within which all actors move in conditions of equality. Private rights, formal equality, and the rule of law are probably not enough to constitute a sphere of rational-critical discourse in an environment of pervasive material inequality. All communications are inevitably constrained, and there is no reason to expect that the better argument can prevail in civil societies that are so penetrated by the market. .... Discourse ethics cannot constitute a democratic public life in an environment marked by political conflict, class struggle, violence, [as well as "savage inequalities" in our schools], and the [overall] structural inequalities of capitalism (Ehrenberg, 1999, 223-4).

6. CRITICAL THEORY, CURRICULUM AND PEDAGOGY

I have written the following in the afterword of my monograph called *The Frankfurt School*.

> The men of the Frankfurt School have given us valuable insights and guidance concerning what is to be done. .... The hope for school reform is not independent of the issues analyzed in this monograph. The focus on intramural, narrowly pedagogical issues reduces almost everyone to an unwitting apologist for the status quo. Those of us who are interested in authentic progressive school reform must educate ourselves on the great issues of our time.... It is important ... to study, involve ourselves in the issues of our town, neighborhood, and workplace – as well as seeking to relate these local (but important) issues to the deeper and broader ones of our historical period (Brosio, 1980, 45-6).

Ultimately, educators must develop their own versions of critical theory, as well as the curricula and pedagogies that are developed logically from the former. I believe that it should include analyses of school success and lack of, in reference to social class, political economy, capitalism as a system, as well as how race, ethnicity, gender, sexual preferences and "other identities" have been used to divide people and punish them through invidious comparison to the "norm." Freire has helped us realize that hopefulness is a necessary, although not sufficient, attitude as we join the continuing historical struggles.

Peter McLaren is correct to stress the changing nature of the capitalist system while cautioning us to remember what has remained essentially constant. "In the spirit of the Frankfurt School he [McLaren] advised critical educators to realize the postmodernist explosion of signs, signals and images that tend to make opaque the real relations of power and privilege during late capitalism"(Brosio, 2000a, 108). I have argued elsewhere in a section called "The Need for Portrayal and Bravery": "The great political and educational challenge of our historical period is to develop representations and portrayals of the socioeconomic and political realities that structure our lives. The crucial link between hegemony and the ungloved iron fist must be revealed through politics, education and artistic depiction. Capitalism's totalizing power seems unrepresentable at this time; therefore, the ability to successfully move the democratic imperative forward upon the State, the school and other sites may be on hold until the achievement of some [better] degree of class consciousness. However, this state of awareness is difficult to achieve, in part, because postmodernist culture is characterized by disconnected and decontextualized images. In Fredric Jameson's view, the postmodernist celebration of randomness, heterogeneity and claims of unprecedented complexity reinforce the difficulty in understanding the, as yet unrepresentable, capitalist totality. Relatedly, the positing [by some postmodernist thinkers] of a decentered, fragmentary and incoherent subject makes opposition to antidemocratic capitalism nearly impossible" (Brosio, 1993, 480). I am convinced that this passage cannot be emphasized enough in these times. Furthermore, conscientious teachers at most levels of instruction can take this call for representation and portrayal as a framework for their own curricular and pedagogic creativity.

Critical Theory and the critical forms of pedagogy that have resulted from it – in addition to other compatible sources – provide many helpful insights for interested teachers. Critical pedagogy is a tool for teachers who wish to empower subordinate students and their parents. Considering the talent and imagination of many teachers, this task could be achieved – if teachers thought it was an important goal. However, the working conditions of teachers need to be improved in order for the many to feel secure enough to engage in such teaching and hoped-for learning. Many teachers who are well-intentioned with regard to weakening the correspondence of students' socioeconomic statuses and "identities" with school success or failure bump up against various structural barriers in the schools themselves – ones that exist also in the society.

The practice of critical pedagogy must be evaluated according to whether it convinces students of its value and relevance, or the lack of, to their own lives. People must participate in their own education and liberation. History is open! Nevertheless, as we know, the openness is no guarantee that we can actually make history just as we like. According to David Livingstone "there is no 'quick fix', no clear road from the discomfort felt by so many today to liberatory social change. The briefest engagement should be sufficient to convince ... [us] that deeper practical understanding ... of the complex layers of ideological forms ... [and] of the material bases of group conflict and co-operation, as they limit both local and wider efforts at progressive ... change in advanced capitalism, is urgently needed" (Livingstone, 1987, 12).

As has been stated, there are many examples and sources of critical pedagogical ideas and practices. This is not to claim that those who view critical pedagogy as relevant and useful draw upon the specific writings of the Critical Theorists of the Frankfurt School. The editors of *The Critical Pedagogy Reader* are helpful in developing further this point.

> The struggle for public democratic schooling in America has been a multidimensional enterprise that has for over a century occupied the dreams, hearts, and minds of many educators. These educators were not only seriously committed to the ideal and practice of social justice within schools, but to the transformation of those structures and conditions within society that functioned to thwart the democratic participation of all

people. Critical pedagogy loosely evolved out of a yearning to give some shape and coherence to the theoretical landscape of radical principles, beliefs, and practices that contributed to an emancipatory ideal of democratic education in the U.S. during the twentieth century.... It constituted a significant attempt to bring an array of divergent views and perspectives to the table, in order to invigorate the capacity of radical educators to engage critically with the impact of capitalism and gendered, racialized relations upon the lives of students from historically disenfranchised populations (Darder et al, 2003, 2).

The editors lay out some of the major influences on the formation of critical pedagogy in the book's introduction. The listing of their inclusions is relevant herein because it provides the reader suggestions for where to find those who have written about critical pedagogy – including descriptions of actual practice. The educators and activists include Myles Horton, the founder of the Highlander Folk School; Herbert Kohl and the open school movement; Jonathan Kozol and Maxine Greene. Samuel Bowles and Herbert Gintis, Martin Carnoy, Michael Apple (all of whom kept the problem of capitalism front and center) are mentioned. Henry Giroux who was a pioneer in using the term critical pedagogy, M.L. King, Angela Davis, Cesar Chavez, Malcolm X, Ivan Illich, Paulo Freire and Augusto Boal, Antonio Gramsci, Michel Foucault, and The Frankfurt School deservedly make the list. The editors: Darder, Baltodano and Torres include also the philosophical principles of critical pedagogy. They include cultural politics, political economy, historicity of knowledge, dialectical theory, ideology and critique, hegemony, resistance and counter-hegemony, praxis (the alliance of theory and practice), dialogue and conscientization. The editors provide also various critiques of critical pedagogy. It must be noted that the various quotes from those who have influenced critical pedagogy placed at the very beginning of the introduction to *The Critical Pedagogy Reader* start off with John Dewey. My book *PSCCDE* includes some of the same writers and activists. The following are some of the book's chapter titles: "Various Reds," "Dewey, the Progressive Protest – With a Whiff of Reconstruction," "Liberationists: Freire and Various Spiritualists," "The Politics of Identity: The Struggle for Human Dignity is Expanded," and "Back to Postmodernism: Problems and Possibilities – With a Touch of Green." Educational practitioners can consider and study this literature as they attempt to help students develop further their human potentials.

The journal, *Rethinking Schools* and *The Rouge Forum News* (online and print) both provide offerings concerning education for democratic empowerment, social justice, respect for diversity and other radical and progressive issues.[5] Both of them are aimed at theory and practice, that is, *praxis!* According to Henry Giroux:

Many writers in the critical education tradition have attempted to challenge the right wing fundamentalism behind educational and social reform [more accurately: reaction] in both the United States and abroad while simultaneously providing ethical signposts for a public discourse about education and democracy that is both prophetic and transformative. Eschewing traditional categories, a diverse number of critical theorists and educators have successfully exposed the political and ethical implications of the cynicism and despair that has become endemic to the discourse of schooling and civic life. In its place, such educators strive to provide a language of hope (Giroux, 2000, xiv).

7. LIVING TRADITIONS

I wish to reinforce in this last section some of what has been argued previously. Democratic Marxism and Critical Theory are living traditions. We can and should help develop further these traditions as historical problems and possibilities take on somewhat different characteristics for us, although remembering that Critical Theory is Marxist in its assumptions. Moreover, in my view, historical Marxist thought that is representative of what Marx actually wrote and said is crucial to any profound and holistic understanding of what is happening presently. This applies also to some of the most important things that can and should be done. David Held (1980) maintains that the Frankfurt School colleagues all considered Marx's work on political economy as of central importance to their own inquiries. However, they concluded that, in spite of the capitalist economy's great importance with regard to politics, society, culture, education and so forth, it was too narrow a base when considered alone for the development of ideas that grew out of Marx's original work!

The Critical Theorists maintained that socialism *and* liberty must be parts of a good and rational society. Furthermore, they believed that the means to achieve this condition must be compatible with the ends. They responded to those who claimed that the ends justified the means with a stinging retort: what justifies the ends? Their emphases on aesthetics and culture were intended to help their contemporaries understand that the economy is not a separate place or zone. As Held has written:

> ...the critique of political economy does not provide a sufficient basis to investigate the increasing encroachment of the market and bureaucratic organizations into areas of life hitherto free of them and that the general interlocking of 'base' and 'superstructure,' of civil society and the polity, seems to make radical alternatives to the present society remote (Held, 1980, 361).

The Frankfurt colleagues and Held might be more alarmed were they to experience and comment on the present state of what they sagaciously foresaw!

Critical Theory takes structure and the impediments it presents to volition as a given; however, its creators sought to study the complex relationships between social practices and structure, as well as the mediation of all the forces at play *within* complex societies and *by* human beings. They recognized that there are no clear demarcations between objective and subjective. These insights are very relevant today because of the "development" beyond what Marcuse and his colleagues had experienced. Although this is not the place to challenge postmodernist thought in depth, my view is that the Frankfurt School members anticipated many of the issues that concern postmodernists; however, the former's commitment to what Marx had achieved constitutes a marked difference between them and the latter. I agree with Held in the following passage:

> The Frankfurt School and Habermas sought to extend and adapt the insights of Marx's work in order to reveal the complex factors that hinder people coming to consciousness of themselves as capable of different action.... They directed attention to the effects of domination not only in production but also in the family, the environment and other areas of life. Consequently, their work transformed the concept of the political; it directed attention to issues such as the division of labour, sexism, ecological problems as well as the central question of ownership and control. This has crucial ... significance that was recognized by sections of the New Left in the 1960s. In short, Critical Theory

took Marxism into a range of new areas.... [This] helped to open up many dimensions of life to critical social analysis and active intervention (Held, 1980, 363).

Teacher educators must ensure that our students can understand passages such as the one from Held. Furthermore, we must strive to help students relate these kinds of ideas to their own curricular and pedagogical goals. Obviously, in the end the classroom teachers at all levels must do something! The same is true for their students! Lesson plan construction must be accomplished with the recognition that there is an important literature beyond "how to".

In keeping with what educators can and should do in these times, I shall reinforce what has been implied and even stated earlier in this chapter. The supposition by many writers during this "postmodernist" period that human beings, as epistemic subjects, are inadequately equipped to know and understand complex phenomena does not bode well for those who claim that current socioeconomic, political, cultural, educational, as well as other processes and institutions we encounter, are devilishly complex, difficult to comprehend as systems – and even opaque. Many observers and writers contend that the combination of epistemic weakness and unprecedented complexity "out there" make any kind of "grand narrative" explanations impossible. These writers have accused the Enlightenment project and related Marxist thought of being just talk and commentary, without any objective grasp of what might be called reality and structure. I have addressed these issues in chapter fourteen, "Postmodernism as the Cultural Skin of Late Capitalism: Educational Consequences," in *RDCCE* (Brosio,1994).

Marshall Berman argues that modernist writers, artists, musicians and others have created educative representations of earlier forms of capitalism. He credits Marx as a great modernist intellectual, writer and *artist*. The very alive, real and convincing characters who appear in Marx's masterpiece *Capital* (1867) were understandable to his contemporaries and to us. Berman's brilliant account of Marx as a great modernist artist can be found in his books, for example, *All That Is Solid Melts Into Air: The Experience Of Modernity* (1988) and *Adventures In Marxism* (1999). Marx's achievement was to explain how capitalism worked as a system and how it must and could be opposed and overcome by working people. He made the grim facts of economic life "come alive" through his understanding and artistry. There are many related sources that are available today, albeit mostly outside of the mainstream media, that can help alert and studious teachers to translate what they have learned into effective teaching practices in their classrooms and elsewhere. Discussions of these issues can be and are in fact organized around the need for teachers to take seriously what their students already know and to help them name the world more effectively, as Freire would have us do. The teachers must be committed also to viewing themselves as life-long students.

My experiences as a teacher educator have taught me how wonderfully inventive teachers can be at any level of instruction, and in each of the subject areas, as they relate the needs of their students to what is best of the various disciplines. Social studies and literature are obvious candidates for such teaching and learning; however, music education, art, speech, theatre, mathematics, science, physical education, and even computer "literacy" can be taught in ways to get beyond the mere imparting of skills. Edward R. Adams wrote a fine paper as part of the requirements in my philosophy of education class in 1990: "The Emergence of Socio-political Themes through Music in Public Education." Here is an excerpt from this relevant work.

> As an art form, music extends inherent, persuasive qualities that transcend social class while lyrics add an additional veneer of response provoking possibility. Utilizing this motivational vehicle, an artistic and socially conscious group of urban intellectuals stimulated a significant segment of American [actually, U.S.] youth from the 1940s through the 1980s.... Their purpose was to arm and equip attitudinally a new generation with empathy and dedication to improve the human condition. That condition was to include a peaceful, non-violent world and nation; ecological sensibility, workplace safety; employment ... desegregation and civil rights; the brotherhood of mankind [sic]; migrant and minority rights; social justice; human dignity; compassion for the handicapped; and varying degrees of gender equity. Their methodology was to bring a democratization process to the arts. (Adams, 1990. This unpublished paper can be had upon request.)

Frederic Jameson believes that culture "cleaves" to the very skin of economic systems; therefore they both must be analyzed in terms of their organic and dynamic relationships. Consequently, it is possible to connect our daily experiences to structural realities and forces that underlie the vicissitudes of everyday life. He contends that a positive definition of ideology allows us to create representations of our local positions in reference to larger realities that initially exceed our ability to relate to and thus understand. The class system that is intrinsic to capitalism – as it is exploited additionally and more specifically by taking advantage of racial, ethnic, gender, sexual orientation, and other "differences" – can be understood in these times by those who work energetically and in long-term disciplined ways. Jameson is correct when he complains that the inability or lack of effort to "map spatially" in terms of power, class, privilege, wealth, access and so forth impedes our abilities to act effectively in order to overcome exploitation and other injustices. Jameson challenges us with the following:

> In the early market stage of capitalism, limited and immediate experiences of people still permitted them to understand in a congruent manner the socioeconomic forms that governed their lives.... For example, if art focused [solely] upon a certain section of London, it missed the connections with colonial India and the whole imperial system that had an increasing impact on the daily lives of Londoners [however, they did come to see the connections because of informal education](Brosio 1994, 605).

Fortunately there are many persons around the world who understand that when the U.S. government has a cold the whole world must sneeze! Educators and others who are interested in a critical educated body politic must understand the barriers and opportunities that exist within the *totality* of the current global capitalist system – one that includes various forms of neoimperialism – in order to do what is best for and with our students.

8. CONCLUSION

Most of us encounter the world as fragmentary and disconnected. We must learn to overcome this disadvantage through the ability to construct cognitive maps that can empower us to relate our quotidian experiences to the totality of global capitalism and its attendant class realities. This is necessary in order for us to become effective political agents who can strive collectively to confront and hopefully overcome what we have succeeded in comprehending. I contend that democratic coalitions must address a dangerous divisive problem, namely the tension between social identity and cultural recognition on the one hand and social-class struggles aimed at remedies for economic injustice on the other. Nancy Fraser has addressed this issue and

> realizes that the political economy and culture are inextricably related, therefore justice requires both redistribution and recognition.... Because socioeconomic injustice is rooted in ... the expropriation of the fruits of one's labour, deprivation due to inadequate standards of living and so forth – it is necessary to restructure radically the divisions of labour, develop more public control and democratic answerability to macro investment policies, push for more progressive redistribution of income, and to insist on greater access to key resources. Cultural injustice is grounded in ... social patterns of representation, interpretation, and communication. Examples include being treated as though invisible, disrespected, "othered," and so forth; therefore remedies for cultural injustice require cultural-symbolic changes, that is, different and better recognition of differences. Fraser realizes however that cultural recognition is ... a form of redistribution; furthermore, redistributive remedies presuppose a conception of recognition, namely, the equal moral worth of everyone (Brosio, 2000b, 397).

The editors of *Rethinking Marxism* (Summer 2002) comment on an article by John O'Kane. They explain that the latter's contribution includes commentary on how culture and economy are now "saturated" in recent or late capitalism. The goal is to make sense of "complex illusions" that have been manufactured as part of the "cultural economy" of today's capitalist system. Once again we learn that such understanding is the sine qua non of successful dissent and opposition. According to O'Kane, culture:

> spawns an aesthetics of choice which mimics the spectacle through a bewildering array of images. Its excessive presence reinforces the experience of choosing as freedom, but this [stage of] capitalism's effective mix of superfluous triviality and reduction of real options blinds us to the social outside. As culture lies apparently independent, commodity consciousness saturates a world shown as a mere catalog of products. Important social concerns are refigured through the englobing presence of markets as one elongated 'Infomercial' that defies systematic understanding (O'Kane, 2002, 17).

Critical educators, within places called schools and extramurally, can and must defy the defiers.

ENDNOTES

[1] I presented a paper – "High Stakes Tests: Reasons to Strive for Higher Marx" - at the Rouge Forum Summer Institute on Education and Society at the University of Louisville in June 2003. Slightly altered versions of this paper can be found in: Notes & Abstracts in American and International Education, Fall 2003, 2, 1-22, and The Journal for Critical Education Policy Studies Vol. 1, No. 2, October 2003. Retrieved January 12, 2004 from http://www.jceps.com/?pageID=article&articleID-17.

[2] For a recent insightful and profound analysis of Gramsci's ideas on the central role played by schooling-education, see Carmel Borg and others (2002), editors, *Gramsci and Education.*

[3] See chapter six, "Liberationists: Freire and Various Spiritualists," in my PSCCDE for some examples of affinity between Gramsci and Freire – along with certain liberation philosophers and theologians.

[4] For an analysis of these eruptions, see: RDCCE, chapters ten and eleven.

[5] I offer this example of Rethinking Schools, Fall 2003, Vol. 18, No. 1, as introductory to the journal. The editors state the following on the backside of the cover: "We stress a grassroots perspective combining theory and practice and linking classroom issues to broader policy concerns. We are an activist publication...." The Rouge Forum, according to its founders, "is a group of educators, community organizers, students, and parents seeking a democratic society. We are interested in questions like these: How can we teach against racism, national chauvinism, and sexism in an increasingly ... undemocratic society? How we can gain enough real power to keep our ideals and still teach and learn?" The RF can be accessed on the www

REFERENCES

Adams, E. R. (1990). *The emergence of socio-political themes through music in public education.* Unpublished paper.
Berman, M. (1988). *All that is solid melts into air: The experience of modernity.* New York: Viking Penguin.
Berman, M. (1999). *Adventures in Marxism.* London: New York: Verso, 1999
Boggs, C. (2000). *The end of politics: Corporate power and the decline of the public sphere.* New York: The Guilford Press.
Borg, C., Buttigieg, J. and Mayo, P. (Eds.). (2002). *Gramsci and education.* Lanham: Rowman & Littlefield.
Brosio, R. A. (1980). *The Frankfurt School: An analysis of the contradictions and crises of liberal capitalist societies.* Muncie, IN: Ball State Monograph Number Twenty-Nine.
Brosio, R. A. (1993). Capitalism's emerging world order: The continuing need for theory and brave action by citizen-educators. *Educational Theory, 43,* 467-482.
Brosio, R. A. (1994). *A radical democratic critique of capitalist education.* New York: Peter Lang.
Brosio, R. A. (2000a). *Philosophical scaffolding for the construction of critical democratic education.* New York: Peter Lang.
Brosio, R. A. (2000b). Issues and arguments concerning class, gender, race, and other 'Identities.' *Educational Studies, 31,* 393-406.
Darder, A., Baltodano, M. & Torres, R. D. (Eds.). (2003). *The critical pedagogy reader.* London: Routledge Falmer.
Ehrenberg, J. (1999). *Civil society: The critical history of an idea.* New York: New York University Press.
Fromm, Eric. (1961). *Marx's concept of man.* New York: Frederick Ungar.
Giroux, H. (2000). Series foreword. In T. A. Osborne (ed). *Critical Reflection and the Foreign Language Classroom.* London: Bergin & Garvey.
Held, D. (1980). *Introduction to critical theory: Horkheimer to Habermas.* Berkeley: University of California Press.
Hoare, Q. and Smith, G. (Eds.). (1971). *Selections from the prison notebooks of Antonio Gramsci.* New York: International Publishers.
Livingstone, D. & Contributors. (1987). *Critical pedagogy and cultural power.* South Hadley, MA: Bergin & Garvey.
Marcuse, H. (1964). *One-Dimensional man: Studies in the ideology of advanced industrial society.* Boston: Beacon Press.
Morgan, W. J. (2002). Antonio Gramsci and Raymond Williams: (eds.). *Gramsci and Education.* Lanham, MD: Rowman & Littlefield.
O'Kane, J. (2002). Capital, culture, and socioeconomic justice. *Rethinking Marxism, 14*(2), 1-23.
Postman, Neil. (1979). *Teaching as a conservative activity.* New York: Delacorte Press.

Postman, N. (1985). *Amusing ourselves to death: Public discourse in the age of show business.* New York: Viking.
Reitz, C. (2000). *Art, alienation, and the Humanities.* Albany: State University of New York Press.
Wingo, G. M. (1965). *The Philosophy of American education.* Boston: D.C. Heath.
Wingo, G. M. (1974). *Philosophies of education: An introduction.* Lexington, MA: D.C. Heath.

BARBARA J. THAYER-BACON

SHARED AUTHORITY IN DEMOCRATIC CLASSROOMS:

Communities-always-in-the-making

Abstract. This project seeks to develop a relational democratic political theory of individuals in relation to their communities, highlighting the transactional relationship that exists between individuals and others while striving to be critical and anti-racist. The larger project involves a study of students from five major cultural areas within the USA: Mexican, African, and Native Americans, as well as Japanese and Chinese Americans. This paper includes a study of site-based visits to indigenous schools in Africa as well as visits to American school/community settings where this cultural group represents the majority population. This exploration serves as a means of better understanding the ways in which minority students from diverse cultures might be best served in a complex and diverse society such as the United States of America. This chapter will draw from the theme of "shared authority" highlighted in Thayer-Bacon's study of African American students.

1. INTRODUCTION

I am studying five major cultural areas with community-focused cultural values, the Mexican, African, and Native Americans, as well as the Asian cultures of Japan and China, to help me in my efforts to develop a sociopolitical philosophical theory that has a transactional individual community focus (individuals affect and are connected to others and others affect and are connected to individuals). I began the development of such a theory in my (1998) *Philosophy Applied to Education: Nurturing a Democratic Community in the Classroom*, with Charles Bacon as contributing author. In Chapter One of that text I considered individualist theories influenced by Locke and Rousseau (also known as classical liberalism), which I argued have had the strongest influence on public schools in the USA. I contrasted individualist theories to socialist theories influenced by philosophers such as Plato and Marx (also known as communitarian theories). I offered a third alternative, democratic theory as developed by John Dewey, which I hoped brought out the strengths of individually and socially focused theories as well as addressed their weaknesses. I argued that the world we live in is a transactional world that is continually in process, it is an interactive, inter-relational world where individuals affect their social groups *and* social groups affect individuals (Dewey, 1916/1966). Dynamic changes take place with the self and the community, because of their interaction with each other. As a result, all are affected.

Great changes have happened in political philosophy and in societies at large since Dewey was writing. We live in times that Nancy Fraser (1997) describes as

K. Cooper and R. White (eds.), The Practical Critical Education, 95–109.

"postsocialist." Today, key underlying assumptions of democratic theory are being questioned and dismissed. Dewey's liberal democratic theory focused on individual freedom and autonomy, even as he offered us the possibilities of moving beyond individualism with his theory of social transaction (Dewey and Bentley, 1949/1960) and, he assumed, an Enlightenment-type of rationalism, even as he showed us how to move beyond this rationalism in his arguments for truths as warranted assertions (Dewey, 1938/1955). Enlightenment rationalism and the idea of a unitary subject have come under serious criticism by postmodernists, feminists, and critical theorists. Fraser (1997) says we live in times when group identity has supplanted class interests and when the need for recognition overshadows the need for re-distribution. She suggests we live in times when no credible vision of an alternative to the present order is available, that the visions we have lack the power to convince because they bracket questions of political economy. The visions she refers to include: radical democracy, multiculturalism, political liberalism, and communitarianism.

My project aims to develop a credible alternative, a relational, pluralistic political theory that moves beyond liberal democracy as well as socialist theories. I also aim to consider how such a credible alternative translates into our public school settings. In order to help me address my own limitations and better understand tough questions and issues a relational, pluralistic political theory must face in our pubic schools, I am spending time in USA schools where the majority of the students historically have been disenfranchised from the USA's "democracy." In particular, I am spending time with Mexican, African, and Native Americans in their schools (whom Ogbu refers to as involuntary minorities: Lomotey, 1990; Romo & Falbo, 1996; Ogbu, 1991). I am also spending time with students who seem to be "making it" within the current school system: Japanese and Chinese American students (model minorities, Nieto, 1992). Additionally, I am going back to the students' countries of origin and spending time in schools there, to give me further comparisons. I have learned a great deal from these school visits. I will use what I have learned to help me recommend school reform that is necessary to translate a relational and pluralistic political theory into educational theory for public schools in the USA. However, I think this project has the potential for implications beyond the boundaries of the USA, as classical liberalism has been imposed or embraced by the educational systems of all countries colonized by England, France and, more recently, the USA. Students from community-based cultural backgrounds, which include the majority of indigenous people, have struggled to succeed in individualized classrooms worldwide. I hope to contribute a relational, pluralistic educational theory that will help *all* students have a chance of actively participating in a democratic society-always-in-the-making.

In this chapter I want to share some of what I learned from my visits to African American and West African schools under the general theme of *shared authority*. I want to consider the key concept of *shared authority* in a democracy-always-in-the-making in contrast to classical liberal, conservative, and radical views of individual authority. An excellent essay written by Henry Giroux (1997) on authority will help with this consideration. I will begin by sharing some stories from my visits to Junior Secondary School (JSS, similar to USA middle schools) and River High School

(RHS). These stories will help us discover how the concept of *authority* translates for different teachers in the schools I visited. I will then discuss the theoretical implications of the practices I observed in the section that considers putting theory and practice together, and the possibilities for getting beyond liberal democracy today. I will show how the emphasis on individual development changes to a transactional view of individuals-in-relation-to-others in a democracy-always-in-the-making.

2. STORIES FROM THE FIELD

In the spring of 2002, I spent the equivalent of one week each at a high school, middle school and elementary school in Tennessee where the schools have a majority African American population. In June, 2002, I spent a week observing a K-3, a 3-5 and a 6-8 school system in a small village two hours from the capital, Accra, of Ghana, West Africa, where I was the first white woman to study their schools, or reside in their village for that matter.[1] These schools graciously opened their doors to me and invited me to visit after I wrote to ask permission. In my letter I explained that I am not a qualitative or quantitative researcher seeking to do an ethnographic field study, but rather, I am a philosopher of education and my project is education political theory writing. However, as a pragmatist and a scholar in Cultural Studies, it is vital that my theory writing be informed by practice, in order to keep my theory grounded in the historical, local, contingent, everyday world. If I do not turn to the everyday world of schooling practice in various cultures, I risk writing a theory that assumes/imposes a universal, abstract perspective as if it were everyone's Reality. A theory that is separated from everyday practice will be unable to actually address anyone's particular reality. This is why I sought to immerse myself in these particular schools.

2.1. Ghana, West Africa

In Ghana, Religious and Moral Education is a regular part of the curriculum in the public schools. The public school I visited was started by a Presbyterian church and it is now run by the state. Even the recycled uniforms the children wear still display badges that say "(name of village) Presbyterian Primary School" from the days when the church supplied the resources for the school. The school day starts with all the children lined up outside their classrooms, singing patriotic songs and saying "The Lord's Prayer." Aside from a daily half-hour class on Religious and Moral Education, the children also participate in Worship for a half hour on Wednesdays, where all the children in the Junior Secondary School come together to sing religious songs, hear Bible verses and a short sermon and give monetary donations to help others. I observed the JSS Religious and Moral Education teacher, Fortune, several times during my week-long visit and would like to share some of my field notes from those observations.[2]

2.1.1.Day 1, Tuesday:

In Fortune's class of 33-57 students (the number varied depending on the day and the class), although the majority of the students are Christians, she teaches them about Christian, Moslem and Traditional religious beliefs (Indigenous beliefs). One day her topic was on the Islamic religion, another day her topic was on taboos for the three religious groups. The students do not leave the room for different classes; instead, the teachers come to them. When Fortune walks into the classroom she announces, "No talking." All the students in unison respond, "Yes, Madam." Again she says, "No talking," and again they respond, "Yes, Madam." Now she is ready to begin. She asks a couple of questions and the students answer for her. When the students answer correctly she says, "Clap for her." "Clap for him." All the students in unison clap a rhythm, "clap, clap, clap-clap-clap, clap." If they say a wrong answer, the whole class, including the teacher, says like a moan, "Ehhh!!" Next Fortune goes over to the teacher's table and picks up a cane. (I wonder, what is the cane for?) She walks up and down the isles, teaching them about Islam. She goes over the five daily prayers of Islam and when they are observed. Each prayer has a name and she has them all repeat the names several times, orally, together. She writes this information on the board, then they copy it down in their copybooks. (This oral recitation-board copying technique occurred in most of the classes I observed, due to lack of books and supplies for the students. Fortune has the one and only religion/moral education book for this class.) She reminds them that for Friday's class they have an exam. They are then asked to take their assignment book and start with the questions on the board. "Any questions?" "No, Madam." "Any questions?" "No, Madam." She puts the questions on the board and they begin to copy them and answer them. "Take your time and write for me. If you misspell, I'll just count it wrong because I can't read it." They respond "Yes, Madam." At 4:30 p.m. Fortune walks out of the classroom while the students work until the dismissal bell rings.

2.1.2. Day 2, Wednesday:

The next day I had the opportunity to see what Fortune does with the cane beside just hold it in her hand or use it as a pointer for what is written on the board. After Worship, the afternoon classes begin with attendance, which takes some time as there are 57 students in the entire JSS afternoon classes, with 2-3 students sitting together sharing each of the desks. Fortune waves her cane and bangs it on the teacher's table to tell them to get quiet. Students organize their copybooks on the teacher's table for her to grade and, while another teacher teaches the students a Vocational Skills class in the room, Fortune sits at the teacher's table and grades the students work. Periodically, as Fortune grades, she lectures to the students but she is speaking in Ghanaian dialect so I do not understand what she says. Then she says, "How do you spell 'prayer'?" "How do you spell 'observed'?" The person spelled it 'prayr' and 'obserrvd'. "Eh!!!" (said by the teacher and the students). She is publicly correcting the students, although she did not name who did this misspelling. The Vocational Skills teacher finishes writing on the board what the students must copy and is done with her lesson. Then Fortune announces, "If you got below *40% - you are going to get lashes*." She waves the cane. She sends a boy to bring her a second cane from another classroom. Then she passes back the copybooks so the students can see what their grades are. Both girls sitting by me received below 40% grades. They start to whimper. I ask them softly, "Is she joking? Does she really mean to hit you with the cane?" They assure me she is not joking. Fortune starts with the row right by where I sit, and asks the students to voluntarily come to the front of the room one by one if they have received below 40%. She canes the students, starting with the two girls sitting right by me. Each child has to come to the front of the room and stand facing the blackboard and she gives them several light swats on the butt and then a hard one on their thighs. Yikes! The number of lashes varies with students, depending on how they respond to them. If they dodge the lashes they get more and if they are too stoic in receiving the lashes they seem to get more too. 1-2-3 times hard. Some boys get 6-7 hard lashes and one on the back. Tears begin to stream down my face and I feel sick. All the kids who got below 40% on their test were caned. I saw eight kids caned before I left at 2:05 p.m.

I talked to the adults we were staying with about caning that evening. I discovered they have all been caned, as have my West African friends in the USA I have learned since returning home. I was told that caning is not allowed in the cities anymore and they're not supposed to do it – but out here in the little villages it is still done. They all talked about how it is needed for discipline, so the kids will be motivated to learn and work harder. They talked about in the cities, such as Accra, where they are not caning, they are now having lots of discipline problems. My colleague here in the USA laughed when I asked him and he said, "I didn't know I was supposed to be traumatized by caning until I came to the West."

2.2. The United States, River High School

The Tennessee high school I observed is a city school on the east side of town, with a 90+% of African American students attending, even though the city is only 6% Black. The school has a long history and is highly regarded by those who have graduated from River High and those who teach there, although it has the lowest test score results in the city. River High was the state champs in football for its division the year I observed and it has an award winning dance and music program. In an effort to increase the White population to River High, a magnet school for the performing arts and a science academy were developed and these programs are located in beautiful, new, state-of-the-art wings that wrap around the old building. I spent several days observing the Band teacher, Ms. Lincoln. River High is on a block schedule, as are all high schools in Tennessee, which means the students have four 90 minute class periods each day instead of 6-7 periods in a day that each last around 50 minutes. A one semester course in block schedules counts as the equivalent to a year-long course in traditional schools. Block scheduling works very well for classes like English, where students can have more time for reading, writing and classroom discussions, but it does not work so well for band classes, as ninety minutes is too long a time for students to physically play an instrument and students need the consistency of a year long course which they lose if they only have Band one semester each year. However, Ms. Lincoln has found a creative way to use the ninety minutes she has with her students. Lincoln went to River High as a child and she has lived in the area her whole life. She taught younger children for years but sought out the Music Teacher position at her alma mater when it became available. She teaches Beginning Band third period, 11:45 am – 1:52 p.m.. Monday, Tuesday and Thursday are for playing instruments, Wednesday is for working on sheet music and "Friday is free for all." There are fifteen or sixteen students in this class, all African American, predominantly male.

2.2.1. Day 1, Wednesday:

From 11:45-noon Ms. Lincoln allows the students to eat and chat and goof around with each other, as they have the last lunch and it is not until 1:20 p.m. (school starts at 8 am). She starts class at noon. She has in her office, right off the band room, drinks and food for the students. They know where the food is and are allowed to help themselves. She makes sure her students do not go hungry. From noon-12:30 p.m. the students get into their band chairs and sit in a semi-circle facing Ms. Lincoln and they chat with her. She sits at the front of the semi-circle, or stands. Her band assistant, a Black male named Nathan, stands near her or pulls up a chair and sits beside her as he joins in the conversation. On this day Nathan congratulates the basketball team on their win and a student tells the class about the first African American man and African American woman to win a gold medal in the Winter Olympics (I observed during the Winter Olympics). The kids are sharing and discussing news stories with each other, as they finish their chips and drinks. When they all start talking at once, Lincoln waves her hand and says, "I can't hear everyone at once" and they respond by going back to talking in turns. 12:10 p.m., now she asks them a Trivia Quiz question from Black History month about a woman like Rosa Parks who was the first woman to refuse to get up in a railroad car. Name: Ida B. Wells. "Who was the founder of NAACP?" Answer: W. E. Du Bois. Lincoln then reminds them: "I hope your teachers have signed you up because I know *all* of you will be at the game on Friday. You're playing at halftime. I want all of you freshmen to show the upper class how to behave at an assembly." There is lots of talking again. Lincoln asks: "Anyone else have something to say? Who's got something on your mind? Anyone not a happy child?" A student shares an inspiration story. There's a yellow tennis ball on the floor. Lincoln picks it up and bounces it a few times. (I wonder what role the tennis ball plays in her class?) Lincoln: "Speak now or forever hold your peace." She asks them what they think about the "Reading Across the Curriculum" program the school is trying out. The students don't like it, it's boring; they need to get better stories. "Put some interesting books there," a boy says. When a student went to interrupt her – Lincoln held the tennis ball up in her hand and aimed it at him and said, "I will, don't interrupt me." Their suggestions for the "Reading Across the Curriculum" program include: "The teacher needs to read with more enthusiasm." Lincoln then asks them how many are up to par in their reading, and about half of them raise their hands. "Do you feel this program will help you?" "No." "Well, then what do we have to do now?" Ms. Lincoln says, "My *mother* was an English teacher." She's showing them how they need help, due to their broken English. There is a phonics discussion. Lincoln: "I don't know if they do that anymore." "Last thing - then we have to move on." "How many of you feel like you got a good foundation at home?" (two raise their hands). "How many had a parent read to you?" (three raise their hands). She wants to hear more feedback and suggestions from others. "Now, you need to get a desk and come to the board." I look at my watch and realize she has invested 45 minutes in "building community" in her classroom and sharing her time with them. It is clear that she views her responsibilities in terms of teaching her students as being beyond the boundaries of music.

At 12:30 p.m., the students get desks and pull them to the side of the band room where there is a portable blackboard. Lincoln settles them in: "What time is it?" They say in unison, "Your time." Lincoln: "It is *my* time so stop playing." They all get quiet and listen to her. She gives them directions. "We will be *reading* today. Isn't that something that we talked about, reading? Somebody read or I'll call on someone." She waits and repeats, "Somebody read." Someone reads the worksheet directions. She instructs them on how to highlight in their notes what she emphasizes and helps them to see what will be on the quiz on Friday. Lesson 2, "Somebody read." Treble cleft. Lines. "Every good boy does fine. FACE." She waits for them to draw a treble cleft, then do the next step. All of the students work on their own. Lincoln: "You can go on if you are ready." A few minutes later, Lincoln: "We can't go any further, this is taking you too long to do." Moaning, they get back to work. Lincoln: "Okay, put your pencils down. Now it is time to be on the board. Guess who's going to be on the board?" She brought up the gal who was not working hard when they were working on their own. Lincoln had her name the lines, and label them on the board. A boy got Lincoln her tennis ball and tossed it to her at her request. After a few minutes she threw it at a boy who was not paying attention, hitting him on the chest. He stopped what he was doing. She shows the gal how to make sure she'll get it ("say the cliché out loud"). Lincoln: "Who else is having trouble? Don't be afraid that you don't know, just say you don't know." She teaches another kid at the board what to do. She then has the other kids call out a letter for them to draw in the note place. She reviewed this again with the cliché and the writing of the letters on the lines, then without the letters there to help them. A third student goes to the board, Jamal. Lincoln is excited: "You've got it!" Then she asks: "Everyone got it? Eliot?" She checked off their folders that they had completed this work and then dismissed them for lunch.

2.2.2.. Day 2, Thursday:

I arrive at 12:15 p.m. The students and teachers are talking, laughing, sharing stories. They're talking about gambling and what high stakes gambling is, double or nothing. Lincoln asks a student: "What job have you got? If you could bet that much money on a card game?!" They're talking about gambling in the school cafeteria. She warns them that if a parent complains they'd be in trouble because there are cameras in the cafeteria, and they'd be able to see them gambling. Lincoln: "It shouldn't even be – better put up the cards." Then someone talks about how money is allocated at the school and how he heard the principal talking about money for the football team.

Two guys must be on the football team, because they both cheer "Yeah!" and high-five each other and one says "New helmets!" Then there is a discussion of GPA and what is needed for eligibility to play sports - overall? semester? Six weeks? Then the same boy who brought up the money issue says, "We need a lottery for education." This triggers a discussion about Hope Scholarships, and what Georgia and Florida are doing for education with their lottery money. Then another boy asks, "What happens to your stuff in your locker when they cut off your lock?" He's advised that they save the library and school books, but they throw away everything else. Lincoln says: "The rest goes to BFI" (BFI is the trash company). Next, the same boy talking about money brought in a book to share with them and he reads them passages from it. It's about racially biased criminology. We learn that the local prosecutor says that 15 % of the crimes committed in the city are committed by Blacks, but that 75% of the crimes reported on the news are about Blacks. After the student reads a passage, Lincoln asks: "What is the point he's trying to make?" They talk about how violence in the cities is taken as a given, but is shocking to Whites when it happens in the suburbs. Lincoln: "Society makes us believe it is us. We don't do those crimes." Then the students and teachers give several examples of awful crimes White people have committed lately, shootings in schools, baby in trash can, drowning of five kids in bathtub. They talk about the shooting tragedy at Columbine High School. They label it "suburban neglect." Lincoln offers the students her opinion on gun violence. And she tells them emphatically that this is just her opinion, they don't have to agree with her. She tells them that she grew up here in the 60's. That she was born in 1957. She tells them how it was in the 80's and 90's when they started having drive-by shootings.

> We were killing each other. Yet the media did not pick this up as important news, as a tragedy, until it hit the White communities. Now it has come around full scope and it's about violence, period, for everyone. I hated the tragedy of Columbine, but I also felt, *Now* you want to do something?

They talked about crack houses and brothels in their neighborhoods. One boy says, "We don't know what it means to say I'm Black and I'm proud. We can see what you went through though."

Lincoln says:

> The 60's were hell on earth. We're saying to you, look at the opportunity *you* have. Especially in education. I remember segregation, riding in the back of the bus, taking food with us when we traveled because we couldn't get off the bus. We want you to be proud, and to take advantage of what you have.

She talks about how they have street skills – there's always a bootleg – a back door that depends on luck. She wants them to count on education to be their ticket to a better life, not luck. Lincoln asks: "Anyone else want to say something?" She thanked the student for the book he brought in to share with them. She talked to them about Blount County having debate teams and she tells them she'd like to see one at River High School. She tells them several of them would be good at it. She reminds them to go hear the brother sing at Bethel, 7 p.m., tonight. "Alright, anyone else?" "Who has their folders today? Bring it up." Now it is time for class work.

Please know that as I move to compare these two teachers' teaching styles, I do not want to pass a negative judgment on Ghanaian teachers. I think their efforts to teach are heroic, for they teach in conditions *no* American teacher *ever* has to face today. There is no plumbing in the JSS I observed, so there is no running water or bathrooms. Children buy water and food from the women venders who come at recess time and set up under thatched roofs, or they bring it from home, or they go without. (It was 90+ degrees the days I observed, which was during the cooler, rainy season.) They use the cornfields for a bathroom. There are no copy machines or computers and printers at Fortune's school; there are only cracked and worn blackboards upon which to write lessons and tests. There are no shelves lined with books, not even pencil sharpeners. Children bring double-edged razors for sharpening their pencils. The teaching conditions are so different that they are beyond comparison. However, the two teachers so clearly model different views of *authority* through their teaching styles and that is what I want to further consider at the theoretical level in the next section.

3. CONNECTING THEORY TO PRACTICE

The USA was founded on a concept of democracy that has its philosophical roots in the Euro-western classical liberal theory of Locke (1632-1704) and Rousseau (1712-1778). For Locke (1823/1960) and Rousseau (1762/1968), the role of government/state is to protect individuals from others and otherwise to stay out of individual's lives and allow them to live as they freely choose. The goal of liberalism is to secure opportunities for individuals to realize their full potentials. Classical liberal democracy emphasizes a negative view of freedom as "freedom from," focusing on individual rights as natural rights and emphasizing the need to protect these natural rights for they belong to individuals prior to the formation of political governments, religious institutions, and social relations. It is an argument for the primacy of the individual over the state (Dewey, 1935). Such a view of democracy is based on a strong assumption of individualism. It is also based on a strong assumption of rationalism, on freed intelligence, that individuals can learn to think for themselves and use their reasoning capacity to critique their government's actions and change the government if it is not meeting their individual needs.

In terms of the classroom, classical liberal democratic theory relies on a concept of authority that is individualized and advocates a child-centered approach. As Giroux (1997) describes liberalism's view of authority, it is one that holds out to us an ideology of "need fulfillment" that casts students in an "othered" role as deviant, underprivileged, or uncultured. It uses authority to promote self-control and self-regulation, in order for the self to be able to reach its full potential. It is based on a psychology that is individualized and child-centered, and views the child as a unitary subject. In my field observations of teachers in the USA working with African American students, I have seen several teachers who reflect this liberal approach. Their pedagogy is one of cordial relations, seeking to keep the students "happy." It amounts to a kind of negotiated agreement between teacher and student that I will not ask too much of you, student, if you do not cause too much trouble and grief for me. As Grioux (1997) rightly points out, the liberal view of authority is silent on the connection between authority, culture and power. Classical liberals emphasize the positive aspects of authority and ignore "the 'messy webs' of social relations that embody forms of struggle and contestation" (99).

From a classical liberal perspective, Ms. Lincoln's job is to make sure her students learn as much music as they can during the time they have with her. Her focus should be on individual achievement, relying on the myth of merit to cajole her students into being highly motivated and hard working so that they will reach their full potential as musicians. Her students walk into her room with whatever natural talents they have inherited and her job is to make sure other students do not impede any individual's progress. What is going on in the students' lives is really not her business. When the students walk into the band room they should be able to bracket out all contextual distraction and focus on the task at hand. A classical liberal would judge Ms. Lincoln as not using her time efficiently, wasting half of her 90 minutes on food and conversation, with no musical education occurring. They would also worry about her efforts to teach students moral lessons that go beyond the boundaries of her discipline subject area. During the time that she does teach music, they would approve of her efforts to reach each student and make sure that all of her students are learning, although they may be concerned that the slow students are holding the fast students behind in their learning. They also may be concerned about her style of discipline/attention getting as being potentially harmful, although they would admire its efficiency at getting the point across without taking any teaching time away from the other students' learning.

In Ghana they have struggled with creating a democracy since the British left in the late 1940's. They have had several coupes resulting in dictators who have rewritten their constitution four times. Still, they are proud that their country is more stable than most in Africa and that they are held up as a model for others to follow. They argue that they are finally starting to get an understanding of what a democracy is. However, in their classrooms and at home I did not observe this. The families, schools and churches are all structured in a strong authoritarian style, with the elders maintaining strict control. The students are not assumed to have civil rights, they must obey, which they do so overall without complaint. From a Ghanaian perspective, Americans overindulge and spoil their children with their child-centered approach. From an American classical liberal democratic perspective, Fortune is viewed in troubling ways. Her approach to teaching is seen as oppressive. She uses corporeal punishment to frighten her students into working harder. She publicly humiliates her students as a way of improving their skills.

Fortune relies on a concept of authority that Giroux (1997) describes in his essay, "Authority, intellectuals, and the politics of practical learning," as neo-conservative. In this essay, originally published in 1986, Giroux situates his discussion within the context of the Reagan era and the new conservatives' fears of "loss of authority." The new conservatives discourse on authority give authority a positive meaning as something to be celebrated as representative of the American Dream, based on hard work, discipline, promptness and cheerful obedience. These are the very values Fortune seeks to teach her students in Ghana. Giroux points out that, unfortunately, this type of authority also supports reactionary and undemocratic interests and I think we can see this concern clearly in how classical liberals might respond to

Fortune's caning of her students as undemocratic. The neo-conservative concept of authority focuses on control, management, and efficiency. With this view of authority, teachers function as clerks, which accurately describes the teachers I observed in Ghana. Like the classical liberal view of authority, the conservative view is also silent on the connection between culture and power. Both views are what Giroux calls "the dominant educational discourse."

Giroux (1997) points out that while neo-conservatives view authority only positively, leftist educators tend to view authority as negative only, as a loss of freedom, connected to a logic of domination, as unprincipled authoritarianism. It is certainly the case that leftist educators would judge Fortune as being an authoritarian. Giroux seeks to move beyond leftist educators' views of authority and develop an alternative, dialectical view of emancipatory authority as a central element in a critical theory of schooling. For him, such a concept of authority is necessary in order for us to be able to analyze the relationship between domination and power. A dialectical concept of authority as emancipatory is necessary in order for us to reinsert into the language of schooling the primacy of the political, a task Giroux has worked on his entire career. With Giroux, schools become an ideological and political terrain; they are not ideologically innocent. He seeks to underscore Dewey's (1916/1966; 1927/1954) vision that public schools can be places where the skills of democracy are practiced.

Giroux (1997) argues that an emancipatory concept of authority will empower students (and teachers and parents) to be critical and active citizens in a democracy-in-the-making. It is my contention that Ms. Lincoln serves as a strong example of a teacher who allows her students to practice the skills of democracy. Lincoln is teaching her students to be active citizens. She knows how to successfully create what Giroux calls "a democratic counterpublic sphere" in her classroom. An emancipatory concept of authority such as Giroux describes emphasizes that authority is "a terrain of struggle." It also emphasizes that teachers can function as "transformative intellectuals," who have the ability to think and act critically, and who can teach their students to do the same. Transformative intellectuals are the bearers of "dangerous memory," and Lincoln certainly serves in that kind of role as she shares with her students what it was like growing up in the 1960's.

While Giroux's (1997) essay on authority helps us to make sense of the difference between Fortune's concept of authority as conservative, and Ms. Lincoln's concept of authority as more emancipatory, there are problems with Giroux's concept of emancipatory authority that hinder us from fully appreciating what goes on in Lincoln's classroom. Giroux's emancipatory authority clings to a view of human subjectivity based on individual autonomy and agency, which is a holdover from modernist democratic theories. His view of human subjectivity creates problems for him as emancipatory authority ends up still placing the teacher in the position of higher authority and students in the "othered" category as somehow lacking power and in need of assistance in gaining power. A teacher who is described as a "transformative intellectual" is still in the role of leading and guiding those who are not as informed and are in need of transformation. The teacher, because she is an intellectual and a bearer of dangerous memory, has more authority than her students and can use that authority in ways that help them, as well as ways that harm them. Emancipatory authority has to work at defending itself against the possibility of the teacher's authority co-opting the students' authorities, taking over and directing their struggles for the end of oppressions.

Feminist theory can help us get beyond Enlightenment's assumption of individuality without jeopardizing the emancipatory political project of describing schools as political terrain that have the potential to be counter-public democratic spaces. What is needed is a transactional view of individuals-in-relation-to-others. I want to argue that what I observed with Ms. Lincoln and her band class was a view of authority as *shared,* that develops from a relational ontology and pluralistic (e)pistemology.[3] A relational ontology describes human beings as always existing in relation to other human beings, at a intimately personal level (Flax 1983, 1990; Noddings, 1984; Ruddick, 1989) as well as at a broader social level (Smith, 1987, 1990). It also describes human beings as always existing in relation to their natural surroundings and the greater world at large, so that it embraces an ecological (King, 1989; Merchant, 1980; Warren, 1990) and holistic (Allen, 1986; Khema, 1999) description of selves-in-relation-to-others. From a relational perspective, there is no such thing as individuality and human agency, key concepts of classical liberal democracy to which emancipatory authority still wants to cling. There is only us-in-relation-to-others, and a recognition that we are continually affecting others just as they are continually affecting us. We exist in a dance together that from a larger perspective is inseparable and indistinguishable. From a pluralistic (e)pistemological perspective there is no such thing as One Answer or One Truth that we can hope to find. There are many truths and many possible standards and criteria that we can rely on to try to make our case for what we think is the right thing to do, knowing full well that our criteria and standards will need to be corrected and modified as our perspectives enlarge and our knowledge expands, through the results of our transactions with others. This is not a naively relativistic argument that anything goes and none of us can claim any authority, but rather a qualified relativistic argument that says all we can ever claim is a limited, situated authority that develops and is enhanced by our relationships with others. Whatever authority we can hope to claim is a shared authority.

From a pluralistic, relational perspective, Ms. Lincoln's style of teaching makes more sense. Ms. Lincoln knows how to create a relatively safe environment in her classroom where students' voices can be heard and contribute to the conversation. How does she do this? First, Lincoln recognizes that her students are growing teen-agers with insatiable appetites and they do not necessarily start out the day with a solid breakfast, due to their economic situations. She knows that her students cannot concentrate in class if they are hungry, so right away she takes care of that problem by supplying them with food to get them by until lunchtime. Second, Lincoln knows that her students must sit still in desks all day and that there is very little opportunity for them to talk to each other or get up and move around the room. She figures she can take care of their need to move, talk and eat all at the same time during the first fifteen minutes of class.

Third, Ms. Lincoln knows that her students cannot leave the context of their lives behind when they walk through the door into her classroom. If she talks to them she will get to know them better and find more ways to connect the curriculum she needs to teach them to their interests and concerns. She also knows, as a Black woman who grew up in the same neighborhood they live in and who attended the same school, she needs to help them become aware of and be able to critique the social forces they must deal with on a daily basis. She wants to arm her students with a critical understanding of racism and how it affects their lives, and help them overcome feelings of inadequacy or stupidity. She wants them to feel proud of who they are, and capable, for she knows that, if her students can feel good about themselves, they will be willing to struggle with learning how to play a musical instrument and have confidence that they can succeed. It goes without saying that her curriculum is culturally relevant to capture her students interests. But, it is not artificially divided into only music. She relies on her students' oral capabilities as she uses a pedagogical style that is in agreement with their auditory learning styles. She uses repetition by calling many students to the board for she knows that repetition will help all her students improve their understandings. In summation, Ms. Lincoln relies on her knowledge of the African American social context of her community and adapts her curriculum, goals and teaching style to that knowledge. From a relational, pluralistic perspective of democracy, she is a fine teacher who is helping her students learn the skills they will need to participate in a democracy-always-in-the-making throughout their adult lives.

Ms. Lincoln models a belief that students have important things to say and they can teach us all a thing or two. If we give them the opportunity to share their views and bring in news and readings to share in class, if we share our authority with them, not only will we get to know them better, but we will be encouraging their communication and relational skills as well as their confidence. We will help them develop their voices and find ways to contribute those voices to their larger society. By opening up her classroom to her students' contributions and even giving them some time together without adult direction, as well as maintaining time for her to teach them directly, she creates a classroom space where the students share authority with her. Notice, she does not give up her authority. When it is her turn to speak she insists on their attention, even if it means using a tennis ball to get their attention. But she gives her students the same attention she insists upon when it is their turn to speak and she keeps asking to make sure everyone has had a turn to talk. Her classroom is a democracy-always-in-the-making and if we attend to her example closely there is much we can learn, not only about the practice of teaching African American high school students, but about a theory of democracy that is ontologically relational and (e)pistemologically pluralistic in its basic assumptions.

4. CONCLUSION

Ms. Lincoln's style of teaching is very different from Fortune's in some ways and very similar in other ways. Both teachers take advantage of their time with their students to not only teach them about their subject area but to teach them moral lessons about life as well. Both are encouraging their students in their own unique ways to work hard and strive to achieve a high quality education so they will have more freedom and choices in their lives. Ms. Lincoln hopes that with a good education her students hopefully will be treated with greater dignity and respect as adults living in a racist society while Fortune doesn't have to worry so much about racism in Ghana where everyone is Black. Fortune has to worry more about job possibilities for her students living in a Third World nation with meager economic resources. Still, I did not observe teachers in Ghana, like Fortune, sharing their authority with their students. The teachers have 2-3 students per desk in rooms that are full to overflowing and they demand silence and obedience, reinforced with a cane if needed. There is no question as to who is in charge. Their pedagogical style is directive and strict. I discovered with Lincoln an African American teacher who is teaching her students about democracies-in-the-making by sharing her teaching time with them and setting up her room so that the students have voices in the class. Ms. Lincoln knows how to create a relatively comfortable, safe place where her students can share their ideas and contribute to the curriculum and instruction. She knows how to develop a classroom where authority is *shared.* She plays music *with* her students, allowing herself to become the student as they teach her, just as they let themselves be taught by her. They are in process, creating music together that is sometimes discordant, sometimes united and sometimes in harmony, but always connected and affecting each other, always in a transactional relationship with each other.

A transactional view of democracy stresses the interaction that goes on continually between teachers and students and how much they affect each other. A transactional view of democracy stresses that democracy is always in process, helping us see how the group must continually adapt and adjust to the needs of individuals as well as the individuals continually adjust and adapt to the needs of the group. It is a view of democracy that is not based on underlying assumptions of individualism, rationalism or universalism that classical liberal democratic theory relies upon, which in the end undermine the very possibility of democracy. A transactional theory of democracy-always-in-the-making is based on a relational ontology and pluralistic (e)pistemology that underscore how connected we are to each other, how multifaceted and diverse we are and that any claims of authority we can hope to make are enhanced by our relationships with others.

ENDNOTES

[1] All names have been changed in the text to protect the identity of the schools and the participants in the school communities.

[2] As the teachers in the JSS in Ghana went by their first names with me, and by the formal title of Madam with their students, I will call Fortune by her first name, and by Madam when students speak to her. At River High School the teachers all go by their last names, even with each other, so I will use Ms. Lincoln, or Lincoln for the teacher I observed at RHS.

[3] I use ( ) around the "e" of epistemology to symbolize a non-transcendent epistemology. I have written about this topic at length in Relational "(E)Pistemologies" (2003).

REFERENCES

Allen, P. (1986). *The sacred hoop: Recovering the feminine in American Indian traditions.* Boston: Beacon Press.

Dewey, J. (1966). *Democracy and education.* New York: The Free Press, MacMillan, (Original work published 1916).

Dewey, J. (1955). *Logic: The theory of inquiry.* New York: Henry Holt and Company, Inc., (Original work published in 1938).

Dewey, J. (1954). *The public and its problems.* New York: Henry Holt and Company, (Original work published in 1927).

Dewey, J. (1935). *Liberalism and social action.* New York: G. P. Putnam's Sons.

Dewey, J. and Bentley, A. F. (1960). *Knowing and the known.* Boston, MA: Beacon Press, (Original work published in 1949).

Flax, J. (1990). *Thinking fragments: Psychoanalysis, feminism, and postmodernism in contemporary West.* Berkeley, LA, Oxford: University of California Press.

Flax, J. (1983). Political philosophy and the patriarchal unconscious: A psychoanalytic perspective on epistemology and metaphysics. In S. Harding & M. B. Hintikka (eds.). *Discovering reality* (245-281). Dordrecht, Boston, London: D. Reidel Publishing Company.

Fraser, N. (1997). *Justice interruptus: Critical reflections on the "Postsocialist" condition.* New York and London: Routledge.

Giroux, H. (1997). *Pedagogy and the politics of hope: Theory, culture, and schooling (A critical reader).* Boulder, CO: Westview Press.

Khema, A. (1999). *Be an island: The Buddhist practice of inner peace.* Boston: Wisdom Publications.

King, Y. (1989). The ecology of feminism and the feminism of ecology. In J. Plant (ed.). *Healing the wounds: The promise of ecofeminism* (18-28). Santa Cruz, CA: New Society Publishers.

Locke, J. (1960). *The second treatise on government.* Cambridge: Cambridge University Press. (Edition used originally published in 1823).

Lomotey, K. (Ed.). (1990). *Going to school: The African-American experience.* Albany, NY: SUNY Press.

Merchant, C. (1980). *The death of nature: Women, ecology, and the scientific revolution.* San Francisco: Harper and Row.

Nieto, S. (1992). *Affirming diversity: The sociopolitical context of multicultural education.* White Plains, NY: Longman.

Noddings, N. (1984). *Caring: A feminine approach to ethics and moral education.* Berkeley, CA: University of California Press.

Ogbu, J. U. (1991) Immigrant and involuntary minorities in comparative perspective. In M. A. Gibson & J. U. Ogbu (eds.), *Minority status and schooling* (3-33). New York: Garland.

Romo, H. D. and Falbo, T. (1996). *Latino high school graduation: Defying the odds.* Austin, TX: University of Texas Press.

Rousseau, J. J. (1968). *The social contract* (M. Cranston, Trans.). Harmondsworth: Penguin Books (Originally published in 1762).

Ruddick, S. (1989). *Maternal thinking: Toward a politics of peace.* Boston: Beacon Press.

Smith, D. (1990). *The conceptual practices of power: A feminist sociology of knowledge.* Boston: Northeastern University.

Smith, D. (1987). *The everyday world as problematic: A feminist sociology.* Boston: Northeastern University.

Thayer-Bacon, B. (2003). *Relational "(E)Pistemologies".* New York: Peter Lang, Inc.

Thayer-Bacon, B. with Bacon, C. (1998). *Philosophy applied to education: Nurturing a democratic community in the classroom.* Upper Saddle River, NJ: Prentice Hall.

Warren, K. J. (1990, Spring). The power and the promise of ecological feminism. *Environmental Ethics,* 12(1), 125-146.

WILLIAM F. PINAR

TEACHING THE QUEER CHARACTER OF RACISM

Abstract. My argument will be straightforward if queer: racism is, in some sense, an "affair" between men. Of course, racism is not *only* an affair between men. Women have been very much victims: White men's assaults on Black women from slavery to the present is, for instance, well known. Nor I am suggesting that "race" can be reduced to gender; it cannot. But it does have to do with sex and desire, as the study of lynching and interracial prisons make plain.

> All race relations tend to be, however subtle, sex relations.
> (Calvin C. Hernton (1988 [1965], 6)

> Is it surprising that prisons resemble factories, schools, barracks, hospitals, which all resemble prisons?
> (Michel Foucault, 1995 [1979], 228)

As a nation we Americans remain submerged in a thirty-year old reaction to the progressive and sometimes revolutionary politics that characterized the 1960s. The majority of Americans remain too conservative and, on too many occasions, downright reactionary. How one would like to believe that, to borrow a phrase first used thirty years ago by the "Right", there is a "silent majority" of Americans whose contempt for official reality keeps them at home on election days. If everyone voted, there might be a majority of Americans who find the Southern Baptist idea of "gracious submission" laughable, for whom race is a positive difference, and queer people are interesting if not cool. If – the power elites will never enact such legislation – all Americans were required to vote, the nonsense of the "Right Wing", dominated now by White Southerners, might quickly fade into an Orwellian past (Black and Black, 1992).

But in Washington, D. C., we are submerged in their fantasies still (as of this writing, January 2004), still ruled by a fragile but effective coalition of religious crazies, right-wing extremists and corporate interests, sometimes intersecting categories. With the help of the mass media, this coalition evidently succeeds in persuading many who do vote that (by the lure of prosperity) American business – and business "thinking" – is our salvation. Many are so thoroughly seduced by this fantasy they evidently think what works for American business ought to work everywhere, even in fundamentally non-business organizational forms such as the schools.

In U.S. public schools, especially, the dominant thinking remains "corporatist," preparing students to live in a consumer economy, an economy which commodifies everything, including ideas, a predictable point given Richard Brosio's thoughtful

111

K. Cooper and R. White (eds.), The Practical Critical Education, 111–120.
© 2007 Springer.

analysis (in this volume). Is capitalism itself related to the racialized culture of its origin? Is capitalism a form of "Whiteness"? Is Marxism (see Weyl, 1979, 37)? While allegations of racism toward Marx and Engels are discredited as right-wing political attacks (which they have sometimes been), allegations regarding homophobia are less easily dismissed[1]. Perhaps both capitalism and Marxism are complex expressions of the European episteme David G. Smith (in this volume) associates with the narcissism and self-centeredness of especially bourgeois North Americans, as well as with the aggressive imperialism of the Bush Administration in the United States.

To attend to anti-racist education requires, I suggest, interdisciplinary humanities curricula understood and taught as forms of social and cultural psychoanalysis (Pinar, 2004). Students, especially "White" students, need to know the gender of racial politics in this country. They need to understand the racialization of gender as well as the gender of racial violence. Parents need not fear some homosexual virus will infect their children if they learn that racism has been in some essential way "queer." The homoerotic "virus" is quite already there, everywhere, since the beginning of time. I would say that the point is to experience it, celebrate it, not to suppress it or push it into some subterranean sphere from which it someday resurfaces, mixed and mangled almost beyond recognition – violent, defiant, no longer love but hate: lynching for instance, or prison rape.

Interdisciplinary humanities curricula conceived as social psychoanalysis teach how nefarious gender totalitarianism is, how the contemporary regime of heterosexism not only victimizes queers but self-identified "heterosexuals" as well, especially women and children (see chapter 13, Pinar, 2001). The contemporary suppression of homosexual desire, its imprisonment and segregation in "homosexuals," not only creates self-delusion as to one's own gender identity and sexual potential, but relocates desire onto others, skewing perception, deforming experience. Self-division leads to the multiplication of "others." And "others" sometimes get "offed."

I am not suggesting that everyone is "naturally" bisexual; from studies in the history of sexuality we can appreciate that that category is too limited, essentialized, finally illusory, like "heterosexuality" and "homosexuality." Probably Freud's notion of "polymorphous perversity" is a more serviceable idea. But "sexuality" – itself a twentieth-century concept, at least in terms of its role in identity formation – is now so thoroughly politicized that we cannot make such statements neutrally, "objectively." As Elizabeth Grosz (1995, 181) has noted: "There is no pure sexuality, no inherently transgressive sexual practice, no sexuality beyond or outside the limits of patriarchal models." Given the hegemony of heteronormativity, "bisexuality" is probably politically progressive. The educational task is not to educate children to understand a pre-historical, biologistic or "natural" bisexuality; it is to understand how their phenomenologically real but thoroughly constructed and variable feelings of desire are implicated in a complex gendered history of racial violence and oppression in America (Pinar, 2001).

What is important to teach now, it seems to me, is that there is a racial politics of masculinity that historically has relegated women to units of currency in a homosocial economy of desire[2]. It may be so that men have, since some prehistorical matriarchal period, not "recognized" women apart from our need for them, including our repudiation of them. It is also true that men have succeeded, to different degrees, in various cultural settings and historical moments, in persuading and/or forcing women into psycho-social and sexual roles men wished women to assume. Footbinding in China is only one obvious example; genital mutilation in Africa is another; the persecution of "witches" in the West is a third; widow-burning in India yet another (Dworkin, 1974).

To what extent have women been complicit in this alienated system of male homosocial desire, even while finding spaces for survival and self-affirmation, creating opportunities to cultivate creativity and fashion love, perhaps cannot be known. The worldwide, if culturally variable, history of misogyny – and women's resistance to and transcendence of it – is a very complicated story. Where it intersects with the tale I have told in *The Gender of Racial Politics and Violence in America* (Pinar, 2001) is that men's commodification of women, and in particular, White men's fictionalizing of White women functioned not to protect women from rape; it functioned to rationalize "heterosexual" male sexual assault ... upon other men. Nineteenth-century White men used White women as provocations to sexually mutilate Black men. Desire denied can become paranoia, Freud knew, and lynching would seem to be an illustrative if complex instance of that point.

Black women were fictionalized as well by White men, slandered as lascivious. The first woman who publicly declined, and in rather spectacular fashion, this fictional status, this reduction to a figment in the White man's imagination, was Ida B. Wells. This is not the place to speculate why Wells was the first. It may have been fortuitous, the simple consequence of the 1892 Memphis lynching "at the curve." She was not the only Black woman who knew that White men were blowing not just steam when they obsessed over Black men raping White women. It is true that Wells had a certain orientation, we might even say "commitment," toward Black men: she assumed some responsibility for her brother who was sometimes in difficulty; she took on an all-male Sunday School class later in Chicago and organized settlement houses there for new and homeless (mostly male) migrants from the South, which is to say she felt some moral responsibility toward Black men. It is clear from her Memphis diaries (Decosta-Willis, 1995) that she was hardly uncritical of men; her skepticism of and refusal to participate in the taken-for-granted romantic customs of the time underlines that.

Nor was Wells uncritical of what the gender system did to women: she did not decline to record how bourgeois Black women (without using that phrase) were sometimes guilty of gossip and pettiness, a phenomenon that undermined racial solidarity as it kept women competitive, isolated, and ornamental. After the British campaign, she did marry and gave birth to four children; she took her duties as mother very seriously. In her autobiography it is clear that her children came first, even before her commitment to crusade for racial justice. Still she found time, however, to continue to fight lynching (see Wells, 1970).

As Hazel Carby (1987) points out, Wells has been called a leader without a movement, "a lonely warrior," a spokesperson for protest in "the age of accommodation," whose life's work can be judged "a limited success" (quoted in Carby, 1987, 108). Many historians regard her as a minor figure compared to Du

Bois and Washington; suffering under such comparison, her political ideas, strategies, tactics, and analyses have been appreciated primarily in relation to the achievements of these men. As Carby (1987) notes, Wells was no imperfect copy of Washington or Du Bois and should not be considered only in relation to either. Perhaps there is a historical through-line here, too; she suffered one hundred years ago because men found her "difficult," which is to say "unladylike," unwilling to compromise her strong voice for the sake of men's comfort (Carby, 1987). She suffers still, in contemporary under-appreciation of her achievement.

A public schoolteacher like Anna Julia Cooper (1988 [1892]), Ida B. Wells found her true calling in protesting with the pen: she became a militant journalist and antilynching activist. For Whites and some Black men, Wells was, as Carby (1987) reminds, an "uppity" Black woman with a strong analysis of the relations among political terrorism, economic oppression, and conventional codes of sexuality and morality. For Carby (1987, 108), Wells' analysis "has still to be surpassed in its incisive condemnation of the patriarchal manipulation of race and gender." Carby finds the influence of Wells' work in the writing of Black women from Pauline Hopkins to June Jordan and Alice Walker who, like Wells, have labored to understand how rape and lynching were used as interlocking tools of political, social, and economic oppression.

Wells' commitment to fighting racial injustice appears to have begun when she was thrown off that Chesapeake and Ohio train, but after the loss of her friend at the lynching "at the curve," she concentrated on the outrage, the crisis, that was lynching. What also might have been at play in her commitment, in her courageous assault on White-male fantasy, was her refusal to accept the imaginary status of women, in particular White women. Like Frances Harper, Wells did not believe that "White women are dewdrops just exhaled from the skies" (quoted in Roediger, 1998, 254). She knew that the White male fantasy of the virginal, morally unreproachable White "lady" was just that, a fantasy; she suspected and discovered that in some cases the "rape" White men were "avenging" by lynching was a voluntary relationship between two consenting adults. And in some cases the White woman had been the sexual aggressor. White women were not ornaments on the shelves of the White male mind; they were, she knew, human individuals with minds and passions of their own. Stubbornly, White men refused to accept this fact, and more than a few White women decided to go against the prevailing White "wisdom" in order to pursue passion and, no doubt, love with men and women who were Black.

White men were not only wrong about White women, they were wrong about Black men and women. Of course, Wells knew that Black men were not brutes, sexual fiends, slaves to their "animal" passions; passions which, White men were sure, focused exclusively on White women. Like the "money shot" in heterosexual pornography, lynching used the presence (however imaginary) of women to camouflage homosexual desire. Not only White women were imaginary in this process; Black men were fictionalized too, and at every opportunity Ida B. Wells contested that "place" in fantasyland to which they had been consigned by White men. By so doing, she contested, too, the place Black women had been assigned. In

England many, especially British female reformers, "saw" her, but back home even northern newspapers condemned her, predictably, as a harlot (Ware, 1992).

As perhaps America's greatest pedagogue, Ida B. Wells realized that her "students" – European Americans – could not learn the lesson she had to teach, not from a Black woman at least. She tried to reach them, but even Northern (White) newspapers would print nothing she had to teach. In the 1890s few European Americans could see how topsy-turvy their world was, as the racial mythology in which they were submerged was too powerful, too totalizing. Undefeated and undaunted, Wells shrewdly appealed to those whom she thought might command a hearing, might shock her resisting, refusing students to confront what they were so determined to deny. She took her cause to the British, Americans' political and, for some, cultural parents (Ware, 1992). With the help of British women reformers, Wells succeeded in persuading many in Britain that lynching was barbaric, that White men were the uncivilized ones, which in the conflations of the period, meant they were not "men." In turn, the British communicated that to their wayward American "children"; it was an allegation that hit home.

It would take another forty years before a White woman would surface who would contest the fictionalized status of women which lynching presumed. Jessie Daniel Ames knew that Southern women were not fragile, passive, helpless victims of Black male desire. She knew that White men's invocation of chivalry functioned to restrict women's freedom as much as it did to prop up an unstable and fragile White male ego. Ames had fought for women's right to vote; after her participation in that important victory, she continued to struggle for women's rights, including the right not to be reduced to an ornament: the Southern White "lady." She tackled this considerable problem bravely, challenging women's relegation to White men's trophy cases while intervening in that murderous practice the possession of such "ornaments" presumably justified: lynching (Hall, 1979).

Men's battle against lynching, what became a primarily Black-male struggle led by the National Association for the Advancement of Colored People (N.A.A.C.P.), de-emphasized the gendered nature of the practice, predictably so, given the invisibility of men as gendered to the male mind (Zangrando, 1980). Walter White (1929) saw the problem as primarily economic, although the explicit gender dimensions of racialization portrayed in James Weldon Johnson's 1912 *The Auto-biography of an Ex-Colored Man* implies that Johnson sensed that more was at stake in lynching than economic manipulation, political power, and White supremacy. The still shockingly absolute refusal of White men to enact federal legislation to end the practice underscores how powerful a symbol of White/Black male relations lynching was. As they had for a century and would continue to the present day, White Southern men led the reactionary refusal to protect the basic civil rights of all Americans, this time disingenuously crying "constitutionality" and "states rights" to prevent federal intervention in southern barbarism (Ferrell, 1986). A masculinized symbol system par excellence, law and legislation were in this struggle symoblizations – disguised tools – of male-male desire (Hocquenghem, 1978; Grossberg, 1990). Southern White men were not about to keep other Southern White men away from Black men's bodies.

These racialized sexual dynamics – camouflaged in Congress by three-piece suits and abstract argumentation over God, country, and states' rights – become unmistakable in U.S. prisons (see Pinar, 2001, chapters 16 and 17). There, heterosexually-identified Black men bypass sexually available Black and White gay men to gang rape, repeatedly, unless they submit to being "punks," straight White men, preferably heterosexually-married young White men. Once sexually submissive, these "punks" are sold to older White men for long-term sexual relationships. When asked by criminologists about the practice of gang rape, informants replied: " Now Whitey knows it's his turn now" (see Scacco, 1975, 51-52).

Nor longer can the social preference of men for men – that sublimation of homosexual desire Eve Kosofsky Sedgwick (1985) coined homosociality – be disguised by the physical presence of women, however imaginary they often remain in many men's minds. In U.S. prisons the fundamentally sadomasochistic and sexualized character of White/Black male relations is unmistakable. It becomes clear that lynching was a kind of rape, a distorted, mangled, nightmarish expression of (White male) sexual desire. In prison, lynching would be avenged.

Interracial prison rape is racial revenge in sexualized terms. In psychological terms, it is, I believe, also an expression of the Western male's unconscious self-structure, a matrifocal structure requiring the repudiation of that symbiotic union with the mother to become something "other" – a "man" (Chodorow, 1978; Gilmore, 1990). Through, rape men act out their internalized structure of self-self relations, performing on women and other men the crimes of gender formation they endured as boys and adolescents in order to become and continue to be "men." Is that why the category is so unstable, so fragile, so imaginary? Compulsory heterosexuality necessarily suppresses an omnipresent homosexual desire, relocating and imprisoning it in "homosexuals," themselves now gender criminals whose fantasized distinctiveness supports the binary between gay and straight, allowing heterosexually-identified men to continue to believe the delusion that they themselves are "normal."

Straight is, presumably, normal, natural, God-ordained. The intensity of the (especially White male) reaction against calls for the protection of the basic civil rights for a fragment of the population the Right Wing insists is only 1-2% suggests otherwise. The protection of the civil rights of gay and lesbian Americans gets recoded as the granting of "special rights," a rhetorical strategy racists used successfully against African Americans one hundred years ago. The lady doth protest too much. The dangers of homosexuality are evidently so powerful, so multiple, so appealing that only constant legal and political suppression can keep them contained. When those who are imaginary "others" must stay "in their place," it is clear that what is at stake is the structure of the White male imagination, recoded as "morality" or "godliness" and most fundamentally as "real." As Alan Sinfield (1994, xi) notes: "In many ways, of course, we already don't have traditional heterosexuality. That is why (neo)-conservatives go on about it so much: urgent ideological work usually signals the failure of a system, not its dominance." When the right wing begins to battle homosexuality, the war is lost. But our victory, perhaps already achieved, is like the light of a distant star: it will take a very long time for the light to reach us on earth. Not in my lifetime, it would seem.

The European-American male self structure, in its repression and self-splitting, constructs a series of "others," each with its distinctive history of suffering and struggle, each with its own casualty list, but sharing a convoluted place in the White male mind. "Prejudice" may be a discredited concept today, but only because it was too narrowly attitudinal, obscured too much of the complexity of those internal dynamics as well as social relationalities, historical and civilizational legacies, economic pressures, and cultural formations that are all visible in any serious study of racialized, gendered, religious, and classed oppression (Allport, 1958; Young-Bruehl, 1996).

Why do "men" create "others"? Could it have something to do with processes of their own identity formation, specifically that they themselves – as "men" – are imaginary? Because they themselves, in order to become "men," are fictionalized, are they then condemned to perceive others in fictional terms as well? The formation of male identity in a regime of compulsory heterosexuality requires repudiation of the pre-oedipal symbiotic identification with the mother (White men projected onto Black men their own matrifocality in debates about the Black family [see Moynihan, 1965]). In so doing, men structure a male self that is dissociated from the body and emotion (except rage and self-pity, it seems), from that viscous, sensual, phenomenological experience which allows one access to, intimacy with, not only separated and individuated others, but to oneself as well. Could it be that this repudiation of the mother and imaginary identification with a relatively absent father – and here I mean not only the father who works but the prototypical, mythological "father" in a patriarchal society which denies him feeling and "femininity" – congeals a state of self-dissociation in which "othering" is inevitable? Does this self-division require the multiplication of others?

In prison we glimpse how these processes and structures of masculine self-deformation get performed in the construction of social reality. Men feminize younger men, not as substitutes for absent women – the research reported makes clear that even when prison officials provide conjugal visits with spouses and girlfriends straight men continue their sexual involvement with other men (Burstein, 1977) – but because straight men need "bitches," a residue of the repudiated, repressed, then projected feminine within. Of course how men construct "the opposite sex" varies according to class, culture, and historical moment; in prison the "opposite sex" to men is still men. "Why can't a woman be more like a man?" echoes Professor Higgins' famous question. Prison is no weird alien planet; prison provides a glimpse, for those who can bear to see, what (straight) men do everywhere. In prison men assume – some voluntarily, many against their will – the roles that in society women are required to play.

In prison we see racial and class hierarchies reversed. In prison it is good-looking, young, heterosexual White guys who are the losers, inverting (as it were) the gendered racial hierarchy outside. But being "losers" in the man's world that is the prison means having been made over into "punks," i.e. "girls," a reproduction of the gender hierarchy on the outside. "Gender and race conflate in a crisis," as Gates (1996, 96) observes, an ongoing crisis at least four hundred years in duration, a crisis that continues to support heterosexually-identified White men's delusion that what they imagine is real. In prison it is Black men's fantasies that become real, that become social reality.

Lynching and prison rape disclose the conflation of gender and race in the White male mind. These two events, key imprinting events we cannot set aside as bizarre and exceptional, require us to reconceptualize how we understand "race" in America. What must be concluded from the intolerable facts of these phenomena is that, to a considerable extent, the gender of racial politics and violence in America is queer. Women have been involved, sometimes complicit, often reworking White men's racism toward their own ends, and in several spectacular cases – Ida B. Wells most prominently – taking leadership in fighting White men's violence. But that violence has been sexualized, homosexualized.

I am not suggesting that racism can be reduced to latent homosexual desire, or that if we could somehow uncork homosexual desire, racism would disappear in an orgy of reconciliation and love. Still, it might help. If White men could allow themselves to experience how their persisting fantasies about Black men are intertwined with suppressed desire, racism would, at the very least, be reconfigured. The racism of White gay men who desire Black men is instructive here (Hemphill, 1991). The focus remains on the Black male body, but now it is revalorized as desirable: the "rapist" is now "stud." Black male subjectivity remains erased as the White male gaze remains fixed onto the same dark skin, the same muscled Black body that those sixteenth-century European invaders of Africa found so amazing and overwhelming that they wanted it for themselves, in subjugation, sexualized subjugation.

To understand the queer character of racism we must appreciate how relations between Black males and White males is that of a "romance" gone terribly wrong, as Leslie Fiedler's (1948, 1966) remarkable analysis makes clear. Not that the Black man ever reciprocated the desire of his pursuer: his enslavement meant he was never free to negotiate the terms of the relationship, at least from the position of social and political equality. But the subtext of desire experienced and rejected gets expressed in the myriad of ways the two "bounce off" each other, as every effort to find a new rapprochement is undermined by the bitter echoes of the past. If we are to "teach tolerance," to engage in any anti-racist education worthy of the name, we teachers – in classrooms, in corporate boardrooms, on the street, in Congress – must appreciate that the educational projects of tolerance and multiculturalism are inextricably intertwined with feminist and queer theory, not just conceptually but historically. The gender of racial politics and violence in America is queer.

ACKNOWLEDGEMENT

My thanks to Chris Myers, Director of Peter Lang, New York, for allowing me to draw upon *The Gender of Racial Politics and Violence in America* in the composition of this chapter.

ENDNOTES

[1] Consider Engels' letter to Marx [Manchester, 22 June 1869]: Dear Moor, ...The pederasts are beginning to count themselves, and discover that they are a power in the state...they cannot fail to triumph. Guerre aux cons, paix aus trus-de cul [war on the cunts, peace to the assholes] will now be the slogan. It is a bit of luck that we, personally, are too old to have to fear that, when this party wins, we shall have to pay physical tribute to the victors. But the younger generation!....Best greetings. Your F.E. (quoted in Parker 1993, 32).

[2] Homosociality recalls Eve Kosofsky Sedgwick's (1985) discussion in Between Men of nineteenth- and twentieth-century Anglo-American male bonding rituals which used – and use still – the abject image of the homosexual to imagine their bonds free of same-sex desire, thereby normalizing heterosexuality and rendering it compulsory. See also Irigaray (1985), Rich (1980), Rubin (1975)

REFERENCES

Allport, G. (1958). *The nature of prejudice.* New York: Anchor Books. [Originally published in 1954 by Addison-Wesley.]

Black, E. and Black, M. (1992). *The vital South: How presidents are elected.* Cambridge, MA: Harvard University Press.

Burstein, J. Q. (1977). *Conjugal visits in prison: Psychological and social consequences.* Lexington, MA: Lexington Books.

Carby, H. V. (1987). *Reconstructing womanhood: The emergence of the Afro-American novelist.* New York: Oxford University Press.

Chodorow, N. J. (1978). *The reproduction of mothering.* Berkeley: University of California Press.

Cooper, A. J. (1988/1892). *A voice from the South.* [Introduction by Mary Helen Washington.] New York: Oxford University Press.

Decosta-Willis, M. (Ed.). (1995). *The Memphis diary of Ida B. Wells.* [Foreword by Mary Helen Washington. Afterward by Dorothy Sterling.] Boston, MA: Beacon Press.

Dworkin, A. (1974). *Woman hating.* New York: E. P. Dutton.

Ferrell, C. L. (1986). *Nightmare and dream: Antilynching in Congress, 1917-1922.* New York: Garland.

Fiedler, Leslie (1948). "Come back to the raft ag'in, Huck Honey!" *Partisan Review* 15, 664-711.

Fiedler, L. A. (1966). *Love and death in the American novel.* [Revised edition.] New York: Stein & Day.

Foucault, M. (1995 [1979]). *Discipline and punish: The birth of the prison.* [Trans. Alan Sheridan.] New York: Vintage.

Gates, Jr., H. L. (1996). *Colored people: A memoir.* New York: Alfred A. Knopf.

Gilmore, D. (1990). *Manhood in the making.* New Haven: Yale University Press.

Grossberg, M. (1990). Institutionalizing masculinity: The law as masculine profession. In Mark C. Carnes & Clyde Griffen (eds.), *Meanings for manhood: Constructions of masculinity in Victorian America* (133-151). Chicago: University of Chicago Press.

Grosz, E. (1995). *Space, time, and perversion: Essays on the politics of bodies.* New York: Routledge.

Hall, J. D. (1979). *Revolt against chivalry: Jessie Daniel Ames and the women's campaign against lynching.* New York: Columbia University Press.

Hemphill, E. (Ed.) (1991). *Brother to brother: Collected writings by black gay men* (xv-xxxi). [Conceived by Joseph Beam. Project managed by Dorothy Beam.] Los Angeles: Alyson Books.

Hernton, C. C. (1988 [1965]). *Sex and racism in America.* New York: Doubleday (Anchor).

Hocquenghem, G. (1978). *Homosexual desire.* London: Allison & Busby.

Irigaray, L. (1985). *This sex which is not one.* [Trans. Catherine Porter.] Ithaca, NY: Cornell University Press.

Johnson, J. W. (1960 [1912]). *The autobiography of an ex-colored man.* New York: Hill & Wang.

Moynihan, D. P. (1965). *The Negro family: The case for national action.* Office of Policy, Planning and Research, Department of Labor. Washington, DC: Government Printing Office.

Parker, A. (1993). Unthinking sex: Marx, Engels, and the scene of writing. In Michael Warner (ed.), *Fear of a queer planet: Queer politics and social theory* (19-41). Minneapolis: University of Minnesota Press.

Pinar, W. F. (2001). *The gender of racial politics and violence in America.* New York: Peter Lang.

Pinar, W. F. (2004). *What is curriculum theory?* Mahwah, NJ: Lawrence Erlbaum.

Rich, A. (1980, Summer). Compulsory heterosexuality and lesbian existence. *Signs* 5 (4), pp. 631-660.

Roediger, D. R. (ed.) (1998). *Black on white: Black writers on what it means to be white* (255-273). New York: Schocken Books.

Rubin, G. (1975). The traffic in women: Notes on the "political economy" of sex. In Rayna Reiter (ed.), *Toward an anthropology of women* (157- 210). New York: Monthly Review Press.

Scacco, Jr., A. M. (1975). *Rape in prison.* Springfield, IL: Charles C. Thomas, Publisher.

Sedgwick, E. K. (1985). *Between men: English literature and male homosocial desire.* New York: Columbia University Press.

Sinfield, A. (1994). Forward to Mark Simpson's *Male impersonators* (ix-xii). New York: Routledge.

Ware, V. (1992). *Beyond the pale: White women, racism and history.* London: Verso.

Wells, I. B. (1970). *Crusade for justice: The autobiography of Ida B. Wells.* [Edited by Alfreda Duster.] Chicago: University of Chicago Press.

Weyl, N. (1979). *Karl Marx: Racist.* New York: Arlington House.

White, W. (1929). *Rope and faggot: A biography of judge lynch.* New York: Alfred A. Knopf.

Young-Bruehl, E. (1996). *The anatomy of prejudices.* Cambridge, MA: Harvard University Press.

Zangrando, R. L. (1980). *The N.A.A.C.P. Crusade against lynching,* 1909-1950. Philadelphia: Temple University Press.

DAVID G. SMITH

NOT ROCKET SCIENCE:

On the limits of conservative pedagogy

Abstract. This paper takes conservative pedagogy to mean forms of teaching and learning that are constructed through a logic of self-enclosure. Drawing on the work of Argentinean philosopher Enrique Dussel (now living in exile in Mexico), the paper seeks to show how, in the Western tradition, this logic arises as the preeminent logic of modernity, beginning in the fifteenth century. Its poverty lies in its inability or unwillingness to face what lies outside the constraints of its own identity. It is also connected to contemporary structures of global inequality. Authentic pedagogy must face the Other of its own identity.

Not long ago I visited a friend living in an upper middle class neighborhood in my city. There, the houses are all well maintained, the streets are wide and clean and in the warmer months, Philippina nannies can be seen strolling the young of many of the two income families of the area. The local elementary and junior high schools have a reputation for attracting the best teachers in the city and many students from across town are bussed or driven by their parents to take advantage of these schools that repeatedly do well on provincial achievement tests.

On the day of my visit, the weather being fine, after lunch I went for a walk. Very soon two women of thirty-something age were seen approaching. It seemed they, too, were on a walk after taking their children back for the afternoon school session. As they passed, I overheard one say to the other, "I don't care if my kid is a rocket scientist or not. I just want him to be able to deal with whatever comes to meet him in life."

What I would like to do in this paper is undertake a kind of meditation on this conversational fragment, unwrapping it carefully to show its multidimensionality and to show how, in its very simplicity perhaps, it is implicated in some of the deepest difficulties we face as teachers in a globalizing world.

On the surface the remark seems fine, quite ordinary, and indeed good on several levels. There is the attempt to be realistic for one's child in terms of future career. Of course, the desire to prepare children for life is a cornerstone of modern education. Who could argue? These are 'motherhood' issues, which this particular mother rearticulated in her own way very well. So what is the difficulty?

I want to ask the hermeneutic question, What does it mean, "to be able to deal with whatever comes in life?" What understanding of "life" is involved in such a claim? For one thing, to claim success, the full register of life's offerings would have to be known in advance, so that success could be checked off. But under such

121

K. Cooper and R. White (eds.), The Practical Critical Education, 121–131.

circumstances, what happens when an encounter with life shatters the register itself? Or, in the pedagogical situation, what becomes of experience, and experiencing, if the appropriate response to every situation is already claimed, even, say, the situation of openness and ambiguity? ("OK Jason, here's how to handle ambiguity!"). Surely in the long run this is a recipe for despair in young people. If the future is not open, why should I go on?

The key difficulty in the mother's assumption, then, is its one-sidedness. That is, it assumes the possibility of full understanding *before* an encounter with the "coming" of life, such that, in the face of an encounter with another (an Other), the Other can be dealt with only in a way that leaves the dealing Self intact. At the conclusion of the encounter, the dealing Self can claim, "I have dealt with it." The consequences for the Other of the encounter are not really of particular concern; what matters most is that I have dealt with them according to the logics of my own self-sufficiency. I am still alive. I did not suffer a death of any sort, whether existential, emotional, material, or spiritual.

It may be suggested that indeed "dealing with what comes to meet me in life" in fact *presumes* the possibility of my own transformation, but if that is so, then it is more the case that life has dealt with me, rather than the other way around. This is a theme I will take up in more detail later. For now, I wish to suggest that cultivating the capacity to deal with whatever comes to meet one in life is essentially a conservative value, based on the desire to conserve oneself, one's life, one's value system at all costs. It is to define for oneself, for one's group, one's neighborhood the conditions by which any encounter might be judged a success, *in advance of* the encounter itself. As such, it is a value system that is inherently violent against the Other, and this violence can take many forms. Relatively benign forms include practices such as simple neglect, fake interest or willful ignorance; more horrific is the case of contemporary American foreign policy, i.e. "Become like us, or we will destroy you. But then if you become too much like us, we will destroy you as well." (McMurtry, 2002, *passim*) Basically this approach amounts to a refusal to see life as pedagogical, as always everywhere bearing a message from beyond the contours of one's own experience, a form of invitation to an ever-deepening human maturity.

In directly pedagogical terms, violence against children arises from a fear of their social otherness, in which case the function of education is to train children into obedience to given norms. This presumption has a long history in Western societies since the Renaissance, and the eventual emergence of Child Study as a scientific discipline in the nineteenth century (Kessen, 1965). Basically it means, "Kids, this is the game we are playing; if you fail, it is because there is something wrong with you, not the game itself." Culturally speaking, for the young it means alienation from the broader life-stream of human experience, arising from an adult refusal to see children as "coming" from any order different from what is already known. For us as adults it means giving up on the means of our own rejuvenation, literally on the possibility of remaining young in heart, mind and spirit (> L. re + *juvenis*, young) through an embracing engagement with what at first we do not understand. Later I will consider how pedagogy might be oriented (interesting word) less violently, and more centrally concerned for our common health as a species. In the meantime, let us turn to a term constituting the other half of the conversation fragment of our neighborhood mother, namely "rocket science".

"Rocket science" has entered the English vernacular to express a pinnacle of human achievement, with the rocket scientist ascribed ultra-high status within the pantheon of desirable professions. The phrase "One doesn't have to be a rocket scientist to know that ..." is a negative qualifier attached to offering an opinion under the double strategy of indirectly linking one's opinion to the exceptional intelligence of a rocket scientist while modestly deferring his/her authority in making claims for oneself. This doubling is apparent in our mother's conversational fragment. My son *might* become a rocket scientist (which of course would secretly please me greatly), or might not, which I can accept too. But the point is, rocket science has become a standard against which other kinds of performance can be measured.

What is rocket science?[1] From its very beginnings in China in the thirteenth century, when Chinese soldiers fought off Mongol invaders with "arrows of fire" powered by "the black powder" now known as gunpowder, rocket science has been a center-piece primarily of military research and development. Today it is also associated with space exploration, but even this is driven by military imperatives, as space surveillance satellites feed the information systems necessary for global military superiority. Even domestically, all television signals used in the world today are controlled by a relatively few satellites put in place through rocket science, which ensures that virtually all contemporary television programming must now pass through the filter of military intelligence and the corporate money chains that support it (Ford, GE, Exxon, the Carlyle Group etc.). Since the 1960s, the government of the United States has fought vigorously to control satellite activity in outer space. The recent explosions of both Brazilian and Japanese rockets during the attempted launch of their respective research and communications satellites are not mysterious when considered in the light of the US government's global imperial aims (Ikenberry, 2002). For the United States, the rockets' "red glare" and the "bombs bursting in air" are taken as signs of national survival, "proof through the night that our flag was still there." Under this imaginary, rocket science is the means for keeping at bay those deep anxieties that the current world order may be crumbling. More on that later.

There are several aspects of rocket science that are worth noting here. According to military science writers Fought and Quilmartin (2002)[2], what distinguishes rocket propulsion from other propulsion systems is that "the thrust produced is independent of the medium through which the vehicle travels." Propulsion engines such as turbo-jets or even gas combustion engines all require intake of oxygen during travel, such that sensitivity to the surrounding environment during the journey is a key aspect of any journey's success. Rockets on the other hand travel independently of their traversing environment. The full stock of fuel must be on board the rocket at commencement, after which nothing further is required. This condition underscores how in rocket science all calculations for success must be determined in advance of the journey, so that the target can be reached predictably. The journey itself, the Way of it, is only important insofar as a calculus of it can be predetermined to avoid failure of reaching the desired destination. The mediating environment is something that must be 'dealt with' so that the aim, target or endpoint can be reached without interference. In this sense, then, we can see that there is a connection between rocket science and our mother's appeal to it as a register for her son's ability to succeed in dealing with life in advance of a real encounter.

Secondly, rockets are *missiles* and hence are linked linguistically both to *missives* and *missions* (> L. *miss*-, send). Rockets are part of a larger cultural repertoire of activities involved in the sending of messages, conveying to others the intentions of the sender. *Missives* have the status of "official letter"(*OED* ninth edition) carrying the full authority of the sender so that the receiver is left in no doubt regarding the seriousness of the message conveyed. *Missions* are delegations of religious authority whose purpose is to lead the other into the mission's Truth hermeneutic. That military operations are often described as missions points to the link, in the Western tradition at least, between religion and militarism. In the five hundred year trajectory of Western imperialism from 1492, the cross and the sword traveled together as symbolic companions (Galeano, 1997). In Anglo-American military operations, the explosive charges that rockets carry are called "ordnance", which is a term originating in the Middle English "ordinance", meaning not just an "authoritative order or decree" but also, significantly, "a religious rite" (*OED* ninth edition): Bombing as a worship ritual.

What I am trying to do here is to take the remark of our neighborhood mother as a kind of cultural artifact, within which are compressed various cognitive, historical, epistemological and existential linkages. Such linkages typically lie beyond or below the purview of direct consciousness, but their sedimentation within active, living, day-to-day language speaks of their ongoing presence, both within structures of understanding as well as more importantly within the structures of life practice itself. Remember the context: upper middle class, everything under control, neat and tidy. OK kid, maybe not rocket science (although that would be nice), but dammit, we'll make sure you can deal with whatever comes to meet you. Our future is at stake, and any decent future should look like the present, thank you very much.

I have been told that when this suburban subdivision was first built in the 1960s, a sign graced the entry to the neighborhood with the words, "A community for normal people like you." Of course the valorization of normalcy was normal in early 1960s North America. The Bell curve ruled just about everything. This was before cracks began to appear in the edifice of (North) American global power (Vietnam War, OPEC Oil crisis etc.), that is before knocks began to be heard from the outside the door of domestic serenity; before any registration on the collective unconscious that the Good Life was actually sustained through a whole series of economic and political dependencies *elsewhere* that rendered (and continues to render) that Life highly problematic and vulnerable. The Good Life is problematic and vulnerable precisely because of its entrapment within a logic of self-sufficiency and its blindness to the suffering of global others, a blindness that makes the delusion of self-sufficiency possible.

This is deep stuff and hard to face for ordinary decent citizens like our two mothers who are simply trying to do the best they can for their children within the horizons of their own self-understanding. To make matters worse, the money chains that support global media systems work tirelessly to ensure that the average citizen living within the Anglo-American power nexus is completely shielded from the realities that call into question the foundations of everyday life. The academy (universities and colleges) are completely complicit in this delusional game too, because the epistemic infrastructure of most academic disciplines is itself built on principles of cognitive self-enclosure that deprive the knowing self of the benefit of encounter with what lies beyond the contours of its own imagination. These are strident claims that demand clarification, a work to which attention will given in what follows. The implications for our understanding of pedagogy will also be considered.

What is the logic of self-enclosure, and how has it arisen? The first thing to say is that self-enclosure is not a universal human disposition, by any means. East Indian political psychologist, Ashis Nandy (1988), has noted, for example, that one reason the British were able to dominate a continent of hundreds of millions with a cadre of expatriate colonial administrators whose number never exceeded fifty thousand is because within Hindu Vedantic understanding, the Sanskrit phrase, *tuam sat asi* – "That thou art" – means that You and I share a single reality. That is to say, the Western Self/Other binary formulation is belied on close investigation. As humans, we are all part of the same reality, even though we may share various and different characteristics at any given time and place. Difference is not a problem to be 'solved', with the Other regarded as grist for the mill of predetermined understanding.

So the arrival of the British in India (after the Portuguese, who came after the Muslims, who came after the Mongols, who came after the Greeks of Alexander the Great in 2 BC) was not an arrival of total strangers, monsters from beyond, but simply another manifestation of reality, not something to be fought against *per se*. To the British it was said in effect, your arrival here is not a problem for us. This experience had its parallel with arrival of the earliest European settlers in Canada who could never have survived without the open generosity of the indigenous population (Weatherford, 1988).

Of course, such arrivals become a problem later, when it is reluctantly comprehended that those who have arrived bring with them a form of philosophy or self-understanding that is preclusive; that is, it precludes the possibility that you, as Other, could have any value beyond what I could assess for you. In other words, you have value only insofar as you are of value *to me*. You have no intrinsic value of your own, or even if you do, that is your own private affair, which has relevance only insofar as it threatens my own self-understanding, in which case I have the means to destroy you.

The contemporary philosopher who has most poignantly tracked the origin and trajectory of the form of self-understanding that has characterized the *imperium* of Western culture for over five hundred years, is Enrique Dussel, an Argentinean now living in exile in Mexico. According to Dussel (1995; 1996) the Western *episteme* consolidated its imperialistic character about half a century after Cristobel Colon (< Eng. colony) first landed in the Caribbean in 1492. The subsequent plunder of 'Latin' America by Portuguese and Spanish conquistadors required a theological justification, and this was worked out in a debate in 1550 between Gines de Sepulveda and Bartolome de las Casas in Valladolid, Spain.[3]

De las Casas had been a soldier in the first wave of conquest, but was so appalled by the slaughter that, on returning to Spain, he became a priest with the intention of ministering among the Aztecs, employing the means that had marked the early Church at its inception in the gentile world of the first century. This involved 'living among' people and re-working one's own self-understanding through the conceptual and cultural understandings of the people with whom one lived.[ii] de Sepulveda on the other hand was the theologian of the Catholic establishment. His argument, which won the day, was based on the premise that since European civilization is superior to all others in every way, Spain is justified in its slaughter of indigenous peoples as part of a 'Christian' strategy of civilizing.

De Sepulveda appealed to the New Testament story of the lord who invited friends to a sumptuous banquet (Luke 14:14-24). When all invitees came up with excuses for not being able to attend, in fury, the lord charged his son to go into the city streets and "invite" the poor to come in. When there was still space left over, he insisted that roads and fields be scoured, and all those found should be "compelled" to come in. At this point de Sepulveda invoked a logical turn first proposed by the theologian Augustine in the fourth century. Human conversion to civilization may contain two stages: first, invitation; second, compulsion. Argued de Sepulveda: "I maintain that we are not only permitted to invite these barbarians, violators of nature, blasphemers, and idolators…. But we may also *compel* them, so that under the bondage of Christian rule they might hear the apostles who announce the gospel to them." (cited in Dussel, 1995, 67) Under this rubric, the anguish of the Other is justified as the "necessary price" of its civilization, and expiation for its "culpable immaturity." (Ibid., 66)

Here can be witnessed what Dussel calls the "gigantic *inversion*" of European modernity: "[T]he innocent victim becomes culpable and the culpable victimizer becomes innocent." (67) Most relevant to our discussion here is the way that the de las Casas/de Sepulveda debate announces the unique strategy of empire to arise out of the mind-set which was clearly evolving by the fifteenth century. This mind-set we now understand and name as "Eurocentrism" (see Said, 1995), and more than any other social or political movement of the last five hundred years, it has defined, at least for itself, but also indirectly everyone else, the basic structure of geo-political affairs. Its end-game is rocket science; its pedagogy begins with invitation but ends in compulsion.

Critique of Eurocentrism has been a staple of humanities departments in most universities since the arrival of "post" theory (poststructuralism, postmodernism, postcolonialism etc.) in the 1960s. What has been lacking in this work, however, is a depth of understanding of *how* Europe came to understand itself as the center of global affairs. As such, the forgotten partners lie silenced on the periphery, fully aware that not only does the center hold its position precisely at their expense, in a relation of inverse dependency, but also that this present set of historically constituted arrangements is and can be challenged and changed. The extraordinary precariousness of this situation has been brought 'home' to the Euro-American nexus by the events of September 11th 2001.

It is Enrique Dussel's contribution to reveal how Europe *became* "the center" in its own global imaginary with the discovery and conquest of "Latin" America. By the sixteenth century, Africa, Asia and indeed America had become established in the European mind as peripheries. By the eighteenth century the philosopher Hegel had consolidated these circumstances into a philosophico-theological ideology in the concept of *Occidental Europe*: "Asia is the part of the world where the beginning is verified as such…. But Europe is absolutely the center and the end (*das Zentrum und das Ende*) of the ancient world and the Occident; Asia is the absolute Orient." (cited in Dussel, 1995, p. 22). Asia in this instance is Asia Minor, constituted by the Muslim empires evolved since the seventh century, as well as the continent from the Sea of the Arabs (Arabian Sea) to the Sea of the South (the Pacific), now named as the Orient. In Europe, "…the Christian principle has passed through the formidable discipline of culture…and therefore the End of Days has arrived; the idea of Christianity has reached its full realization." (p. 23, 24) Embodying the spirit of Christian liberty, Europe is now "the flag of the world" and from it, "universal principles of reason have developed….Custom and tradition are no longer of value." (Ibid.)

The circumstances through which "North" America and other countries like Australia and New Zealand come to fall under the name of Europe need not concern us here. The point is that all are inhabited by the spirit of Self centeredness, that is, the spirit that names its own terrain as the center around which all other identities circulate as peripheries, and against which those identities are compelled to define themselves. Not only that, but this set of arrangements bears the marks of sacralization. Christ = God = Europe (including Europe's children in North America and elsewhere). Of course, today the Occident has been secularized, but its cultural interstices are saturated mnemonically with its theological origins.

What remains now is to work out the implications of demythologizing Eurocentrism and bring that work back to a consideration of how pedagogy might proceed without the violence inherent in its contemporary presuppositions. Every mother's child deserves not to be trapped within the cage of his or her own subjectivity, given what is happening in the world today. More than anything else, what is required for *species* survival, not just ethnic, tribal, national or sectarian survival, are new forms of openness to one another, personally and collectively as well as a conjoint approaching of the table of deliberation regarding the shared human future. The boundaries and constraints that we typically draw around ourselves as forms of self-security and self-protection need to be shown for what they really are, which is, always and everywhere inevitably permeable, and always and everywhere "hinging" (i.e. like a hinge, to use a metaphor from Freire) on the reality of others. Pure seclusion behind constructions of identity is a delusional idea, as the Great Wall of China attests. A monumental and extraordinarily majestic work of engineering, certainly, designed to keep out the hoards of Mongol invaders of the late Middle Ages (to borrow a Eurocentric time frame), but ultimately the wall was a failure, a tragic hymn to paranoia that has equally monumental and equally futile contemporary exemplifications, *pace* homeland security policies sequent to 9/11. What the age of globalization demands is a consideration of how, and in what ways, persons may live with the inevitable fluid contingency of every identity. Indeed, among other things, identity itself is a mask (> L. *persona*, mask) that can be used to hide the fear of one's own insignificance, or indeed mortality (Becker, 1975; Loy, 2003).

The timeliness of Dussel's deconstructions becomes apparent when considering the multiple ways the Euro-American empire is currently in a state of chronic devolution (Bello, 2001, 2002; Gray, 1998; McMurtry, 2002). Massive financial indebtedness, increasing moral illegitimacy in the international sphere, collapse of social infrastructures within home territories, rising expectations from that eighty percent of the world's people who live externally to the Euro-American power nexus – all this plus the intimately intersected nature of today's global economy, conspires to evacuate the means by which the empire can sustain itself. Eurocentrism is finished, in reality though not yet in imagination, as the words of our neighborhood mother serve in reminder. It is to this imaginal context that I wish to turn in examining the challenges to pedagogy that the end of 'Europe', and now the end of 'America' as the inheritor of Europe's imaginary, brings forward.

Subjectivity is the marker of the Age of Europe, suggests Dussel, and it is tied to the condition of wealth accumulation spawned by the almost unimaginable riches that flowed to Europe from Latin America beginning with the first Spanish conquests, and then from Africa and Asia. Euro-American wealth from the petroleum of the Middle East in this century is only the latest in a long genealogy of resource conquests throughout the world: the invasions of Afghanistan and Iraq part of an intended extension of this conquest into Central Asia (Brzezinsky, 1997). Material wealth is the condition under which theories of the Self flourish most vigourously. After all, if I am rich, I must be doing something right, at least by my own calculations. More broadly, this basic association is what enabled Europe to articulate and nurture its multiple forms of Self aggrandizement as theoretical and philosophical possibilities, beginning, say, with Descartes (1596-1650), consolidating with Kant (1724-1804), Hegel (1770-1831) and even Adam Smith (1723-90), and culminating with Darwin (1809-82). Indeed, the philosophical infrastructure of the Western imaginary is largely defined by these gentlemen even today, and their habitation extends deep into the webs of the pedagogical theory being pronounced daily in faculties of education the world over as forms of universal truth. The reign of Europe is through its intellectual traditions as much as through its more naked aggressions. Descartes' *cogito* provides the assurance that I can think myself into a security of being. ("OK kids, THINK!!" [Otherwise you don't exist, you're a nobody]). From Kant, I gain confidence that the way I reason is the same everywhere and that all reasonable people are just like me. If they are not, then they are not human; it's as simple as that ("Boys! Stop fighting and be REASONABLE like proper gentlemen!). Hegel? We heard from him earlier in this paper ("Now children, Jesus can help you overcome ALL your difficulties, because he has overcome everything already, as our wonderful life attests!"). For Adam Smith, self-interest is the deepest character trait of a human being ("Dear Graduating Class: Take care of yourselves, and the world will be taken care of"). Darwin gave us the White European Man as the pinnacle of human evolution, an evolution solidified pedagogically through Piaget and child development theory which announces logico-mathematical thinking as the climax beyond which any form of human cognition is impossible. The mother was right after all, rocket science rocks, man! Five hundred thousand Iraqi children dying of malnutrition and disease as a result of US/NATO bombing and sanctions directed from Washington since 1992 is "worth it", according to President Bill Clinton's Secretary of State Madeleine Albright (McMurtry, 2002).

In teacher education, and many Euro-American graduate programs in education, these multiple forms of subjectivity theory have coalesced into multiple ways of celebrating individual expressivity and self-claiming, whether as narrative research, story telling, phenomenology or features like "expressive objectives" in curriculum. Actually, there is nothing at all wrong with these *per se*. Indeed they still have an important place within the canons of teaching and teacher education. The central problem is that they are based upon an incomplete equation: My Experience = My Experience. Within Dussel's understanding, a fuller equation would read, My Experience = My Accounts of My Experience + Everything Else. Of course, to be meaningful Everything Else needs concrete elaboration, although even without such elaboration it can serve as a place-holding reminder that my experience is *never just* my experience, it *always* borders on that of others who are or have been impacted by it, and whose interpretations of what I say about myself could be at variance with my own. Perhaps even more importantly, Everything Else stands for what in the new ecology theory is called "the implicate order" (Griffiths, 1989) – the whole planetary and cosmological life that is *implied* in every single life. Within this imaginary, at the very least, I must give my own accounts of experience always with the greatest modesty and humility, never as triumphalist tales with my Self as inexorably the hero.

In a more tragic sense, what has been lost in the blind celebration of Subjectivity within modernity are the historical reasons why Subjectivity should come to be celebrated as such. That is, celebrating Subjectivity is a pushing off from something, indeed from historical conditions in which persons were persecuted and oppressed by hierarchical religion, monarchies, and more lately, industrial culture. Subjectivity therefore marks a refusal of individual helplessness, an announcement of my significance, in spite of all evidence to the contrary. This surely is a positive accomplishment, but it is only so as long as the broader socio-cultural and historical circumstances remain part of the equation. When or if those drop off, then Subjectivity becomes, as Max Weber said, "a cage." (cited in Baum, 1976). The Self, as my identity, becomes frozen within a static interpretive frame that ensures my own infantilization as historical processes move beyond me.

When I forget the historical forces that contributed to bringing my own sense of Self into being, so do I also forget that Others are coming into being as a result of their own circumstances. Indeed it is this forgetfulness of Others, especially suffering Others and my forgetfulness of being 'implicated' in that suffering, that constitutes the central problematic of the Eurocentric imagination. Yawning self-sufficiency carries the seeds of its own demise.

For teaching and teacher education, what needs to be recovered more than anything else, is a broader sense of World which can free young people from the cage of subjectivity that their own more immediate environments (including class, tribe or nation) has constructed for them. Inevitably this will result in clashes with the forces that would banish all Difference under the privilege of the Same, i.e.

forces that would attempt to make all Others like Me personally and collectively. Most radically, educating children and young people to be able to "deal with whatever comes to meet them in life" must, to be honest, prepare them for death, without which life has no meaning. Here, death does not mean a morbid tragedy without solace, but an acceptance of the fact that for life to have a chance, certain things have to die, and usually this means the things that I hold most dear as a way of securing myself in my own imagination or within my inherited group. How to do this requires attention to those who carry about them a spirit of human wisdom in its deepest senses, wisdom born of great loss, great suffering, and who bear witness to the multiple ways the mighty always fall on the sword of their own self sufficiency. Without learning to 'let go', a hand cannot grasp what is extended to it from beyond itself as the possibility of a new beginning. As Enrique Dussel has said, "The problem today is the exhaustion of a 'civilizing' system that has come to an end." (1999, 19) What is next? A better question might be, What is being forgotten?

ENDNOTES

[1] For an excellent brief history of rocket science, see the extended essay by Fought and Quilmartin (2002). I am indebted to their work here.
[2] For an elaborated version of this debate, see Dussel (1995), pp. 66ff.
[3] See Morton Enslin (1956), Christian Beginnings, New York: Harper and Row, for a discussion of how the earliest Christian missionaries engaged Greek philosophy to reformulate their own self-understanding

REFERENCES

Baum, G. (1976). *Religion and alienation: A theological reading of Sociology*. Mahwah NJ: Paulist Press.
Becker, E. (1975). *Denial of death*. New York: Harper and Row.
Bello, W. (2001). *The Future in the balance: Essays on globalization and resistance*. Oakland CA: Food First Books.
Bello, W. (2002). *Deglobalization: Ideas for a new world economy*. London: Zed Books.
Brzezinski, Z. (1997). *The grand chessboard: American primacy and its geostrategic imperatives*. New York: Basic Books.
Dussel, E. (1999). Beyond Eurocentrism: The world-system and the limits of modernity. In F. Jameson and M. Miyoshi (eds.), *The cultures of globalization*. (3-31). Durham NC: Duke University Press.
Dussel, E. (1996). *The underside of modernity: Apel, Ricoeur, Rorty, Taylor and the philosophy of liberation*. E. Mendieta (Trans. and Ed.), *Atlantic Highlands*. NJ: Humanities Press.
Dussel, E. (1995). *The inventions of the Americas: Eclipse of "the Other" and the myth of modernity*. New York: Continuum.
Enslin, M. (1956). *Christian beginnings*. New York: Harper and Row.
Fought, S. and Quilmartin, J. Jr. (2002) Rocket and missile systems. *Encyclopedia Britannica* (Software Version), no page numbers.
Galeano, E. (1997). *Open veins in Latin America: Five centuries of the pillage of a continent*. I. Allende (Trans.) New York: Monthly Review Press.
Gray, J. (1998). *False dawn: The delusions of global capitalism*. London: Verso Books.
Griffiths, B. (1989). *A new vision of reality: Western science, Eastern mysticism and Christian faith*. Springfield IL: Templegate Publishers.
Ikenberry, G. (2002). America's imperial ambition. *Foreign Affairs*. 81(5). September/October, 44-60.
Kessen, W. (1965). *The child*. New York: Wiley.
Loy, D. (2003). *Great awakenings: Buddhist social theory*. Boston MA: Wisdom Publications.

McMurtry, J. (2002). *Value wars: The global market versus the life economy*. Toronto ON: Garamond.
Nandy, A. (1988). Reconstructing childhood. In *Tradition, tyranny and utopia*. Delhi: Oxford University Press.
Said, E. (1995). *Orientalism*. New York: Vintage Books
Weatherford, J. (1988). *Indian givers: How the Indians of the Americas transformed the world*. New York: Fawcett Columbine.

PART THREE:

CRITICAL LEADERSHIP FOR A DEMOCRATIC EDUCATION

While leadership tends to be situated within a specific set of skills, Critical leadership tends to not differentiate between formal and informal leadership. As a result, leadership is not necessarily the sole province of administration but can be characterized through individual and group collective action. Thus leadership, particularly Critical leadership, can easily become attributes of teachers and students, as well as of interested and involved members of the society at large. But what is a Critical leader? Does Critical leadership subscribe to a particular set of tenets?

Because Critical pedagogy is typically, traditionally and historically a grassroots kind of movement, "Critical leadership" is almost an anomaly. With a perspective that questions power differentials, Critical leadership seems, at first glance, to run counter to the prevailing notion of what a leader is. Perhaps it is more to think of what a leader *can* be that helps to advance the notion of Critical leadership.

Of course, a Critical leader must be cognizant of, knowledgeable about, and be predisposed to a leadership role. A Critical leader must also be literate in a politically Critical sense and must have amassed a certain fund of learnedness to draw upon. From here the goal of the Critical leader, no matter what his or her position in any organization, is to work towards the goals that support authentic democratic values. The result of these efforts may be to develop a strong propensity for the capacity building of human agency in order to promote social justice through positive social change.

The third and final section of this volume seeks to understand what leadership within a Critical framework entails. This section discusses effective practical strategies in the continuous development of the leader who is at once Critical, reflective and democratic. The following contributors point to the possibility for the reconceptualization of leadership in dimensions that are at once Critical and strongly supportive of and actively advocate for human agency and voice.

Chapter 9, written by Duncan Waite, Susan Field Waite and Sharon Fillion, is entitled "Duplicity, democracy and domesticity: Educational leadership for Critical democratic action." This chapter deals with the contexts within which Critical democratic leadership transpires, the processes involved in such leadership, and the actions incumbent upon such leaders. This chapter describes the parameters of effective Critical democratic leadership. Waite and his co-authors discuss the factors and influences that delimit Critical democratic leadership. These authors question how such leaders will be known as well as behavioural traits that they will exhibit. The authors employ a Critical sociocultural lens and advocate that leaders engage in Critical hermeneutics – personally and with their constituencies. Such a forensic approach is necessary in order to deconstruct the duplicitous rhetoric of democracy. Waite et al maintain that this is especially true in today's society where conditions of new public management are creating not only stultifying accountability regimes but other conditions that are indeed questionable to the public good.

Noah de Lissovoy and Peter McLaren contribute their ideas in Chapter 10. Entitled "Ghosts in the procedure: Notes on teaching and subjectivity in a new era", this article discusses teaching as a space of material, ideological and subjective struggle and transformation. This struggle suggests a terrain in which the political and spiritual commitment of the educator must contest intensified control and domination of current educational processes. It is this terrain that exists in the context of a newly energized and exploitative contemporary global capitalism. The authors argue that educators need to challenge the hyper-racism of official schooling, as well as their own ideological construction as pacified citizen subjects. Furthermore, the enforcement of this construction, which occurs through fear and fatalism, must be interrogated, dismantled and eradicated. In this regard, contemporary changes in the material conditions of public schooling are examined. Such material conditions include the effects of recent neo-liberal reforms and it is suggested that these changes necessitate a corresponding modification in the subjective and political strategy of Critical pedagogy. Such a pedagogy should focus greater attention on global struggles against imperialism, as well as a collective resistance to the alienation enforced by professional educational identities. De Lissovoy and McLaren call for a more decisive break with official school culture through the practice of "oppositional teaching", as well as a more sophisticated awareness of the complexity and discontinuity of student identity.

In the third chapter of this section, Chapter 11, Hilary Janks and Maselele Paulina Sethole show us some of these principles in action. Entitled "Reaching out and reaching in: "We had to develop ourselves first, before anybody can develop us", the authors recount how a poor, under-resourced primary school in a Black African township was changed from an object of pity to an institution to be proud of. It is here that the principal of this school reveals the profound difference between "leadership" and administration. Janks and Sethole describe the entire process of developing the schools' potential and thereby building greater capacity for literacy and learning, beginning with internal issues. Visitors' workshops, school development plans and leadership training courses followed. What makes this story so compelling is the clarity of purpose, the dedication and the ultimate success of the project, not only on its own terms but in terms that the greater society can see and appreciate. The ultimate turn-around of this school, due to the efforts of the principal, is a model of interrogating one's own assumptions, building capacity and moving forward in as direct a line as possible. This requires a shared vision and unwavering commitment to the students, teachers and the surrounding community in order to develop a distinctive, positive ethos, school and community participation and a reaching out to the surrounding area. This reaching out and reaching inwards has resulted in a kind of organic leadership that is as distinctive as it is Critical.

Chapter 12, "Opening the text: Voicing a future", written by Terry Wrigley, continues the theme of complexity and discontinuity of student identity by examining how schools typically close down on learning. The author suggests that the voice and agency of the learner are systematically denied through the organization and its disciplining of relationships, the curriculum as a selection of content and through the preferred modes of teaching and learning. Wrigley exchanges the idea of "orderly schools" for the term "respectful schools". He suggests that the curriculum is largely taught in isolation of historical analyses such as racist oppression and the disempowerment of marginalized groups. Not only must the curriculum include the location of human activity within history, it must also situate the individual within a larger frame of "social totality", investigate the roots of conflict grounded in opposing interests and make connections to the work of "the human social making of relations and products". Through this, Wrigley reaches out to the pedagogical denial of voice and agency by examining textuality and readership. In this way, the author strives to inform the reader as to the necessity of locating seminal texts that promote Critical thinking. By way of summary, Terry Wrigley suggests that Critical leaders need to engage with current norms at all levels. Improving existing schools is not enough – we need to *rethink* education

For the reader, it is hoped that these accounts serve to create an atmosphere in which one can begin to ponder what it means to be Critical. Having begun with a question of this nature, perhaps it is fitting to end with a question of a similar nature. The question asks how one can recognize, investigate and challenge values, assumptions and the influences acting upon the individual in order to develop a capacity that will nurture a Critical approach to literacy, learning and leadership.

DUNCAN WAITE, SUSAN FIELD WAITE AND SHARON
FILLION

DUPLICITY, DEMOCRACY AND DOMESTICITY:

Educational leadership for democratic action

Abstract. This chapter deals with the contexts within which critical democratic leadership transpires, the processes involved in such leadership, and the actions incumbent upon such leaders. Basically, what affects critical democratic leadership? How will such leaders be known? How will they behave? The authors employ a critical sociocultural lens and advocate that leaders engage in critical hermeneutics–personally and with their constituencies. Such a process is necessary to deconstruct the duplicitous rhetoric of democracy, especially under conditions of new public management and its stultifying accountability regimes, among other conditions.

1. READING THE SITUATION(S)

Influenced by shifting cultural dynamics and by cumulative acts of corporate and governmental duplicity and educator complicity, public schools are relinquishing their democratic mission for an economic, instrumentalist one. Educators' roles as leaders are being co-opted and subverted. Cultural and political forces are reshaping educators' roles and spheres of influence in ways that are slowly eroding state and local control over public education, while simultaneously expanding federal and corporate influence.

Our purpose here is to illuminate the complex, competing forces at play on the school principalship and on other types of school leaders, whether or not those leaders occupy a formally-designated leadership position or lead without a legitimizing bureaucratic authority. With an understanding, a critical reading, of those forces, we proceed to lay out an initial sketch of the possibilities for action. Our thrust in this chapter, then, is at once both theoretical *and* practical. We are concerned, above all, with the day-to-day actions and strategies of the politically-astute school leader. What is a leader to do with the knowledge and insight gained from a critical reading of his/her situation? How might such leaders both survive and make a difference in the lives of teachers and students, if not throughout society at large?

We begin with what we feel is essential to leadership, however it is practiced and no matter by whom it is practiced: That is, we think it fundamental that the critical leader develop his/her skill at reading the situations in which he/she operates with a critical eye. As we develop our thesis we will argue for a leadership skill that we refer to as a critical hermeneutic skill. Such a skill—an ability to 'read' between the

137

K. Cooper and R. White (eds.), The Practical Critical Education, 137–149.

lines, see behind the façade of social, historical, political situations—is a fundamental skill if one is to change the status quo.

Changing the status quo is essential. Among the numerous and often competing aims, purposes, or goals of education, we believe that education is, above all else, concerned with liberating the human potential in everyone. We feel schooling today seldom accomplishes this. Schooling today merely perpetuates inequities (Bourdieu & Passerson, 1977; Thomson, 2003) under the guise of content standards, standardization and technological "progress."

2. CURRENT SOCIAL, CULTURAL AND POLITICAL CONTEXTS OF SCHOOLING

In countries that provide free public education, education becomes a common shared cultural currency, and, as such, always carries the differing hopes, dreams, desires and ends of many. The dynamic discursive field of public education, however, has taken on a somewhat more instrumental, monolithic and authoritarian tenor of late. We see troubling shifts in the dominant conceptions of public education, in whose voices are given legitimacy in the field, in corporate and federalist governmental infringement upon state, local and professional governance of public education, and the roles of public school teachers.

We understand that education and schooling are complicated and complex—with counter-discourses always at play with/among the dominant discourses. However, given today's near total obsession with 'accountability,' measurement, and testing, the functionalist and instrumentalist purposes of school have, to our minds, asserted their hegemony over schools, children, teachers and administrators. Indeed, such functionalist purposes have so hypnotized the public that they have become, in the public's eye, the raison d'être for schools, their reason for being. That is to say, that schools and schooling have come to have little other purpose in the public discourse than simply raising test scores—something Ball (2000) describes as performativity, and which Waite, Boone, and McGhee (2001) equate with Goffman's notion of impression management.

In our darkest, most cynical moments, we are concerned that schools today do nothing other than teach test-taking. Borrowing concepts from the symbolic interactionists and ethnomethodologists, we think that children today are simply 'doing school,' rather than receiving an education in the broadest sense of the term. By extension, we fear teachers, too, are simply doing school rather than educating children and, further, that colleges of education and teacher education programs have come to instruct/teach prospective teachers not to teach for learning's sake, but simply are giving these budding teachers the tools necessary so that they, too, can 'do school.'

The obsession with testing and 'performing' combine with other, more global sociocultural forces to work against the liberatory project of education. Global economic problems, including tight money (i.e., economic recession, un-employment, etc.) and lean state budgets provide state, regional, and national legislators ample political cover for apportioning embarrassingly paltry sums for education at all levels. These social and economic forces intermingle with (i.e., both produce and are the products of) global trends identified with New Public Management (Dempster, Freakley & Parry, 2001), wherein, among other things, both federal and state governments provide fewer and fewer funds for public education while exerting more and more bureaucratic sanction and control over schools, colleges and universities. Today, local educators are given fewer resources while simultaneously relinquishing more autonomy.

There is an economic 'squeeze' on the locality, the municipality and, ultimately, the individual for funding public services like education. In public education in the US, especially, costs are being passed on to the individual. In many districts and schools, parents are being asked to pay fees for their children's participation in extracurricular activities, such as band and sports. In some places children are charged locker fees, supply fees and transportation fees. These fees can easily add up to hundreds of dollars per child per year.

The public's attitudes toward, and knowledge of, government may be another influence on what happens to and in public education. When over 50% of U.S. high school students think that it is okay for the government to censor newspapers and the Internet (Knight Foundation, 2005), it is unlikely that these citizens will resist ever more intrusive federal control of public education.

Global and national pressures and trends impact the local school and the local school leader. We remain cynical about most efforts to 'reform' schools, whether these efforts are locally targeted or are more systemic (Sarason, 1990). Generally, school reform or improvement efforts emanate from a functionalist epistemology and, therefore, are unlikely to address deep-seated and, to our minds, truly important issues—issues like learning, social justice, liberation and the realization of the potential of each individual child, no matter what direction that might take. Rather, to our jaundiced eyes, most school reform agendas are instrumentalist and corporatist in nature. For us, they seek to regiment students into roles as obedient producers and consumers, into 'knowledge workers,' in today's terms. Little time or attention is given in today's curriculum to fostering in children the skills, values, and dispositions necessary for them to take an active part in a democratic discourse. As we have written above, students today, for the most part, are engaged, not in education or schooling, but in 'doing school.' Teachers are as well. School has become a simulacrum.

Much has already been written about the deskilling of teachers (Apple, 1986), though rarely, if ever, has this concept been applied to the concomitant deskilling of school leaders, though surely this is the case. Administrators in today's schools, at least throughout most of the English-speaking world, become mid-level managers, petty bureaucrats whose days are filled with tests, test scores, and the so-called accountability data (McGhee & Nelson, 2005). Teachers are compliant (Waller, 1932). Administrators are not known for their bravery or their audacity. Whether through selection, socialization, or out of a sense of survival, administrators, on the whole, tend to be risk averse. For the most part, the institution of schooling serves to domesticate teachers and administrators, creating easy targets for corporate and federal raiders.

3. DOMESTICITY AND DEMOCRACY

Educational leaders have not only abandoned the wilderness for the false security of pens and barns of their own making, they have left the barn door open and invited the fox and the wolf inside. As Cuban (2003) has argued, educators' complicity in the corporate-led duplicity of school reform has historical precedent. To accomplish their school reform agendas, corporate leaders and governmental policy makers have needed the compliance of educators and the general public. As Marx and Engles once wrote, every political revolution needs an accompanying cultural one that convinces people of its necessity:

> For each new class which puts itself in the place of one ruling before it, is compelled, merely in order to carry through its aim, to represent its interest as the common interest of all the members of society, that is, expressed in ideal form: it has to give its ideas the form of universality, and represent them as the only rational, universally valid ones. (1845/1947, 40)

Corporate leaders, and others, assume it's their privilege to direct education and educational policy, partly because they engage in a form of rankism (Fuller, 2003); wherein those of a socially-constructed higher status or rank, or those who are successful in one social domain, feel it is their prerogative to dominate those of lesser rank, status or achievement, even outside of their area of expertise. From a sociology of knowledge perspective, education and educators are almost always of a lesser status.

Public schools are not mere businesses. Tanquay (2003), in arguing that universities, tertiary educational institutions, are not analogous to corporations, cited this passage from a speech by former Yale University President A. Barlett Giamatti:

> A college or university is an institution where financial incentives to excellence are absent, where the product line is not a unit or an object but rather a value-laden and life-long process; ... not profit or proprietary rights but the free good of knowledge; not efficiency of operation but equity of treatment; not increased productivity in economic terms but increased intensity of thinking about who we are and how we live and about the world around us. In such an institution, leadership is much more a rhetorical than a fiscal or "strategic" act. While never denigrating the day-to-day, never scorning the legitimate and difficult chores of management, never pretending that efficiency is useless or productivity irrelevant, leadership in such an institution must define institutional shape, that is, define its standards and purposes—define the coherent, sustainable, daring, shared effort of learning that will increase a given community's freedom, intellectual excellence, human dignity. (50-51)

When only one truth is told and legitimized, we are made to want what a duplicitous corporate culture promises, and so we barter one more piece of the democratic ideal, one more aspect of our roles as educators in hopes of attaining the promised land. In 1927, Dewey warned that, "[r]ule by an economic class may be disguised from the masses; rule by experts could not be covered up. It could be made to work only if the intellectuals become the willing tools of big economic interests" (1927/2000b, 169). In many ways, educators have been the complicit tools of corporate culture in its appropriation of public education. Too many educational administrators and teachers seek ways to accommodate to yet another set of external demands rather than to critically and publicly interrogate and engage the complex forces driving, for example, the advocacy of a particular set of "research-based strategies." In doing so, the integrity of public education and the integrity of educators are compromised. We would do well to remember Dewey's (1939/2000a, 167) comment that "there is no substitute for intelligence and integrity in cultural life. Anything else is a betrayal of human freedom no matter in what guise it presents itself."

Educators simultaneously are being relegated to a narrowly constructed domestic sphere, similar to the constructed "women's sphere" of the early 1800s. As Cott (1977) and others have demonstrated, the economic and social changes between 1780 and 1830 promoted the development of a "cult of domesticity," in which women's roles were redefined and constructed to meet the perceived economic and social needs of the time. Conduct manuals for women proliferated, as the roles and values of "true women" were delimited. The "bonds of womenhood" (Cott, 1977) of two hundred years ago can be compared with the bonds of teacherhood today, when the role of the teacher is to be a selfless expert in subject matter, interested only in the worlds of his or her own classroom, tied to other teachers through a "right" set of values, with no economic or political interests, with no desire to venture outside of the defined sphere, with meek acceptance of the scripts written for him or her. The bonds of teacherhood, which bind teachers into superficially pleasing forms for the public, ultimately cripple teachers, though the socialization process happens so gradually that it seems almost natural. As we socialize novices to these norms, we ourselves are complicit in reproducing schooling.

4. LEADERS AND THEIR RESPONSIBILITIES

Educational leaders have a responsibility to promote and engage in dialogue on critical issues in education, such as what counts as "scientific research." Educational leaders must not abdicate their role in educating themselves, their colleagues and the general public on issues in ways that are critical, public, participatory and intellectually honest. Instead of trying to "win," or provide staff development workshops to help others to win the name-shame-and-blame game of high-stakes testing, educational leaders have a responsibility to expose the duplicity of it. As Dewey (1927/2000b, 170) noted, "The world has suffered more from leaders and authorities than from the masses."

It is the exceptional administrator who assumes the mantle of the instructional leader (Waite, 2002b) and, even when possible, for only short bits at a time and only if his/her school is beneath the radar of the central office because it produces acceptable test scores. Leaders, on the other hand, take risks; democratic leaders, more so: "A crucial feature of democratic leadership is its oppositional character" (Woods, 2004, 12).

School leaders are variously situated within complex webs of power relations (Zipin & Brennan, 2003). As middle managers, they touch and are influenced in turn by many people and constituent groups. As educators, administrators' primary concern is (or should be) with the safety and well being, indeed the growth of the children who are their charges. School leaders must juggle multiple obligations; they are, after all, servants of the state. It is, therefore, a difficult, risky task to counter or otherwise resist state and district mandates that are believed to be detrimental to the interests of children (McGhee & Nelson, 2005). And who are the administrators courageous enough, politically aware enough to, first, see those contradictions, those duplicities, and, second, to counter them?

Lest we come off as too nihilistic, too negative, we must acknowledge that, at heart and as educators, we truly kindle the spark of hope and optimism in our souls (Hargreaves & Fullan, 1998). But we practice what we advocate here for other educational leaders: we employ a critical hermeneutic. We must first remove the blinders from our eyes if ever we are to improve our situations and those of our charges, the children for whom we are responsible.

5. THE CRITICAL HERMENEUTIC

To understand and to operate successfully in any given social situation, a person must be able to 'read' the situation, including the explicit and implicit contextual cues. What kind of situation is this? These cues are given off by the actors in the situation, just as there are larger contextual cues provided by the physical space and its arrangement/architecture, the sociohistorical contexts (e.g., antecedents), the interactional contexts and so on ad infinitum (Erickson & Shultz, 1981). Ability to read the various social situations one encounters and the ability to act appropriately according to the demands and expectations incumbent in them have been considered one's social repertoire or register (Scollon & Scollon, 1995).

Some have suggested that leaders would do well to employ anthropological techniques (Fulginiti, 1986), especially those of observation and analysis, in seeking to understand the schools where they work. Another recommends 'an ethnographic disposition' (Waite, 2002a, 35). These methods would work well for the common administrator. However, we suggest that more critically- and politically-inclined leaders employ a critical hermeneutic. Some already do so instinctively; others might need to be invited, even taught, how to do so explicitly.

Hermeneutics derived from the age-old method of philology, which was the method used in the interpretation of ancient sacred texts. Hermeneutics itself became the method of choice for textual interpretation. This method takes into account the social conditions (i.e., contexts) of a text's production, its meaning within such contexts, as well as the meaning such texts might hold today or in other, more contemporary contexts. Ricoeur (1973) allowed for the use of hermeneutics for the interpretation of action, where, for him, action can be read as text:

> My claim is that action itself, action as meaningful, may become an object of science, without losing its character of meaningfulness, by virtue of a kind of objectification similar to the fixation which occurs in writing. By this objectification, action is no longer a transaction to which the discourse of action would still belong. It constitutes a delineated pattern which has to be interpreted according to its inner connections. (98)

For Ricoeur, interpretation of action through application of hermeneutics necessitates a commitment on the part of the person:

> As the model of text-interpretation shows, understanding has nothing to do with an *immediate* grasping of a foreign psychic life or with an *emotional* identification with a mental intention. Understanding is entirely *mediated* by the whole of the explanatory

procedures which precede it and accompany it. The counterpart of this personal appropriation is not something which can be *felt*, it is the dynamic meaning released by the explanation which we identified earlier with the reference of the text, i.e., its power of disclosing a world.

The paradigmatic character of text-interpretation must be applied down to this ultimate implication. This means that the conditions of an authentic appropriation, as they were displayed in relation to texts, are themselves paradigmatic. Therefore we are not allowed to exclude the final act of personal commitment from the whole of objective and explanatory procedures which mediate it. (116-117, emphasis in original)

A critical hermeneutics, in the way are using the term, would allow for an alternate reading of the contexts, situations, actors, policies and so on that together make up the lived world of the school leader. This reading or interpretation would be much more than a surface appraisal, taking things at face value. The language used in a situation, such as school, and that used to speak about it would similarly be subject to an in-depth interpretation. We must raise a note of caution here, however. Just as Eco (1992) noted that there is interpretation and over-interpretation, so, too, can someone read too much into something like a situation, a policy, or an action. That said, we believe critical hermeneutics offers the best hope for seeing beyond the veil that is the verbiage, the rhetoric surrounding schooling, and that which occurs in the conduct of schooling.

In this sense, the use of a critical hermeneutic lens is strikingly similar to the 'misreading' advocated by Garfinkel (2002) as the sine qua non of the research method he fostered and proposes: ethnomethodology. Of misreading, Garfinkel wrote:

I don't mean by misread, read incorrectly. I mean read *alternately* so that the reading, the second reading, if directions are available in the first reading, then in the second reading, in an alternate reading, that the readings are incommensurable. (112, fn. 36, emphasis in original)

Use of a critical hermeneutic doesn't bind the school leader to any particular course of action, it simply informs those actions he or she might take. In this sense, critical hermeneutics is not prescriptive. It does give the leader more complete information with which to inform her actions and decisions. It allows her to see beyond the obvious to possible hidden agendas, ulterior motives, and obfuscated political mechanizations.

For example, a school leader, using critical hermeneutics, might decide that the testing and accountability system in place in her district and in her local school are not really helping children achieve academically. A critical hermeneutic might allow this school leader to see past the rhetoric and come to the realization that, in this case—for her, her children and the school she leads, achievement and accountability systems inculcate in children narrow behaviouristic, surface-level training and that the systems in place to teach to the test are actually harming children and are in no way worthy of the name 'education.' Furthermore, she might realize that all the talk in her district, maybe across the entire nation, is nothing more than empty, shallow rhetoric. She probably knows of schools that get high test scores, but where the curriculum is entirely geared to the test and where every extra minute of a student's time is spent on drill and rote memorization, including any 'extra' time in elective classes and special area classes such as physical education and art. She knows these things, she sees these things, because once people on the ground have their eyes opened and begin to look critically, reflectively, their power begins to be unleashed.

6. BUT WHAT TO DO WITH THIS NEW FOUND KNOWLEDGE?

There are three general avenues which the response of the leader in the hypothetical situation above might take (though we recognize that the variations are nearly infinite, owing to the contextual particulars): Acquiescence—simply playing the game; active, open resistance; and a middle road—something along the lines of operating below the radar screen while trying to do what's right for the children and their teachers. As we have said, a critical hermeneutic is not prescriptive. The leader's response depends on how s/he reads the situation, to be sure, but it also is influenced by the amount of power the leader wields, other resources at his/her command, the degree of 'followership' enjoyed by the leader, the history of the school and district, the make up and disposition of the school's community, the skill set the leader brings to the situation, and other contextual variables too numerous to mention.

Acquiescence for the critically aware leader in such a situation carries a heavy psychic burden (Hargreaves, 1998; Nelson, 2002). Resistance, too, has its risks and costs. The middle way requires that a leader be constantly vigilant and keen as to its effects and consequences while he/she strategizes, reads the constantly shifting landscape and adjusts his/her tactics. Truly, there are downsides to any of the paths a leader might travel. It is not for us to say here what is right for any leader in any given situation. She must follow her conscience. All we can advocate, indeed all we are advocating, is that leaders employ a critical hermeneutic or whatever means they find most suitable to uncover and reveal as much about their situations as they can and act on their convictions.

Or take another example: School leaders, especially principals and district superintendents in the US, complain that they are hampered in carrying out their duties by educational bureaucracies (Public Agenda, 2003), their policies and requirements. Others have suggested that, "American schools are bureaucracies" (Clark & Meloy, 1989, 275). We might assume that a local school administrator employing a critical hermeneutic finds that his or her work and that of the teachers is inordinately constrained by the district and state education bureaucracies. That this is the case is unremarkable, since, as we have shown, numerous administrators— superintendents and principals—around the US find bureaucracies daunting and frustrating. The Public Agenda data do not, however, provide us with a fine-grained analysis. In fact, Garfinkel (2002) would suggest that *no* research done in what he terms the formal analytic tradition ever could provide such detail.

All that these types of coarse data can provide is cause for chest-beating and finger pointing. In a sense, these types of data contribute to the further domestication of the principals and superintendents. First, they provide a convenient 'out' or excuse for leaders' inaction ("I'd be more of a leader, or I'd do the right thing in this situation, but the gosh-darn school bureaucracy won't permit me to.").

Second, such findings as those of Public Agenda (2003)—their surface-level data and findings concerning bureaucracies in education—combine with the prevalent positivistic mindset of many (but not all) administrators to make bureaucracies into social things, unalterable social facts. The ubiquitous nature of bureaucratic structures throughout educational (and other) institutions/organizations makes changing them a daunting task, seemingly impossible, a fool's errand. One might as well learn to live with it, because you certainly can't change the system.

Administrators who fall prey to this faulty reasoning, who are seduced by the positivist and instrumental/rationalist rationales of bureaucratic school organizations, delude themselves into thinking that it can't be otherwise, when it can. Such administrators dodge the more pertinent questions having to do with the role they themselves play in sustaining and perpetuating the hegemony of educational bureaucracies. As Weber (1946) observed, bureaucracies are self-perpetuating and tenaciously hold onto the power that they wrest from the social world. Bureaucracies are antithetical to democracy.

More complex analyses of the bureaucratic aspects of educational organizations, such as those supplied by Ingersoll (2003), or those which might occur to a leader through application of a critical hermeneutic lens, would reveal functional and dysfunctional aspects of such bureaucracies—their strengths and their weaknesses. A more complete understanding permits educational leaders to counter dysfunctional bureaucratic tendencies, processes, and policies strategically.

Someone employing the methods and procedures of the formal analytic tradition, whether quantitative or qualitative, would have difficulty teasing out the nuances of bureaucratic functioning. A leader using these methods might perceive the bureaucracy, might even find the bureaucracy to be a problem, but someone applying formal analytic procedures could not tease out the nuances of just how the bureaucracy is problematic for administrators and other school leaders. This is why a 'misreading,' in Garfinkel's terms, is necessary.

Such a misreading, like the critical hermeneutic advocated here, would begin to lay bare the lived, enacted processes and structures that are operant, and just how they operate, for the bureaucrats and for the practitioners who suffer under them.

We must be clear that Garfinkel (2002) demanded more of ethnomethodology than a simple misreading. For him, ethnomethodology's aim is to provide instructions of action (as opposed to instructions *for* action). That is, when properly done, an ethnomethodological study would result in finding what actors themselves must know and be able to do in order to produce and reproduce social structures and their processes. In this sense, they are members' instructions. Garfinkel wrote that ethnomethodologists' descriptions:

> were written by design to be read praxeologically—i.e., to be *mis*read—as work-site-specific instructions for their observability, followability, completeness, sufficiency, their bodily/equipmental intertwining, their in-course evolving elaboration, their autochthonous coherence, their autonomous criticism, and the rest in *procedurally enacted coherent details of structures*. (112, emphasis in original)

Garfinkel (2002) was adamant that ethnomethodology is not (mere) interpretation. Ethnomethodology, he wrote, "is not in the business of interpreting signs. It is not an interpretive enterprise. Enacted local practices are not texts which symbolize 'meanings' or events. They are in detail identical with themselves and not representative of something else" (97).

We would hope that leaders would undertake full-blown ethnomethodological studies of their and other's actions and of the social structures they both contribute to and otherwise are a part of. However, this would be an unreal expectation, when even full-time social scientists find the task difficult. If not a full-blown ethnomethodological study, then perhaps the most we can expect at this time and from the majority of those school leaders who seek to be mindful about their work is the critical hermeneutic we recommend. (Of course, we would suggest that if school leaders cannot undertake ethnomethodological studies on their own, that they at least use or read such studies and apply that knowledge as a part of a wider critical literacy project—whether a personal or collective one.)

Without a critical hermeneutic, by simply applying a formal analytic procedure, leaders are left with a coarse analysis of the situation. As in the example above, such leaders might leap toward two opposing conclusions and courses of action—both equally misguided. The first course of action might be resistance, seeking to thwart or buck the more onerous impositions of the educational bureaucracies. The other, opposite conclusion and course of action might be acquiescence.

Fukuyama (1999) suggested that humans need hierarchical organizations and associations: "human beings *by nature* like to organize themselves hierarchically" (227, emphasis in original). Weber (1946) saw bureaucracies as one way that modern and modernizing societies could organize their labor to overcome the abuses of rank-based privileges and those based on birthright, nepotism and cronyism. For Weber, bureaucracies were more systematic, more rational than many traditional forms of organization. Bureaucracies were functional and efficient, and, of course, promulgated standardization within themselves and attempted to do as much in the areas of social life they affected. But there are alternatives to bureaucratic organizational forms and structures.

The bureaucratization and corporatization of schooling steals decisional authority away from educators. Recent scandals in the boardrooms of many major US corporations demonstrate that they can't police themselves. Bureaucracies came into being to stamp out variance, difference and individuality, thus stifling creativity, an essential human capacity. Leaders who employ a critical hermeneutic or are otherwise able to 'mis-read' their situations are more likely to imagine workable alternatives to bureaucratic stultification.

7. ACTION

Democratic leadership in schools involves more than simply reading situations, however critically. Leadership involves *phronesis*, or right action (Habermas, 1973). Communication is a type of action, and a necessary, though insufficient, condition for democracy to obtain (Young, 1985). Democratic communication structures must be interaction- and information-rich. The information or knowledge members of a democratic organization or structure must have access to and knowledge about how society actually works, hermeneutical knowledge (i.e., knowledge about how the society's or organization's intersubjective understandings are created), ideological knowledge and emancipatory knowledge.

Woods (2004) reminds us that there are at least four types of democracy; or democratic rationalities, in his terms—decisional, discursive, therapeutic and ethical. Decisional democratic rationality has to do with "*distribution of externalized authority* (i.e., distribution of authority in external, collective decision making)"; discursive democratic rationality has to do with "the possibilities for open debate and dialogic democracy"; therapeutic democratic rationality deals with "the creation of well-being, social cohesion and positive feelings of involvement"; and ethical democratic rationality addresses "the aspiration of truth and veridical meaning, and who and what is counted as legitimate in contributing to this" (11-12, emphasis in original). Democratic leaders ideally attend to these four types.

Leaders are those who read the situation and are able to translate their reading for their colleagues and constituents, imbued with their vision for the future and their strategy for attaining that ideal future (Gardner, 1998). School leaders deal with complex, sometimes contradictory people and situations, and must tailor their actions accordingly. For example, it might be strategically unwise to openly communicate one's liberatory agenda to any and all constituent groups. Leaders must take others into their confidence judiciously. Unfortunately, this selective fashioning of the leader's communication is really no different than the psychic labor teachers and school leaders are otherwise engaged in (Hargreaves, 1998). A recent loss in the first author's family and the subsequent familial dynamics surrounding that loss served as the genesis for a realization on his part, perhaps commonsense to other, more astute educators, that you should not ask of someone more than he or she is able to give. Democratic leaders need to read their colleagues in such a way and need to be able to read their hierarchical superiors in this way, too: What are others able and willing to give to realize democratic educational means and ends? How can the democratic leader help them to do so?

Democratic leaders—and that includes everyone in a true democracy—as activists, can and should push and test the boundaries of prescribed bureaucratic roles. Democratic educational leaders should not acquiesce, and should resist domesticity. A critical hermeneutic reading will reveal bureaucratic, organizational, even societal fault lines, fissures and pressure points where strategic counter-pressure and action might result in more desirable democratic outcomes and practices.

Right action, *phronesis*, necessitates that the democratic leader operate out of more than a functionalist, instrumentalist episteme. Such leaders are guided by their evolving, though contingent ethics, by their concerns for social justice, and, we might add, by their instincts and emotions.

Democratic leaders are asked to do more than simply manage a school; and yet, they do so with little promise of reward and at a great risk to their career and longevity in their position. Such leaders need to be ontologically secure (Giddens, 1990). They are pushed to do what is right regardless of the risks. They realize, perhaps, that a job for life is an anachronism.

We are reminded that democracy is of at least two general types—representative and participatory (Starratt, 2001). Democratic educational leaders strive to foster

148 DUNCAN WAITE, SUSAN FIELD WAITE, SHARON FILLION

participatory democratic processes and structures at the local level, while working to secure their and their school's representation at other levels.

Democratic educational leaders demonstrate vitality, openness and acceptance, integrity, and the courage to look deeply into the dark recesses of their own hearts, just as they exhume the openly-hidden unspeakables in their schools. The task is difficult and the path toward democratic school organizations is never a straight one. But we cannot demure from so arduous a task simply because it is difficult.

It is not for us to prescribe for others. A large part of what we have written here—from our analysis of current situations, to our understanding of what is needed—is informed by our own experiences. As such, it perhaps says more about how we see our responsibilities in re-shaping the educational bureaucracies we have been part of, as it does about what others can or might do. We simply extend the invitation to others to engage with us and with their colleagues in democratic action.

REFERENCES

Apple, M. (1986). *Teachers and texts: A political economy of class and gender relations in education.* New York: Routledge & Kegan Paul.
Ball, S. J. (2000). Performativities and fabrications in the education economy: Towards the performative society. *Australian Educational Researcher,* 27(2), 1-24.
Bourdieu, P., & Passerson, J. C. (1977). *Reproduction: In education, society and culture.* London: Sage Publications.
Clark, D. L., & Meloy, J. M. (1989). Renouncing bureaucracy: A democratic structure for leadership in schools. In T. J. Sergiovanni and J. H. Moore (eds.), *Schooling for tomorrow: Directing reforms to issues that count* (272-294). Boston: Allyn & Bacon.
Cott, N. F. (1977). *The bonds of womanhood: "Women's sphere" in New England,* 1780-1835. New Haven: Yale University Press.
Cuban, L. (2003). *Why is it so hard to get good schools?* New York: Teachers College Press.
Dempster, N., Freakley, M., & Parry, L. (2001). The ethical climate of public schooling under new public management. *International Journal of Leadership in Education,* 4(1), 1-12.
Dewey, J. (2000a). Democratic ends need democratic methods for their realization. In R.J. Terchek & T.C. Conte (eds.), *Theories of democracy: A reader* (167-168). New York: Rowman & Littlefield. (Original work published 1939).
Dewey, J. (2000b). The public and its problems. In R.J. Terchek & T.C. Conte (eds.), *Theories of democracy: A reader* (168-171). New York: Rowman & Littlefield. (Original work published 1927).
Eco, U. (1992). *Interpretation and overinterpretation.* Cambridge (UK): Cambridge University Press.
Erickson, F., & Shultz, J. (1981). When is a context? In J. Green & C. Wallat (eds.), *Ethnography and language in educational settings* (147-160). Norwood, NJ: Ablex.
Fukuyama, F. (1999). *The great disruption: Human nature and the reconstitution of social order.* New York: The Free Press.
Fulginiti, J. M. (1986). Ethnography in school administration. *Practicing Anthropologist,* 8(3/4), 20-21.
Fuller, R. W. (2003). *Somebodies and nobodies: Overcoming the abuse of rank.* Gabriola Island, BC (Canada): New Society Publishers.
Gardner, H. (1998). The intelligences of leaders. *International Journal of Leadership in Education,* 1(2), 203-206.
Garfinkel, H. (2002). *Ethnomethodology's program: Working out Durkheim's aphorism.* Lanhan, MD: Rowan & Littlefield Publishers.
Giddens, A. (1990). *The consequences of modernity.* Stanford, CA: Stanford University Press.
Habermas, J. (1973). *Theory and practice.* (J. Viertel, trans.). Boston: Beacon Press.
Hargreaves, A. (1998). The emotional politics of teaching and teacher development: With implications for educational leadership. *The International Journal of Leadership in Education,* 1(4), 315-336.
Hargreaves, A., & Fullan M. (1998). *What's worth fighting for out there?* New York: Teachers College Press.

Ingersoll, R. M. (2003). *Who controls teachers' work? Power and accountability in America's schools.* Cambridge, MA: Harvard University Press.

Knight Foundation. (2005). *The future of the first amendment.* Retrieved March 30, 2005 from http://www.knightfdn.org.

Marx, K., & Engels, F. (1947). *The German ideology.* (R. Pascal, Ed.) New York: International Publishers. (Original manuscript published 1845).

McGhee, M. W., & Nelson, S. W. (2005). Sacrificing leaders. villainizing leadership: How educational accountability policies impair school leadership. *Phi Delta Kappan, 86,* 367-372.

Nelson, S. W. (2002). *Oppression, conflict, and collusion: High-stakes accountability from the perspective of three social justice principals.* Unpublished doctoral dissertation, The University of Texas-Austin.

Public Agenda. (2003). *Where we are now? 12 things you need to know about public opinion and public schools.* Retrieved 09/16/03 from http://www.publicagenda.org/specials/wherewearenow/wherewearenow.htm.

Ricoeur, P. (1973). The model of the text: Meaningful action considered as a text. *New Literary History,* 5(1), 91-117.

Sarason, S. B. (1990). *The predictable failure of educational reform.* San Francisco, CA: Jossey-Bass.

Scollon, R., & Scollon, S. W. (1995). *Intercultural communication.* Oxford (UK): Blackwell.

Starratt, R. J. (2001). Democratic leadership theory in late modernity: An oxymoron or ironic possibility? *International Journal of Leadership in Education,* 4(4), 333-352.

Tanguay, D.M. (2003). Inefficient efficiency: A critique of merit pay. In B. Johnson, P. Kavanagh, & K. Mattson (eds.). *Steal this university: The rise of the corporate university and the academic labor movement* (49-60). New York: Routledge.

Thomson, P. (2003). (Guest Editor). Democratising schools: Applying Bourdieu to the educational field. *Special issue of The International Journal of Leadership in Education,* 6(4).

Waite, D. (2002a). Critical new directions in educational leadership. Education and Society, 20(1), 29-42.

Waite, D. (2002b). Is the role of the principal in creating school improvement over-rated? *Journal of Educational Change,* 3(2), 161-165.

Waite, D., Boone, M., & McGhee, M. (2001). A critical sociocultural view of accountability. *Journal of School Leadership,* 11(3), 182-203.

Waller, W. W. (1932). *The sociology of teaching.* New York: J. Wiley & Sons.

Weber, M. (1946). *From Max Weber: Essays in sociology.* H. H. Gerth & C. W. Mills (trans., eds.). New York: Oxford University Press.

Woods, P. A. (2004). Democratic leadership: Drawing distinctions with distributed leadership. *International Journal of Leadership in Education,* 7, 3-26.

Young, T. R. (1985). The structure of democratic communications. *Mid-American Review of Sociology,* 10(2), 55-76.

Zipin, L., & Brennan, M. (2003). The suppression of ethical dispositions through managerial governmentality: A habitus crisis in Australian higher education. *International Journal of Leadership in Education,* 6, 351-370.

NOAH DE LISSOVOY AND PETER MCLAREN

GHOSTS IN THE PROCEDURE:

Notes on teaching and subjectivity in a new era

Abstract. This article discusses teaching as a space of material, ideological and subjective struggle and transformation, in which the political and spiritual commitment of the educator must contest the intensified control and domination of current educational processes in the context of a newly energized and exploitative contemporary global capitalism. The authors argue that educators need to challenge the hyper-racism of official schooling, as well as their own ideological construction as pacified citizen subjects, and the enforcement of this construction through fear and fatalism. In this regard, contemporary changes in the material conditions in public schools are examined, including the effects of recent conservative reforms, and it is suggested that these changes necessitate a corresponding modification in the subjective and political strategy of critical pedagogy. This pedagogy should bring together a greater attention to global political struggles, a collective resistance to the alienation enforced by professional educational identities, a more decisive break with official school culture in the practice of oppositional teaching, as well as a more sophisticated awareness of the complexity of student agency and participation.

1. INTRODUCTION

Research and writing on pedagogy, even from critical perspectives, has often ignored fundamental shifts in the sociopolitical processes and meanings of public schooling that are presently taking place. These include an intensification of structural and procedural violence against working-class students and students of color, often under the guise of new conservative reforms. High stakes testing, scripted curricula and "zero tolerance" disciplinary rules all seek a dramatically more intimate and repressive control and coercion of black, brown and poor children (on the negative effects of new testing regimes, see McNeil, 2000; on disciplinary policies, see Dohrn, 2001). These shifts in turn need to be understood in the context of a greater understanding of the function of capital, and a rearticulation of the characteristic operation of its hegemony toward increasing intervention and coercion (Gowan, 2003). This offensive is evident in social processes within core capitalist countries and include the field of education, as well as imperialist processes globally. These changes pose very particular problems to pedagogical theory and educational leadership in critical pedagogic traditions. We argue for a corresponding modification in oppositional teaching and leadership involving, in particular, an investigation of the unprecedented contemporary assaults on possibilities in educational spaces, a deliberate linking of North American experiences in this regard with other global instances, as well as a more decisive break with the official culture of schooling.

151

K. Cooper and R. White (eds.), The Practical Critical Education, 151–163.
© 2007 *Springer.*

This essay also seeks to connect a reflection on the changing material conditions of schooling to a consideration of the subjective dimensions of teaching. Teaching, in general, is usually thought of as something going on outside the person of the educator, externally and publicly. But how is the *going outside* that is necessary in teaching also a *going inside*, a journey among and within our selves, an articulation not only of positive identifications but also of openings and indeterminacy? The space of teaching and the creative possibilities of cooperation in it for meaning, growing and knowing come forth from the cracks and gaps in our subject positions which desire and creativity unsettles and expands toward new articulations, new melodies, new names. The possibilities of our selves and our relationships as educators are traced by the shape of this creativity. But the space of this inner movement and transformation is itself politically organized, and is as much a matter of struggle as "external" conditions are. Thus, we also consider below what a meditation on the subjectivity of the teacher, in the context of the material conditions of school and society and in relation to student identities, can offer as we imagine new forms of oppositional pedagogy.

In the following sections we discuss the changing political landscape of schooling in relation to the larger context of capitalism and imperialism, and we outline some of the pedagogical implications of transformations at this level for oppositional educators. We also discuss the reflection of these same political processes at the level of the selves that educators are allowed to become and the revolutionary subjectivities they might collectively work to imagine and create. In these discussions, we suggest a range of orientations and practices that might serve as starting points for educators committed to critical teaching and critical leadership. We do not offer a checklist of steps in this regard, but rather develop some general directions. Critical work is context-specific and depends ultimately on the creativity of students, teachers and administrators in their own settings. Furthermore, transformational education and political action are not a matter of following recipes, but rather of exploring fluid and ever-changing possibilities. Nevertheless, particular experiences are mediated by common processes and problems, and we believe that our reflections here are broadly relevant to all who are compelled to struggle *to not accommodate themselves* and their relationships to students to the dominative and exploitative organization of what it generally means, officially and institutionally, to be an educator.

2. GHOSTS IN THE PROCEDURES

Paulo Freire (1998) warned against a tendency toward fatalism among educators and showed how this tendency is complicit in producing a teaching without possibility:

> In reality, this is the most convenient position, but it is also the position of someone who quits the struggle, who quits history. It is the position of those who renounce conflict, the lack of which undermines the dignity of life (45).

However, anterior even to this fatalism, and perhaps even more sinister, is a place of *numbness* at the center of educational practice and thought generally. This numbness seems to overwhelm even defeatism, and in the place that it claims, an absolutely instrumentalist grammar organizes official pronouncements and the discourse of educational "reform." This grammar is enforced in public discourse and even schools themselves. In this strange space, students and teachers, ostensibly the living protagonists of education, become no more than ghosts whose spectral presence only serves to justify the rapid spread of new forms of repression and control.

The condition of blankness at the core of schooling for working-class students is a space of erasure that has been (seemingly) definitively severed from the social violence at its origin (Fine, 1987)—an erasure that appears to have rendered the meaning of what goes on in schools absolutely opaque. In this world, procedures take the place of actual feeling and of the possibility of feeling, and a kind of impersonal and inhuman optimism works through the discourses and performances of official culture to occupy the place of meaning-making and to celebrate the complete instrumentalization of pedagogy. Meanwhile, under cover of apparently "well-intentioned" policy initiatives (e.g. California's *Public Schools Accountability Act*, or the U.S. federal *No Child Left Behind Act*), capital seeks finally to exhaust the last margins of human creativity at work in schools, to soak up the remaining reserve in students' and educators' own humanly productive identities (De Lissovoy & McLaren, 2003). It is precisely the possibility of authentic accountability, which would reveal the damage wrought by such reforms, that these so-called "accountability" initiatives seek to pre-empt and replace.

The bright face that is put on energetic new initiatives and reforms in education (e.g. the fanfare surrounding new performance indexes, teacher "merit" incentives, etc.) can be seen first of all as a false mask that hides the shabby truth of institutionalized neglect and subjugation. But there is a deeper process at work here as well: the naturalizing force of this hegemonic optimism *reconstructs* the experience of schooling for the public (and often educators themselves) so that the most blatant instances of deterioration, neglect, coercion and racism acquire a kind of cheerful everyday-ness. In California, students of color in urban areas must attend schools that are frequently in terrible disrepair and lack basic supplies, from paper to working drinking fountains and bathrooms (Friedlaender & Frenkel, 2002); almost a third of the state's teachers report vermin at their school sites; the same proportion do not have enough books for students to take home (Harris, 2004). This reality does not prevent district officials from touting the successes of "accountability" based on high stakes testing, or teachers from rationalizing these conditions into a routine. We are not arguing against the need for real accountability in schooling—it is precisely the lack of such accountability that permits the deterioration and dismantling of public schools. Our point is that it is necessary to understand how completely this language has been captured and reconstructed by elites. If official practice is a false mask, it is a disguise that is wrapped around the skeleton itself of school culture, and not merely something added to the outside. In other words, if this discourse tricks us about the meanings and purposes of educational practices, it is a trick that is repeated so continuously and fluidly that it starts to act like a kind of truth. As Althusser writes, people "'live' their ideologies...*not at all as a form of consciousness, but as an object of their 'world'*—as their '*world*' itself" (1996, 233).

These processes should be examined against the background of the re-organization of imperialism worldwide, in which the ideological envelope is likewise pushed to its absolute limit: rather than amounting to simple distortion, the psychological operations of the powerful aim at the outright replacement of one universe by its logical inverse. For example, as the situation in the Middle East deteriorates further into chaos and violence, and as occupying forces press their offensives with ever-greater brutality, we are told that all is under control and that freedom is "on the march." In Haiti, a democratically elected president is removed from office through a U.S. engineered coup and this is described as a victory for democracy. Throughout Latin America, neoliberalism presses its relentless agenda of "belt-tightening" against the empty bellies of the poor; these efforts are naturalized as the most banal and everyday economic rationalism, as the necessary disciplining of undisciplined and immature pre-civilizations. The point here is not merely that exploitative conditions are normalized, which has always been the function of bourgeois ideology. In the current moment, we are witnessing a relentless effort to discursively replace an entire social reality with its opposite; not merely to bend the meanings of lived experience in the interests of the powerful, but to erase and remove these experiences altogether and to put in their place a set of discourses whose only claim to truth is their absolutely prolific and incessant repetition.

Once the "proper" image of reality is asserted in this way (e.g. the insistence that occupied Iraq is gratefully receiving lessons in democracy from North America, or that new testing initiatives are whipping schools into shape), corresponding social practices must then be aggressively reshaped to match the new reality. In the case of public schooling, teaching and learning are replaced by the enactment of procedures (e.g. the curriculum of test preparation), and living is replaced with simply existing through duration. This is not merely a process of dehumanization. It would be more accurate to describe this as a kind of pernicious *re-humanization*, a retooling of the very meaning of the "human" as the condition of being inserted into contemporary systems of control and surveillance (Foucault, 1977). Even the repertoire of students' resistant or emotional gestures has already been organized beforehand by schools, so that these "behaviors" end up filling slots in the charts of pathologists, as Lisa Delpit (1995) and others have pointed out. In order to make a space for students' potential anger and love, powerful emotions of the educational process, we must first acknowledge the reality and legitimacy of these feelings. In a space whose positive constitution is the unceasing work of dominant logics, reading the traces of spirit and life means first of all attending to its edges and corners, to the *ghosts* that refuse to be recuperated into this theater of "deviance" and control.

3. CONTEMPORARY OPPOSITIONAL PEDAGOGY

In the context of these pervasive procedures of erasure, which transform the terrain of school and classroom, the shape of oppositional teaching is also necessarily altered. The possibility for the dialogical processes of naming and intervention that Freire (1996) proposes becomes foreshortened by the colonization of the very space and time of the pedagogical encounter. Even mainstream teaching is *occupied* by this invasion: Linda McNeil (2000) has shown how standardized assessment systems dramatically distort and foreshorten the curriculum in favor of a focus on narrow test-taking skills. Furthermore, while current "reforms" disguise themselves in terms of "strictness" and "skills" to appeal to the popular consciousness, in fact they are motivated by quite different purposes. Rather than seeking to "keep students in line," contemporary high-stakes testing and retention initiatives aim to keep students always *below and behind* the line, always ultimately unable to attain it. They aim likewise to keep the resource of the teacher's time and imagination always in debt and unable to meet its obligations to the arbitrary and totalizing criterion of the test (De Lissovoy & McLaren, 2003). In this way, pedagogies that can truly and fully engage students and build skills (and thus in fact be authentically accountable to students themselves) are thereby foreclosed.

The opportunity even for the old contest between an old-fashioned "banking education" and a liberatory pedagogy is thereby continuously attenuated and deferred. This over-control, which aims to defeat rather than to discipline, keeps students and teachers perpetually on the defensive, perpetually scrambling for a breath of air in which to even begin to see themselves as in a social situation at all, rather than as the material of a purely instrumental procedure. As even traditional understandings of the properly educational give way, like vanishing terrain, to the deterritorialized mechanisms of standardized instruction and assessment, any impulse toward a critical pedagogy comes up against immediate and apparently insuperable limits. As scripted curricula more and more occupy the space of any potential dialogue, as dialogue of any kind appears immediately deviant, any movement toward the Freirean space of encounter and possibility looks like insurrection. Seemingly, the dilemma that is increasingly encountered by teachers is either to capitulate or to defy. In this context, the horizon of critical dialogue dangerously recedes. "Critique," with its implication of dialectical thrust and counter-thrust of negotiation and recomposition would seem less *accurate* to current conditions. We need to struggle to protect all such oppositional possibilities, while also thinking newly about how to respond to changing educational circumstances.

Thus, to the extent that we are faced with a new set of conditions, we need to imagine a new response. We suggest that what is called for now is an *insurgent pedagogy*. The first responsibility of this pedagogy would be a determined disinvestment from "schooling as procedure" and the creation of a space of critical teaching against the encroachments of dominant "reforms." However, it is not a matter simply of going back to previous conditions. The hyperdominative and racist procedures of contemporary public schooling are the sign of a deeper sociopolitical movement in education. In trying to roll back the last wave of tests, we need to appreciate as well the underlying reality these policies reveal: a carceral drive in schools, itself connected to a changing balance in the organization of capitalism away from the pole of consent and toward that of coercion.[1] In this light, an insurgent pedagogy would not seek simply to recreate a previous set of possibilities, but also to propose a new response to a newly configured social reality.

Such a contemporary oppositional pedagogy would be characterized by the following key emphases:

- By deliberately juxtaposing images and events from across the globe, it would upset the normative cultural geography that allows those in the U.S. both to exile the suffering endured by victims of U.S. imperialism abroad to the mental space of "far away," while domesticating the flagrant abuses experienced "at home" (for example by inmates in the prison system or by victims of police brutality) as "anomalous." Placing such disparate experiences in communication for students, this pedagogy would seek to trouble common senses of "citizenship" as the exercise of rights and responsibilities within the framework of the nation and, instead, to provoke global identifications with others everywhere (Said, 1993), indeed with the mass of humanity, outside and against national borders.

- This pedagogy would involve attending to the political organization and stakes of teacher subjectivity—the costs to teachers themselves (and to the teaching they can imagine) of the professional identities they are forced to inhabit. Struggle, in this connection, would need to involve an unraveling and re-imagination by educators of their very selves, away from official forms and identities.

- Furthermore, an insurgent pedagogy would crucially juxtapose larger political processes with students' own experiences and, in particular, with students' experiences *in school*. It would take as crucial curriculum content the specific processes of subordination and violation enacted by the administrative, security and pedagogical apparatuses of the school itself. It would thus be distinguished from more familiar critical approaches by a determined reflexivity as to the process and politics of teaching itself.

- This reflexivity would be the starting point for a more sophisticated engagement with students' own autonomous forms of opposition and a re-negotiation of the collaborative relationship, in resistance, of student and educator as we will discuss further below.

At the same time, then, that it focuses attention on conditions in the world outside, such a pedagogy would attend immediately to relationships and processes within the space of schooling itself, as a crucial site for struggle against oppression—including our relationships to ourselves. Love in teaching, before it is expressed outwardly, is an internal journey, a flame across fields of potential for ourselves as subjects, a flare of desire; not simply to be or even to become, but rather to produce, to act and to be made and unmade in living and being with others.

4. TEACHING AGAINST VIOLENCE

As Antonia Darder writes, love in teaching must be "rooted in a committed willingness to struggle persistently with purpose in our life" (2002, 34). But it must also be lyrical, which is not to say merely aesthetic, but rather a matter of production or patterning: the choosing up of a position against a context, the proper displacement of the constituent parts of what a person *is* against the backdrop of the real. This lyricism in teaching, which is the same as joy in the work (a dangerous joy to the extent that it finds itself opposed to the predominant hopelessness of schools), is also what opens it up as a genuine horizon for students. Teaching should be not only virtuous, democratic and sound; even more, it should be *beautiful* — so that students will want it and need it. This is how we ought to understand love in teaching: not as an anodyne substance, nor as an obligatory sentimentality, but rather as a political process — the cracking open of the place of self and identity (hooks, 1994) and the complementary unfolding of the world as a social space, a space of struggle.

This desire, this love and struggle in teaching always add up to much more than any simple collection of best practices since, before any positive pedagogy is proposed, educators need to learn to read the force, the violence, against which their work must be a constant and nimble struggle (Bartolomé, 1994). An important part of teaching is reading that violence as it rains down upon and courses through the word, the text, the classroom, the school, the society. More than a criminal inadequacy of basic resources, more than an ideological hidden curriculum, more than a culturally racist and colonialist pedagogy and disciplinary regime, this assault is the systematic coincidence of all of these aspects, braided together into the logic that grounds education as an institution. A constant bombardment, striation, cross-hatching, this violence remains invisible because it is unnamed and systematic: an effect of a set of social and political structures that never seems to be enacted in broad daylight. But its rays, that the official lenses seem not to record, pierce the possible subjects of desire that students are and disfigure the classroom in a kind of incarceration. Because of this, to enact a critical pedagogy is not an easy project. To do so is to engage in a struggle against an overdetermining force that not only slants education in a repressive direction but also *cooks* it continuously — falling unrelentingly onto the social possibility that education might represent and smashing the tentative solidarity that the educator labors to imagine with students.

Intervening against this force means attending to its enactment in the procedures and processes of schooling and to the articulation of these processes within larger social and political logics. Within this praxis, for example, students and teachers might investigate school security and disciplinary procedures and challenge the institutional rage that is often channeled through these structures against students of color in particular. (A study question: Who gets to surveil the security guards? Who gets to discipline the police when they intrude upon campus to interrogate students without anyone's consent?) Similarly, standardized and high stakes tests should not just be downplayed, but rigorously examined and critiqued not only for what they don't accomplish (meaningful assessment) but for what they reproduce: demoralization among students and the pernicious representation of working-class communities and communities of color as forever "failing." Or educators and students might organize protests against military recruitment efforts on campuses and investigate the ideological function of routine rituals like the pledge of allegiance. Such discussions would need to broaden the meaning of the U.S. flag and other patriotic symbols for students, by pointing to their historical associations of conquest and exploitation for oppressed peoples globally.

While these suggestions are similar to the kinds of practices that have been envisaged by educators in the tradition of critical pedagogy, they are distinct in foregrounding for students the importance of the procedures of schooling itself. They also shift earlier critical emphases in attending to instances of *violation* in students' lives and elsewhere and make explicit the connection of these events not just to contradictions in "democratic" society, but to imperialism as a global process. An insurgent pedagogy requires the naming of imperialism and the investigation of it as an organized, ongoing and pervasive process in North America and throughout the world.

5. THE ART OF ESCAPE

So if it is true, as Paulo Freire says in discussion with Donaldo Macedo (1987), that we can struggle with students against oppression from within the oppressive institutions of schooling (however tenuous our margin of possibility may be), it is important to recognize the scope of the struggle and the kind of determination it must call forth. It is also necessary to recognize the *artistry* required in the act of commitment of the teacher who struggles on the side of students, an artistry that learns to live and breathe in a field of hostile patterns and purposes.

This is why the love that teaching requires should be "armed," to use Freire's metaphor (1998, 40). This is truer now than ever before, as capitalism hurries to foreclose the last possibilities, sew up the last tears and rents and perfect the alienation of its subjects through complete submersion and oblivion. As neo-liberalism organizes an aggressive offensive on a global scale, the effects are more and more evident in schooling, both in terms of an expanding drive for privatization and a more urgent interventionism (McLaren & Farahmandpur, 2001). But if this is true of the social space of schooling, it is just as true of the social space of the subjectivity of the educator. To begin to be able to see, to act and to know with students, we have first of all to summon the strength to imagine ourselves newly, as opposed to our constitution and enclosure by contemporary capitalism.

The pitfalls in our efforts to teach come first of all from a fear that long ago occupied the ground upon which we are able to imagine any public, social or educational self. This fear is the foundation that anchors the house of the subject, keeping it in thrall to the social order. Althusser (1971) showed that we are only known by ourselves or others through this very *fixing* and naming of us by the power of the State. In other words, our sense of our selves as selves at all is immediately ideological. Our own subjectivity is not merely private, nor merely socially produced, but fundamentally and at its origin a political matter with deeply political stakes. Thus, to confront the organization of our own selves and subjectivities means to confront not just habit or neurosis, but orders of power and apparatuses of enforcement that, at a basic level, are tied to the political structure of society.

To escape the clutches of this political structure and this fear, to pull free a few inches or a few moments from its grasp, requires great agility, imagination and audacity. We have to realize that we are in fact truly pursued and even captured; that these are the terms under which we are permitted to inhabit ourselves and so to discover other possibilities means to plot an escape. If this is true generally, how much truer is it for teachers and administrators who spend their days in the heart of perhaps the state's most important ideological apparatus? Our chance of *escaping ourselves* depends upon envisioning a utopic distance, a depth that opens backward into the self as social artifact, devouring its boundaries. This place of openness outside our determined existences is the imaginary starting-point from which we can begin to approach other selves and initiate a collective struggle against a captured form of living.

For educators committed to a contemporary critical/insurgent pedagogy, this means stepping outside of our ghost-selves as we live them in the official procedures and processes of schooling. It means creating communities, not only of action, but of support, solidarity and self-exploration. It means engaging in dialogue with each other in regard to the cost, to our persons, of the alienation and subordination that organize our professional identities. It means seeing the connections between our struggles and struggles elsewhere, and challenging our fear with attention to the sacrifices of others worldwide, including many teachers who have paid a steep price for their commitment to liberation. It means refusing the temptation to imagine or style ourselves as heroic and instead acknowledging the necessity of assistance, of collective efforts and of collective identities.

Specifically, in the contemporary context, critical educators need to take active steps to form communities or study groups outside of schools in which they can dialogue about the effects on their own bodies and minds of the institutions in which they work, and support each other to explore ways of enduring, resisting and transforming these institutions. In these communities, it is possible to: 1) share and strategize in regard to specific struggles that educators face in their practice; 2) propose ideas for resistant teaching and curriculum; 3) undertake collective readings of critical texts; 4) create spaces of emotional support for the whole persons that educators are and which schools increasingly deny. Such communities are places not only in which to imagine and plan critical teaching and action, but also for study and reflection. In addition, they are crucial occasions for self-healing and rejuvenation — indispensable processes in a struggle which incessantly wears down those on its front lines.

6. VOICES LISTENING

Being faithful to the strange discomfort of teaching and learning now necessarily means breaking dramatically with what seeks not only to constrain but even to destroy it. To choose education as a political, social, cultural and spiritual space of transformation means first of all to betray a set of implicit solidarities with dominant schooling regimes. While such a choice includes an activist and ethical commitment to teach "against the grain" (Cochran-Smith, 1991), it implies a further step as well. It means teaching against teaching as officially constituted, educating against education as injury and confinement. For educators, this means interrogating not only the "hidden curriculum" of dominant knowledge and practices which teaches students from oppressed groups the "rationality" of their own subordination. Further, critical pedagogy should entail confronting, above all, the aggressive institutional procedures and processes of schools, including hyperdisciplinary security details, the complex shuffling of students through multi-track year round schedules, standardized tests and high school exit exams, all of which *act* directly on the bodies and persons of students. Such a confrontation necessitates a difficult dialogue in the classroom but suggests other tactics as well, including organized protest, at school and elsewhere.

Furthermore, in challenging the violence done to the persons of students, we should resist the tendency to substitute for this destruction our own construction of student identities. In striving to defend a radical humanism, we ought to inflect our conception of it with a sensitivity which recognizes that the struggle must be for an even wider freedom than the idea of the human has so far allowed (Appiah, 1997). To struggle in this way would mean to explore the entirety of student strategy and response, including those forms that tend *away* from the space of the formally and informally pedagogical, and away from the positivistic moments even of critical teaching (De Lissovoy, 2004). We need to listen more attentively to what is both said and not said, to begin to hear what so far hasn't been. Without idealizing them, we can begin by respecting what students are telling us through their forms of participation and "non-participation" in schools. We might, then, pay more attention to the negative moment in the morphogenesis of revolutionary consciousness — what Freire described as the refusal of the oppressed to read the word of the oppressor: "The refusal to read the word chosen by the teacher is the realization on the part of the student that he or she is making a decision not to accept what is perceived as violating his or her world" (Freire & Macedo, 1987, 123).

This pedagogy would require, then, a more careful attention to students and to the complex forms of identity, activity and agency they create, both with and without their teachers. This sensitivity suggests a questioning of classroom procedures and processes. Thus, teaching implores not so much the "participation" of students, but rather the students' choice to participate — to live. This choice to live necessarily means a choice *against* the forces and forms that exist to cut them down; this choice represents an "'astuteness'... as a way to protect themselves against the dominant" (Freire & Macedo, 1987, 137). This is why teaching is not easy: its accepted (and often even "progressive") practices generally reproduce this oppression. For a teacher to choose a truly critical or oppositional pedagogy, then, means to fight both against oppression generally and, in a sense, to fight against oneself; to refuse both external and internal structures which organize students' identities and educational possibilities from an elite and authoritarian distance. In the opening that this pedagogy allows, students' autonomous actions and interpretations can become starting points for both a restructuring of classroom relationships and for new forms of resistance.

The reactionary teacher attacks the student for his or her "failure." The liberal looks for ways to entice and cajole students to a tepid collaboration with instruction. The left-liberal questions mainstream curriculum while for the most part maintaining an allegiance to its underlying purposes. The *revolutionary* educator makes explicit the fundamental purposes of schooling and their connection to global domination and exploitation, exploring all productive possibilities of critique and resistance. In addition, such educators begin with a respect not only for "who the students are," but for what they are saying *and not saying* in the context of systematic institutional oppression and exploitation. The purpose and direction of teaching cannot be determined arbitrarily before this attention. The conversation is not proposed by the teacher, but is already happening.[2] The question is whether the teacher will be able to hear and offer a response, itself called forth by the word/silence, movement/stillness of students.

This does not mean that educators should not assume their own proper authority, or that teaching should not be organized and purposeful. Rather, the same courage that calls critical teachers and leaders forth to the classroom projects they envision should be able to become the courage that can listen and learn from interruptions. This is crucially important in the present, in the context of the overdetermination of the teacher's power by the intensified control that characterizes conservative curricular and instructional reforms. In a productive sense, "for educators, critiquing the underlying assumptions of our discipline and examining our pedagogy in light of such critiques may be the entry into our own uncomfort zones" (Obidah, 2000, 1059).

- Concretely, educators can pay close attention to student interventions in class, not only for how they comment on the explicit focus of instruction but also for what directions they propose for further and different dialogue and curriculum. This means listening imaginatively and energetically since such proposals are often made only indirectly.

- Educators need to reflect on the patterns of speech and silence in class and the culturally and gender-coded distribution of voice, not so that they can command participation for those who appear non-participative but rather so that they can learn how to create space for all students to contribute and learn in a variety of ways, including silence, and so they can use their own silence effectively (Montoya, 2000).

- Educators can teach students, in a systematic way, to question not only the content of the knowledge that the teacher proposes, but the very standpoint, in an epistemological sense (Hartsock, 1983), from which it emerges. This means frank discussion of the assumptions that ground mainstream and critical curriculum and the way that this knowledge is socially and politically situated in particular historical experiences.

7. CONCLUSION

Teaching is a very personal matter if, by "person", we mean more than a mythical and pure interiority—if we mean rather the fully contextualized social apparatus of being that lives us. That is why even the most "impersonal" and "traditional" educators are caught in the closest intimacy, though they don't realize it. These teachers and administrators, refusing to see that their persons are crucially implicated in their work, hope to navigate the space of teaching and learning as a "pure outside" in which they meet their students as cold externalities. These educators believe that their *selves* are safely *inside* and invulnerable. They don't realize that the self walks in front of us, in public, whether we see it or not.[3] In this essay we have tried to show how the self of the educator and the social context of schooling are crucially implicated in one another. Pedagogical explorations need to recognize the inescapably political character of the educator's subjectivity, his/her relationship to students (and imagination of them), and the institutional terrain upon which this relationship is created. Paradoxically, a meditation on the "inner" spaces of teaching implies an attention to the unfolded "outer": the dimension of global society, oppression and resistance.

The being together of educators and students, and of students with each other, is a gesture toward the larger togetherness of all those who struggle against oppression. Each occasion of true teaching is a passage toward the eventual articulation of the oppressed in connection and communication. It means threading ourselves, having our words in each other, and it is too close for comfort. Rather than emanating from the teacher in encompassing force, love in teaching and in the world is the tentative reply to another/others. In particular, hearing and seeing the suffering of those who are "far away" as well as close by (and thus our own responsibility to them) is the kind of discomfort that must be the starting point of contemporary oppositional teaching. In the face of the violence of official education, this oppositional conversation would organize its attention and energy, and between the dominant spaces of teaching, learning and living, it might suggest a way *against, around, through* and *over*—into the unimaginable zero degree of a different world.

ENDNOTES

[1] These two poles, coercion and consent, constitute the parameters of Gramsci's (1971) model of hegemony in capitalism. A mature capitalist society functions mainly through the willing cooperation of its citizen subjects; however, the increasing repressiveness of U.S. society should remind us that the use of force remains an indispensable tool in the State's enforcement of its rule.

[2] This point has been demonstrated empirically in the work of Kris Gutiérrez and her colleagues (e.g. Gutiérrez, Rymes, & Larson, 1995) who have shown that classrooms are rich with a "heteroglossia" that includes extended and independent student discourses, as well as the official "script" of the teacher.

[3] "The human body is the best picture of the human soul" (Wittgenstein, 2001, 152).

REFERENCES

Althusser, L. (1996). *For Marx* (B. Brewster, Trans.). London: Verso.

Althusser, L. (1971). Ideology and ideological state apparatuses (Notes towards an investigation), *Lenin and Philosophy and Other Essays* (85-126). New York: Monthly Review Press.

Appiah, K. A. (1997). Is the "Post-" in "Postcolonial" the "Post-" in "Postmodern"? In A. McClintock, A. Mufti & E. Shohat (eds.), *Dangerous liaisons: Gender, nation, and postcolonial perspectives* (420-444). Minneapolis, MN: University of Minnesota Press.

Bartolomé, L. I. (1994). Beyond the methods fetish: Toward a humanizing pedagogy. *Harvard Educational Review*, 64(2), 173-194.

Cochran-Smith, M. (1991). Learning to teach against the grain. *Harvard Educational Review*, 61(3), 279-310.

Darder, A. (2002). *Reinventing Paulo Freire: A pedagogy of love.* Boulder, CO: Westview Press.

De Lissovoy, N. (2004). Affirmation, ambivalence, autonomy: Reading the subaltern subject in postcolonial historiography and critical pedagogy. *Journal of Postcolonial Education*, 3(1), 5-23.

De Lissovoy, N., & McLaren, P. (2003). Educational "accountability" and the violence of capital: A Marxian reading. *Journal of Education Policy*, 18(2), 131-143.

Delpit, L. (1995). *Other people's children: Cultural conflict in the classroom.* New York: The New Press.

Dohrn, B. (2001). "Look out kid/it's something you did": Zero tolerance for children. In W. Ayers, B. Dohrn & R. Ayers (eds.), *Zero tolerance: Resisting the drive for punishment in our schools* (89-113). New York: The New Press.

Fine, M. (1987). Silencing in public schools. *Language Arts,* 64(2), 157-174.

Foucault, M. (1977). *Discipline and punish* (A. Sheridan, Trans.). New York: Pantheon Books.

Freire, P. (1998). *Teachers as cultural workers: Letters to those who dare teach* (D. Macedo, D. Koike & A. Oliveira, Trans.). Boulder, CO: Westview Press.

Freire, P. (1996). *Pedagogy of the oppressed* (M. B. Ramos, Trans.). New York: Continuum.

Freire, P., & Macedo, D. (1987). *Literacy: Reading the word and the world.* South Hadley, MA: Bergin and Garvey.

Friedlaender, D., & Frenkel, S. (March 2002). *School equity study documentation.* Oakland: Social Policy Research Associates.

Gowan, P. (2003). U.S. hegemony today. *Monthly Review,* 55(3), 30-50.

Gramsci, A. (1971). *Selections from the prison notebooks* (Q. Hoare & G. N. Smith, Trans.). New York: International Publishers.

Gutiérrez, K., Rymes, B., & Larson, J. (1995). Script, counterscript, and underlife in the classroom: James Brown versus Brown v. Board of Education. *Harvard Educational Review,* 65(3), 445-471.

Harris, P. Research Group (2004). *Survey of California Teachers.*

Hartsock, N. (1983). The feminist standpoint: Developing the ground for a specifically feminist historical materialism. In S. Harding & M. B. Hintikka (eds.), *Discovering reality: Feminist perspectives on epistemology, metaphysics, methodology, and philosophy of science* (283-310). Dordrecht: D. Reidel Publishing Company.

hooks, b. (1994). *Teaching to transgress: Education as the practice of freedom.* New York: Routledge.

McLaren, P., & Farahmandpur, R. (2001). The globalization of capitalism and the new imperialism: Notes towards a revolutionary critical pedagogy. *The Review of Education/Pedagogy/Cultural Studies,* 23, 271-315.

McNeil, L. M. (2000). *Contradictions of school reform: Educational costs of standardized testing.* New York: Routledge.

Montoya, M. (2000). Silence and silencing: Their centripetal and centrifugal forces in legal communication, pedagogy, and discourse. *University of Michigan Journal of Law Reform* 33(3).

Obidah, J. E. (2000). Mediating boundaries of race, class, and professorial authority as a critical multiculturalist. *Teachers College Record,* 102(6), 1035-1060.

Said, E. W. (1993). *Culture and imperialism.* New York: Vintage Books.

Wittgenstein, L. (2001). *Philosophical investigations* (G. E. M. Anscombe, Trans.). Oxford: Blackwell Publishers.

HILARY JANKS WITH MASELELE PAULINA SETHOLE

REACHING OUT AND REACHING IN:

"We had to develop ourselves first, before anybody can develop us"

Abstract. This is a story of leadership that triumphs against the odds. While this triumph is largely due to the principal's ability to define a vision that addresses the needs of the school community and that provides a 'path to a new future' (Hallinger and Heck (2002, 12), the story analyses the contribution of the school's social responsibility partners to whole school transformation in a short space of time. In 1999, at the time that the principal of Phepo school assumed office, the school was riven by internecine struggles, mistrust, explicit threats and fear. 'Developing trust in an organization that doesn't have it is a huge challenge' (Fullan, 2003, 45). This case study sets out to understand how this can be achieved.

1. INTRODUCTION

This is a story of the relationship between Phepo School[1], a poor under-resourced, primary school in Atteridgeville, a black African township west of Pretoria and St Mary's Dioscesan School for Girls (DSG), an elite, independent, church school in an affluent Pretoria suburb. In 1987, a time of intense political struggle against the apartheid State, characterized by guerrilla warfare, national states of emergency, detentions without trial, political assassinations by the State, massive civil upheaval designed to make the country ungovernable, school boycotts and violence, particularly in black townships, St Mary's DSG initiated its Outreach programme.

In South Africa, the term *outreach* is used to refer to social responsibility work, where institutions, usually privileged by virtue of class and race, reach out to disadvantaged communities. At first, St Mary's DSG Outreach chose to focus on teacher In-service Training and Learner Enrichment[2] sharing its educational and material capital with schools in black townships. In 1997, Outreach shifted its focus to whole school development and began concentrating its efforts on schools in Atteridgeville. The whole school development project provided courses related to school management on topics such as leadership, organizational change, financial management and fundraising, and facilitated school-based workshops for staff to enable them to work together to build and implement a shared vision. These workshops were run by Outreach facilitators[3], also known as field workers, who were assigned responsibility for particular schools. They visited their schools regularly to provide support and advice and to consult with the staff. The facilitator assigned to Phepo School was also responsible for designing and delivering the courses on leadership and organizational change. Capacity building is a key issue in post-apartheid South Africa, where so many citizens have been subjected to poor quality education and training in a segregated and unequal education system. The

165

K. Cooper and R. White (eds.), The Practical Critical Education, 165–178.
© 2007 Springer.

work of Outreach was important as it was the only training available to the Head of Department (HOD) (subsequently the school principal) at that time (Interview with Principal, April 2004). DSG Outreach continues to work in Atteridgeville schools; it began working with Phepo Primary School in 1995, one year after the first democratic elections in South Africa.

Janks' relationship with Phepo School began after she heard Maselele Paulina Sethole, the school principal, talking about her garden project on the radio; she visited the school in 1999 and began working in the school, with teachers, on a literacy research project concerned with children's multimodal representations of place. Speaking from outside the field of school leadership and administration, Janks hopes that this article written together with Sethole, a practicing principal, will meet the need for 'pictures of principals as embodied subjects dealing with complex and shifting situations', as articulated by Thomson (2001). In addition, the article responds to Fullan's assertion that

> leading schools require principals with the courage and capacity to build new cultures based on trusting relationships and a culture of disciplined enquiry and action (2003, 45).

and that:

> developing trust in an organization that doesn't have it is a huge challenge. But [...] this is the point: There are cases where this has been done. We need to learn from these schools. (2003, 45).

Phepo is one such school.

Prior to 1994, Phepo School fell under the authority of the Department of Education and Training, responsible for black education in South Africa. A history of colonial and apartheid neglect and limited allocation of resources to black education produced bleak, overcrowded and dilapidated schools with limited material and human resources for the provision of quality education to students. In 1997, according to the Outreach audit, the school had 462 students and 12 teachers with an official average class ratio of 42:1. As some of these teachers were needed to support the management and administrative functions of the school, class sizes exceeded 50 students. All the teachers had a Grade 12 matriculation qualification and either a teaching certificate or a diploma, but only two had University degrees. There were eleven classrooms that were 'not in a state of good repair'. 'The most frequent issue [was] holes in the floors, the need for the painting of walls and broken windows'. Teachers complained that it was 'difficult to do group work because of the desks which take up too much space in a crowded classroom'. The school had a well-kept garden around the administration block but 'the rest of the school grounds were unkempt and dusty'. The teachers reported a shortage of textbooks and writing materials. There was no library and there were only a few library boxes with books.

Although Phepo is only one of thirty-five schools that Outreach has worked with, as a case study it has much to teach us about development work, about leadership and about the complexities of reaching out and being reached. To understand this story, I interviewed the school principal (February, 2002; April, 2004) and the facilitator from Outreach who worked with Phepo School (December, 2002)[4]. I also analyzed the documentary evidence on file at Phepo and Outreach. This includes:

letters to and from the Department of Education, correspondence between the School Governing Body and the parents and the School Governing Body and the teachers, anonymous handwritten letters, Outreach evaluation reports and audits, School Governing Body minutes and a transcript of a focus group conducted by the Outreach facilitator with the Phepo staff (October, 2000). This focus group did not include the principal. I also consulted the principal's records of developments at the school which include photographs, newspaper clippings, photocopies of award certificates as well as a written commentary. These records, protected in A3, plastic envelope, flip files and in an A4 hardcover notebook are called the *School Profiles*.[5]

Here is the story in outline as reported in *Phepo: Evaluation of the Outreach Whole School Change Project*, (Outreach, 2000).

> [Phepo] has worked with Outreach since 1995. During this year the school attended the Visions Building workshops being offered by Outreach. In 1996 Outreach worked with the school on a support basis and began introducing the idea of a School Development Plan. In 1997 the Head of Department and a staff member attended the Leadership and Management Training [courses] and the HOD[6] plus two staff members attended the school development team training. During this same year an attempt was made to draw up a school development plan with the staff. However this did not prove to be a successful exercise. The school was experiencing many internal issues which were exacerbated with the retirement of the principal and the appointment of the HOD as principal. After many attempts at getting the whole staff on board with the project it was decided to terminate the contract with the school and to provide the new principal with support. In 1999 the school, through the initial efforts of the principal, turned itself around. During this year the school re-contracted with the programme and although the management were invited to attend training this did not happen. However the school did draw up a school development plan. The school also attended fund-raising training and financial management training.

Several aspects of this outline need further discussion in order to understand the particular achievements of the principal in this school and the conditions of possibility of different kinds of Outreach work. The 'internal issues' including 'the retirement of the principal and the appointment of the HOD as principal' set the context for the Outreach interventions:

- visions building workshops,
- the school development plan,
- training courses on leadership, management, fundraising and financial management, and
- support for the principal.

Given the turmoil in the school, further analysis is needed to make sense of:

- 'the school turn[ing] itself around' and 'the initial efforts of the principal'.

2. INTERNAL ISSUES

The description of what was happening in the school at the time as 'internal issues' is the euphemistic language of sensitive reports. By April 1998, when Outreach terminated its contract with the school, the school was dysfunctional. The infighting that resulted from the appointment of the HOD to the principal's post was destructive and potentially dangerous. Staff feared bewitchment and poisoning and the principal received death threats. Referring to threats received by the principal, the facilitator says:

> But [what] she went through those few years and it was really, really terrible and God knows nothing happened to her. But there was a time when her treatment was in (pause). Teachers talk, they say certain things; I mean you must have heard the legendary story about her two garden beds that she dug[7]. The staff told her one of these days we going put you in there (Interview with facilitator).

In the focus group, one of the teachers says:

> I remember when I first came to this school, you wouldn't just eat food that just came from anywhere. But now we eat together and it is easy for me to take food from one teacher to another (Focus group transcript).

There were secret meetings, factions, 'bad talk' and threats. Before her appointment, staff accused the principal of 'fraud' (A letter from the Chairman of the School Governing Body, December 1, 1997). The principal describes her pain:

> Principal: Its terrible, and its hell. I must say, it is hell! School has come to a stand still ... You know what used to happen? I would get up and dress beautifully ... I would put on stockings and my best shoes and my beautiful handbag. But before I go to school, I would cry bitterly and after crying I would say, "God, you are going to lead me and you are going to close my eyes and I am not going to see anything that I am not supposed to see. I am not going to open my mouth where I am not supposed to open it and please don't make me hear what I'm not supposed to hear" ... During the week it would be gossip, I don't know how you put it in your language.
>
> Interviewer: Put it in your language!
>
> Principal: Go goieya diskempe
>
> Interviewer: Now try and translate.
>
> Principal: You talk about me to somebody whilst I'm listening. Talk badly.
>
> Interviewer: So is it like talking to somebody about you as though you not there?
>
> Principal: Yes as though I'm not there.
>
> Interviewer: Its not like it's behind your back, it's in front of your face?
>
> Principal: Yes to make me feel the pain. It went on and on.
> (Interview with Principal, 2002).
>
> Teacher 1:   I think it is because, it goes back to that thing we fear what has ...
>
> Teacher 2:   Yes.
>
> Teacher 1:   ... happened [and we never want to see it happening again you know it is so painful ... some one who was not there, like Teacher 7 and Teacher 4, they might think that it was something very light but it destroys lives so we are fearful those who were there.
> (Focus group transcript).

But it was not all just harmful talk. Most of the staff supported the following actions to oppose the principal's appointment:

- a teacher 'chalk down' and 'go slow'[8] (Letter from Outreach to the Department of Education, dated April 14, 1998).

- 'anonymous letters written to the parents' about the principal (Notification of a School Governing Body meeting, February 21, 1998).

- declaration of a dispute with the Education Labour Relations Council against the filling of the principal's post (Letter to staff from the Education Labour Relations Council, March, 1998; Letter to the principal from the Gauteng Department of Education, April 24, 1998).

- challenging the South African Democratic Teachers Union's representation of the staff's position on the appointment of the principal by taking the matter up with the Department of Education (Letter to 'colleagues' from 'Phepo colleagues', handwritten and undated).

It is clear that this context was highly problematic for whole school development work that requires the co-operation of all the staff working as a team; this is the very antithesis of the trust and discipline that Fullan (2003) describes as necessary for building a new culture. The general consensus of the staff at both Phepo and Outreach was that no real progress was made during this time and, in fact, that it is not possible to do organizational development in contexts where factions deliberately sabotage co-operative efforts. Here, I argue that while the politics in the school prevented the staff from taking their ideas forward at the time, many of the ideas generated then provided the principal with direction once the garden project – the project she used to turn the school around – provided the means for organizational change. The visions and plans generated at this time provide an important backdrop for understanding the principal's subsequent achievements.

3. VISION BUILDING

In 1995, staff produced the following vision as a result of the Outreach vision building workshops:

> We as the community of Phepo are committed to developing the child into a meaningful, responsible, successful adult who can contribute meaningfully to the community. In order to achieve this, the staff will work as a united team, being exemplary, dedicated and professional whose teaching will be effective, relevant and learner centred. The parents will be involved in the education of their children and the community in school activities. The school will be managed by those with a keen interest and concern in matters of the school and education as a whole (School Governing Body meeting, September 11, 1997).

It is important to consider this vision so that it can later be compared with the vision that grew subsequently out of the 'initial efforts of the principal'. Here the vision simply articulates what is by definition the responsibility of a school: the education and development of its students. There is nothing distinctive about this vision; nothing that sets it apart from other schools. Even the means to achieve this – a dedicated and professional staff working together as a team, parents who are involved in the education of their children, a community that takes part in school activities and a management team that can be trusted – are what all schools value.

However, given the situation at the school, one can recognize that this statement does represent a vision, an ideal to strive towards, rather than a reality, as many of these practices were not, in fact, in place.

Hallinger and Heck (2002, 12) argue that a vision is able to 'identify a path to a new future'. This vision clarifies where the staff would like the school to go, the desired new future, but it does not provide a path. It is more like a wish and is thus difficult to realize. This articulation of 'the gap between a current status and a desired future state' (2002, 18) is what Hallinger and Heck define as a goal, rather than a vision.

4. SCHOOL DEVELOPMENT PLAN

The development plan managed to identify school needs and actions that could be taken in relation to them. Most of the needs were for equipment (photocopier, fax machine, wall screens, overhead projector, 'computer for admin', video machine, television set, film projector); three related to facilities (school hall, 'sporting facilities e.g. chess boards', playgrounds with lawn, media centre); two to the development of human resources (parent involvement, fund-raising strategies and training); one addressed the need for a children's feeding scheme as an add on to the government scheme (Phepo School Development Plan, July, 1997).

The action plans which were mundane, included getting quotes and exploring maintenance costs, looking for donors, fund raising and setting up parent committees. Because of 'conflicts between the staff, the lack of motivation and commitment ... very few staff were involved in the process' (Pullen and Sethole, 2000). While few of these needs were met at that time, during the period of upheaval, it is interesting to see how many of these plans came to fruition once the school 'turned itself around' and refocused its vision.

5. TRAINING COURSES

It is hard to gauge the impact of the course workshops. It is clear from the data that there was staff resistance to these workshops and to the involvement of Outreach, so few staff availed themselves of the opportunities they presented. The principal attended all the workshops and learnt a great deal about management, vision building, fundraising and financial management, leadership, and conflict resolution that were to prove crucial to her ability to effect change, despite the odds stacked against her.

In 2004, in an attempt to reconstruct what the principal learnt from these workshops, she and Janks went through all the old course materials to ascertain what she remembered of them. What became clear was that she remembered almost nothing of the course details, not even the course activities; nevertheless, many of the principles continue to inform her practice. These include, among others, the importance of recognizing and valuing teachers' work; finding areas in which each member of the staff can excel; creating space in which that staff can grow; the importance of shared ownership of visions and projects; connecting the school to a wider community; developing partnerships and the importance of fundraising.

Located in psychological theories about human resource management and organizational change, discourses which she did not have full access to, the principal extracted some useful ideas for thinking about her current and future actions. The workshops clearly supported some of the needs she had at the time, as she negotiated the right to continue attending these workshops even after Outreach withdrew from the school as a whole. While whole school development was difficult for Outreach to achieve at Phepo, developing the principal as an individual and helping her to develop some skills and principles continued and may have contributed to her ultimate success.

Foucault (1970, 114) emphasises the importance of chance events. The break-through came with a chance occurrence that showed the principal what she might do; something that she could emulate. The Outreach workshop on fundraising happened to be held at Sizanani[9], a Catholic seminary. It was here that the principal saw, for the first time, raised vegetable beds bordered by bricks.

Principal: After the Sizanani thing, I just felt, I'm going to do something and I'm going to start with the gardens.

Interviewer: The Sizanani was like a real inspiration.

Principal: Definitely, definitely. It was my turning point.

(Interview with principal, 2002).

This was the first germ of the idea to establish a vegetable garden at the school. It was as if the need articulated in the school plan for a feeding scheme required material embodiment; as if vision building needed tangible evidence of what the vision might look like in the real world, as opposed to the world of ideas and wishes. While seeing this 'food' garden could be ascribed to chance, recognition of the potential it suggested may well have depended on the prior articulation of the need. The sighting of the garden suggested 'the path to a new future' (Hallinger and Heck, 2002, 12). Because the Phepo staff had experience of properly equipped offices, they could see what they needed, both literally and metaphorically. But, until they could 'see' a 'food' garden, they could not imagine growing food for their feeding scheme project; they could not even list the things they would need. This suggests that real life examples which give material form to possibilities for transformation and change, which give flesh to ideas, and possible pathways to realization, need to be incorporated in capacity development work.

In the same month, September 1998, the principal was approached by BMW, a global motor car manufacturing company, to join their School Environmental Education Development (S.E.E.D) programme. This programme, one of many BMW social responsibility programmes, includes among other things, the development of sustainable organic vegetable gardens. It provides schools with the know-how, the basic material necessities and the support to initiate and run a sustainable garden project. With the help of BMW, the school caretaker and the parents, the principal organized the clearing of part of the school grounds and the planting of the first vegetables.[10]

6. SUPPORT FOR THE PRINCIPAL

In April 1998, when Outreach decided that it would not continue working with Phepo School, the principal asked Outreach to continue supporting her.

> I had to approach DSG and say, "guys I am glad as an individual to take up your courses and I need your support" and they did that. They fully supported me, they come to school, and when [the facilitator] came to school, they were looking at [him] with suspicion and say we are talking about them. We are gossiping. And when [he] came to school, I would close the door and cry, I needed a shoulder to lean on, and I felt, I'm not going to go down and cry to these people, because now I would be failing as a teacher. I needed somebody that I would say, "These are my problems" (Interview with principal, February, 2002).

The facilitator, concerned about her safety and her isolation in the school, promised Outreach's continued support as well as his personal support.

> I just said [to Outreach] ..., there is no way you can leave [the principal] now. You cannot end the support for her. I mean I felt almost responsible, we worked with the school and we were part of that mess, and there was just no way [we] could leave her. Anyway that was the most terrible thing [to] tell her [that Outreach was withdrawing from the school] because she would burst into tears and cry and wept. Basically what I then did was that well, I'm here for you, this has got nothing to do with working of the program. I will meet with you basically twice a month or once a week or when ever you need me, just to offer you support (Interview with facilitator, December 2002).

There is no doubt that this support was key to her survival and her ultimate triumph in an untenable situation. The facilitator became her mentor, her 'therapist', her friend and her ally. She used him as a sounding board and advisor, while all the time remaining her own person. It is a significant strength of this principal that she is able to benefit from her involvement with others. She is not afraid of expertise; she is always keen to learn; she understands the importance of a support network and she always reciprocates. The relationships she establishes are never one-sided and she gives of herself in return.

> For me, she has a real sense of making connections with people, networking. Everything above board, as far as I can feel. I don't ever feel manipulated by her in a way that I don't know. I feel like what I give to [her] is because of the reciprocal up-front thing (Interview with facilitator, December 2002).

The internal politics in the school seem to have been more about power and status, competition and rivalry, than they were about the principal's interpersonal skills.

7. THE TURN-AROUND

'The school, through the initial efforts of the principal, turned itself around' Linguistically, the formulation – 'the school turned itself around' – suggests that change just happened without causes or agents. Some agency is attributed to the principal, although what she did is nominalized as 'efforts', thus losing the specificity of her actions. In September 1998, the principal began a garden project, working closely with BMW. Only one member of staff was willing to work with her – the caretaker/groundsman – so she worked with the parents and the children. There is excellent data on the development of this work, as record keeping is a BMW criterion for success on the project. The documented records and photographs, the *School Profiles*, are concrete evidence of the principal's ability to transform vision into practice.

> These documents, which [the principal] calls the *School Profiles* are central to the production of positive effects. They show in pictures and text the transformation of the school from a 'haven of snakes', both literal and metaphorical, to an energised community that has visibly altered its space. The once overgrown school property now has eighty vegetable plots, with hail netting. ... The *School Profiles* provide a tangible history of the school's transformation of its space, a history of the achievement of this community. Every time [the principal] uses them to talk about the school, she is reminded of where they have come from and what they have achieved in only four years. Every time the children see them being used, they are reminded of what is possible. In the use of these profiles to talk about what has been accomplished, the power of a community project to seed much more than food - to seed pride and dignity and independence is clear (Janks, 2003).

In the BMW project every participating school has to articulate its own vision for its garden project[11]. Returning to a need, originally articulated in the school development plan, Phepo formulated its vision for this project as 'Feed the child, feed the nation'.

> We at Phepo, enhance learning programmes with a focus on the environment by encouraging respect and love for the environment, what we can do for the ENVIRONMENT and what the ENVIRONMENT can do for us.
>
> In doing this, we believe that we would be feeding the CHILD who is hungry, the COMMUNITY that is hungry and thereby feeding the NATION ... The nation shall never be hungry again.
>
> We shall be empowering people by teaching them sustainable food gardening to overcome malnutrition and hunger (School Profiles).

The school now grows enough vegetables to provide its 780 students a hot meal every day. The children are taught to practice the saying 'reduce, re-use, recycle'.

> Children 'pay' for their food by bringing recyclable materials. On different days of the week they are expected to bring vegetable peelings for the compost heap – 'the gardens feed us so we must feed the gardens'; two litres of grey water – dirty soapy water which acts as an insecticide in an organic garden; tins sold to collect-a-can; paper for recycling; and half bricks scrounged from the township for bricking both beds and paths (Janks, 2003).

What the *School Profiles* do not capture is the critical nature of this intervention and the way it worked to transform subjectivity and to change the destructive relations of power within the school. For the first time parents and students are given ways of taking up positions as agentive subjects who can act to transform their material environment in ways that affect both body and place. The vision differs from the previous vision in other important ways:

1. Feed the child, feed the nation, is a more focused vision because it is tied to a specific and tangible project, the school garden, such that the project provides the path for realizing the vision and the vision gives meaning to the project, effecting an

organic relationship between means and ends. According to Fullan, the starting point for changing our context:

> is our immediate situation, change the situation and you have a chance to change people's behaviour in the short run as well as beyond (Fullan, 2003, 2).

He draws on Gladwell:

> It is not the heroic act of tackling complex societal problems that count; instead the power of context says that what really matters is the little things. ... (150) Most of us will be better [people] on a clean street or in a clean subway than in one littered with trash and graffitti (168) (Gladwell, 2002 quoted in Fullan (2003).

Making a garden is just such a little thing compared to the complexity of the issue of food security in Africa; it is a little thing compared to the big vision of feeding the child and thereby feeding the nation.

2. The focus on the children and the community addresses the material conditions of their lives – poverty and hunger. The bigness of this vision makes the internal rivalries in the school seem small, and the 'moral imperative' (Fullan, 2003) that underpins it, makes it impossible to contest. This draws the teachers in. According to Hallinger and Heck (2002):

> The power of a personal vision lies ... in its potential to energise others. A clearly formed personal vision shapes our actions, invests our work with meaning and reminds us why we became educators. When a personal vision is shared by others it can become a catalyst for transformation (10).

3. It is distinctive. This brings the school under a positive spotlight and attracts recognition in the form of prizes, monetary awards, accolades, status. Success breeds success. Using the *Profiles* to show what the school has achieved and strategies learnt in the fundraising course she attended, the principal has been able to attract extensive donor funding. This funding, together with prize money, has enabled the school to build three new classrooms and a media centre, to purchase four rainwater storage tanks, two fax machines, two Photostat machines, two video machines, two overhead projectors, five television sets, to acquire two state-of-the-art computers for the administration staff; it has also received hail netting for the garden beds from BMW as a further incentive to continue performing well. In addition, the school was given one fully operative computer laboratory by Microsoft at the behest of the Minister of National Education and one online computer laboratory from the Gauteng Department of Education. While these are primarily for students to use, the provincial department is also providing training for the staff. Part of the playground has been concreted and now has a chess board. The indigenous garden has some lawn. What is interesting is how many of these needs were articulated in the 1995 School Development Plan.

4. It produces participation. Parents were involved in clearing the ground and later in preparing the food; students were drawn in to collect water for recycling and organic waste for compost and they continue to work in the gardens, preparing and maintaining the vegetable beds; the community benefits from the sale of vegetables and from employment opportunities created by the building projects. Slowly, one by one, the teachers offered to assist on the project – either in the gardens or with the feeding programme. They also began to use the garden to develop the curriculum,

turning the gardens into a living classroom built around what I have come to call, 'the edible curriculum'.

5. It reaches out. In addition to the staff reaching out to the children, the project is used to teach children to reach out to others and the school has its own out reach programme. It has donated trees to its neighbours to help transform the neighbourhood, it has developed vegetable gardens at a local old age home and at a school for children with disabilities, and it shares its expertise with other schools in the township. Underlying the project is an ethics of care both for the environment and for people.

This is how the principal explains the change in staff attitudes:

> The real change occurred when the school got recognition for the gardens and began winning prizes and awards for our work. I used these moments to bring the staff together to share in the awards and the recognition. Slowly, but very surely ... the staff became more and more involved in the garden project and as they did, the barriers between themselves and between themselves and myself slowly started to melt. Teachers developed a sense of pride in the school and their commitment to improving the school increased (Pullen and Sethole, 2000).

With a project that enabled the staff to focus on their achievements rather than their problems, to put the needs of the children and the community ahead of their own disputes, they found a way to move forward. The transcript of the focus group conducted by the facilitator with the staff at the end of 2000, shows a sense of ownership of the project ('it's all hands on deck', the word 'we' is used extensively); a sense of direction ('we now are having a vision and goals'); a changed atmosphere ('I was always absent but these days I am positive'); a sense of achievement and pride ('there is a lot of recognition from the community ... everyone is coming here to find out'); improved interpersonal communication ('people have become straight talkers'); and a sense of feeling valued ('if you do something good you are applauded'). The teachers also pay tribute to the principal.

> Teacher 5: She's an exemplary. She does things. She doesn't say teachers do this and that and she stays back. She does them that is why we are so enthusiastic to do a lot of things at school because she has given us courage - a lot of courage (Focus group, 2000).

> Teacher 1: I think our principal was very determined in what she was doing ... and she was very motivated and when she had ... I think she had ambition about what she was doing. So, if you see something like that, why not jump in and join the thing (Focus group, 2000).

> Teacher 2: I just want to copy what she has done positively, not because I am jealous. I just want to imitate what she has done very good and so forth and, by so doing, we just join in (Focus group, 2000).

8. REACHING OUT AND REACHING IN

The focus group interview with staff was conducted in October 2000, two and a half years from the date when Outreach terminated its contract with Phepo. Although from September 1998, BMW became the main support for the principal, Outreach

1999. In September 2002, the principal accompanied the director of Outreach to the United Kingdom to visit schools and to report on the work of Outreach at her school. Recognizing the 'failure' of the whole school development project, the Outreach director concluded that re-established its contract with the school in April

> Interventions in social systems such as schools, must [rather] be people centred, building on the personal attributes of leaders (Pullen and Sethole, 2000).

The facilitator in his evaluation report October, 2000 draws a similar conclusion:

> Outreach contributed to the development of individuals within the school however the process of school development planning was not particularly successful at the school. It took the school community to come up with a solution that would enable them to make the changes needed. Phepo is a clear example of how the process of whole school development needs to take an individualistic approach with each school and that to attempt to implement school development planning within a school that is experiencing many internal problems is not appropriate.

This is perhaps better expressed by Teacher 5 in the focus group:

> Teacher 5: We had to develop ourselves first, before anybody can develop us (Focus group, 2000).

The data suggests otherwise. The development happened, but before it could be used productively, the principal had to find a way of getting the staff to pull together. All the courses in leadership, fundraising and conflict resolution gave her the knowledge she needed to do her job and the support at the human level gave her the strength to continue. The work on vision building and needs analysis gave her enough direction to make the most of the opportunity presented by Sizanani and BMW; it is no accident that the idea of feeding the child was there, in embryo, in the original school development plan. The principal was able to reach out to others, the staff, the parents, the community and the children in part because her social responsibility partners had reached out to her. But we should not underestimate her own courage and determination, the effort it took to put on her 'stockings and [her] best shoes and [her] beautiful handbag' and to face down her opposition, nor the generosity of spirit that enabled her to embrace and trust those who had tried to destroy her and to share the glory. Only by reaching deep within, could she find the strength that feeds her laughter; the laughter that is her trademark and that fills the school. Only by reaching in, was she able to reach out and to establish reaching out as a fundamental part of the school's ethos. In 2002 she was named Woman of the Year by the Premier of Gauteng and in 2003 she received the National Lifetime Achievement Award from the Department of National Education. What matters most is that her staff could celebrate this achievement with her.

But this and-they-all-lived-happily-ever-after conclusion is not a fitting place to conclude this chapter because it fails to recognize that school development is ongoing. It is a dynamic process which constantly has to be negotiated by a changing community of staff and students in an ever-shifting context. In 2004, the improvements that have been effected in the school make it increasingly difficult to attract funding in a context where there are so many schools that need so much; development requires periods of consolidation, which are less glamorous than new projects; success also breeds envy and new rivalries; and new government policies threaten independent fundraising on the part of schools. Teacher 1 recognizes that they have all learnt from the bad experiences of the past and that the principal helps them in this. The principal

> tries by all means. When she sees something leaking she tries by all means not to let it go on ... [and] for you to remember and say let me sort it out if you do something wrong (Focus group, 2000).

In a school where there is never a leaking faucet and where the conservation of natural resources is at the heart of its vision, avoiding leaks is the perfect metaphor for ethical vigilance which is at the heart of leadership that is committed to the ongoing positive transformation of an institution and the people who work in it. The principal would be the first to acknowledge that she could not have achieved this on her own, which is why she values and nurtures her relationships with organizations that have supported the school and her principalship. Embued with her understanding of Ubuntu – umuntu ngu muntu[12] – the principal pays them the highest compliment. She calls them 'family'.

ACKNOWLEDGEMENTS

Janks and Sethole wish to extend their appreciation to Priscilla Langa-Mtintsilana for her collation of the documents that form the basis of this research and to Alex Hassett for agreeing to be interviewed and for sharing his knowledge of the school. Janks wishes to record her appreciation to Buzz Bezuidenhout and Esther Langa of BMW and to DSG Outreach for their trust that she would not hijack their projects.

ENDNOTES

[1] 'Phepo', which means 'feeding' in Setswana, is a pseudonym for the school.
[2] Outreach began by offering enrichment programmes to promising students selected from schools in the townships at St Mary's DSG on Saturdays. This was later seen to be benefiting individuals without contributing to school change, necessitating the introduction of the Whole School Development Project. Although the learner enrichment programme continues, it is not the subject of this paper.
[3] The management discourse used in this paperfollows the language found in data: "development plans", "vision building", "leadership", "training", "organizational change". This is not meant to suggest an uncritical acceptance of this discourse.
[4] When interviewed, the facilitator was no longer working for Outreach nor was he living in South Africa.
[5] Comments on the paper were received from the current and former directors of Outreach and from the school principal; the concerns they raised have been addressed.
[6] At the time Outreach began working at Phepo School, there was one Head of Department. She subsequently became principal in the face of hostile opposition.
[7] At the start of the garden project, the principal asked the school caretaker (groundsman) to dig two garden beds to illustrate the principles of organic vegetable gardening to the parents of the school whose support she needed.
[8] A 'chalk down' is a teacher's strike; and a 'go slow' is where workers do as little work as possible.
[9] The word 'sizanani' means 'let's help one another'
[10] Janks (2003) *Seeding change in South Africa: New literacies, new subjectivities, new futures* provides an analysis of the garden project and Phepo's relationship with BMW. For more information on BMW South Africa's social investment policy, see http://www.bmw.co.za.

[11] Each of the schools in the programme produces a different embodied vision which results in each school becoming a resource for the other schools; they become mutually informing resources of vision and know-how.

[12] Translated into English this means 'a person is a person through other people'. Ubuntu, a cornerstone of African values is reaching out to others as a way of life.

REFERENCES

Foucault, M (1970). The order of discourse. Inaugural lecture at the Collège de France. In M. Shapiro, (ed.). (1984) *Language and politics*. Oxford: Basil Blackwell.

Fullan, M. (2003) *The moral imperative of school leadership*. California, USA: Corwin Press.

Gladwell, M. (2002) *The tipping point*. Boston: Little, Brown.

Hallinger, P and R. Heck (2002) 'What do people call 'visions'? The role of vision, mission and goals in school improvement'. In K. Leithwood and P. Hallinger (eds). *Second international handbook of educational leadership*. Dordrecht: Kluwer Academic Publishers.

Janks, H. (2003) Seeding change in South Africa: New literacies, new subjectivities, new futures. In B. Doecke, D Homer and H Nixon (eds). *English teachers at work*. South Australia: Wakefield Press and the Australian Association for the Teaching of English.

Outreach (1998) Phepo primary school organizational audit.

Outreach (2000) Evaluation of the Outreach Whole School Development Project, October 2000.

Pullen, D. and Sethole, P (2000) *An individualistic approach to the transformation of a school*. Paper presented at the Technology Trust Annual Conference 29 November to 1 December, London, England.

Thomson, P. 'How principals lose 'face': A tale disciplinary tale of educational administration and modern managerialism. *Discourse* (22)1, 5- 22.

TERRY WRIGLEY

OPENING THE TEXT:

Voicing a future

Abstract. This chapter uses the concepts of voice and agency to compare traditional schooling and critical education. It examines the ways in which traditional school cultures restrict learning and development through disciplinary regimes, choice of curricular content and teaching methods. It then describes some practical and adaptable approaches to critical pedagogy in various curriculum areas. The discussion is situated against the prevailing wind of a pragmatic but uncritical attempt to 'improve schools'.

1. INTRODUCTION

School development is high on the political agenda. The hegemonic approach known as 'School Effectiveness and Improvement' is pragmatic but largely uncritical (Slee and Weiner,1998; Wrigley, 2003). In pursuit of higher and higher test scores, it asks few questions about the direction of change or the kind of society we wish to live in. It is supposedly concerned with school 'culture' but fails to question the antidemocratic norms which permeate our schools. It has much to say about 'value-added' but little about social justice. For all its talk of 'vision', it is largely silent on the big issues of our time, such as poverty, environmental degradation, or imperialism. By contrast, most writings on 'critical pedagogy', while directly addressing the political and ideological issues, are proudly unpragmatic and often connect poorly with life in the classroom. Because this genre of writings is so remote from the here and now, it is difficult to deploy in any project of radical change.

It is my intention, in this chapter, to address issues of concern to the *practical* critical educator, connecting present to future and schools to society. I will try to deal with school ethos, curriculum and pedagogy in a joined-up way, but with particular focus on learning and teaching. In contrast to much current discussion of 'school culture' in management texts, I want to raise some fundamental questions about the rituals, language and relationships of traditional schoolwork. The first half of the chapter is a critique of traditional practice, and the second an outline of practical approaches to critical pedagogy.

The key terms in this discussion are *voice* and *agency*. These are connecting terms, and it is important to hold on to them both. Schools typically close down on learning at three levels of operation:

K. Cooper and R. White (eds.), The Practical Critical Education, 179–194.
© 2007 *Springer.*

- the organization and its disciplining of relationships;
- the curriculum, as a selection of content;
- the preferred modes of teaching and learning.

The *voice* and *agency* of the learner (and particularly those from working-class and ethnic minority communities) are systematically denied on all three levels in traditional schooling. Freire's great contribution was to imagine and mount a combined challenge to all three forms of oppression – disciplinary, curricular, and pedagogical. As illustrations of what is at stake in each of these fields, I will briefly outline some historic contributions to our understanding of them from a British academic tradition.

Socialist historians of British education such as Brian Simon (1960, 1965) have provided substantial evidence of the disciplinary work of schooling from the 19th Century onwards. Reforms have since taken place, partly due to social changes which have made heavier forms of regulation unacceptable, but also through the efforts of progressive teachers; there is still much, however, within the structure and ethos of British schools, which would be seen as barbaric in Scandinavian countries, with their more democratic educational histories. The impact of disciplinary repression, and the negative reaction of working-class boys, for example, was studied by sociologists such as Willis (1977), and recent work has developed this critique with regard to race (Sewell, 1997). It is important to move beyond critique and engage with working-class communities in demands for an improved environment for learning.

Substantial attention was given to ideological distortions in the curricular content of university education, for example by Raymond Williams in his challenge to the 'selective tradition' of 'English literature' in England. His critique was not only in terms of what had been omitted from the canon, but also in his internal analysis.

> Neighbours in Jane Austen are not the people actually living nearby; they are the people living a little less nearby who, in social recognition, can be visited. What she sees across the land is a network of propertied houses and families, and through the holes of this tightly drawn mesh most actual people are simply not seen. To be face-to-face in this world is already to belong to a class (Williams, 1973, 166).

Too little challenge has been mounted about the 'selective tradition' of school curricula, and it has been difficult to mount a popular campaign against the standardized curriculum imposed by government.

The deep grammar of teaching and learning styles has received far too little attention. Though educators such as Douglas Barnes (1971, 1976) had major influence when focusing on the asymmetry of classroom discourse – the dominance of teacher voice, those phoney questions to which the teacher already knows the answer – little has changed to this day. The debate about classroom language patterns was only implicitly political, being restricted to questions of classroom learning and pupils' language development. The issue of *voice* was not usually related to that of *agency* – the ways in which school learning positions young people as inactive – adults-in-waiting, whose ideas 'may come in useful *one* day' but just 'sit still for now and learn this to do well in your test'!

It is my intention in this chapter to look at all three levels at which agency and voice are suppressed, while spending most time on modes of teaching, within the limited space available. Though writing from a British context, I hope it will prove useful to critical educators in many different situations.

2. THE DISCIPLINARY REGIME: SILENCE AND INERTIA

The disciplining of young people no longer takes the form of beatings, but its current forms – enforced immobility, the regulation and division of time and space, a disconnection from activities which are valued by adults and exclusion of those who break these rules (with all its long-term consequences) – are equally deserving of the term 'discipline'. To some extent, control of behaviour and relationships is essential in the strained compression of young bodies we call school, since learning cannot take place in too chaotic or hostile an environment, yet it has serious ideological impact in socializing young people into silence and inaction. In fact, it is this sense of necessity that makes the disciplinary regime work like other ideologies – an exercise of power whilst denying that power is being unjustly exercised, since 'common sense' demands it.

Opposition to the disciplinary regimes of modern schooling is problematic. From a genuine desire to improve conditions for learning, and also to avoid the embarassment of appearing 'out of control', teachers have rushed to embrace the latest techniques of 'assertive discipline' – an ostensibly civilized approach involving the systematic application of rewards and sanctions for even minor infringements of classroom norms. The effectiveness of such control does not mitigate the arbitrariness of the rules which it enforces, and pupils' acceptance of its 'fairness' may inadvertently teach an acquiescence to authority. The system depends on extrinsic rewards and is rarely accompanied by reforms of curriculum or pedagogy which would bring greater intrinsic satisfaction in learning. Even for those on whom it works, it reinforces dependency.

Even the most 'advanced' techniques can collapse in inner-city schools, for a mix of reasons: because the conflicts and issues in troubled neighbourhoods seep into schools, because the students have fewer role models of success as a result of academic learning, because many parents have had bad school experiences themselves. Disciplinary measures are more likely to meet resistance here because of the greater cultural gap between teachers and students. This can result in misunderstandings of students' verbal styles and body language (see Sewell, 1997), in real prejudice against black or working-class students; or in well-intentioned teacher actions being read as hostile and demeaning. In such schools, teacher-student conflict is over-read through the filter of a wider social conflict (class or race) and teacher actions, which are simply accepted as 'normal' in other schools, take on the cultural significance of the disciplining of workers by the boss, or of ethnic minorities by a white majority. This dynamic is overlooked by those who see 'assertive discipline' as the answer.

Independent schools of the British Victorian tradition were places of harsh discipline, but with a different dynamic, because they provided a real passage to high status positions in society. Care was taken, after the subjugation of younger pupils, to promote 'leadership' in the older ones through institutions such as prefects and competitive sport. It is no use trying to emulate this complex power structure in a different age, and with very different populations who have less reason to believe that pain now will lead to pleasure ever after.

Although the School Effectiveness literature is right to shun chaotic schools, its insistence on 'orderly schools' is misleading, since there are many different kinds of 'orderly'. In researching successful inner-city schools (Wrigley, 2000), I found that the key word was 'respect', not 'order'. This respect emerged in many ways in the school culture:

- the display of children's photographs and their work;
- the quality of personal relationships;
- a reaching out to parents – even if they had not turned up on consultation evenings;
- a respect for heritage and youth cultures; an involvement of the students in writing the behaviour code;
- a refusal to write off difficult youngsters;
- the creation of social spaces.

I remember my surprise when a fifteen-year-old calmly walked into the deputy principal's office and picked up the telephone – he was organizing a conference on child labour in Britain and Asia (Wrigley, 2000, 56). In one school I visited, which had quadrupled the number of students gaining five higher-level certificates, the principal and deputies had chosen to remove barriers between management and students, teachers and parents by relocating into an empty classroom and removing the door! (Wrigley, 2000, 8) From then on, nobody had to argue his or her way past a secretary into the inner sanctum of a principal's office. This was a dramatic and highly significant redistribution of power in the school.

Each school chooses its own route to success, but, especially for schools serving marginalized communities, critical and creative attention has to be given to the culture. The School Improvement literature has, quite rightly, emphasized school culture as significant in determining success, but so far there have been few studies which can genuinely be described as ethnographic or ethnomethodological, and too many fleeting research visits which have produced apolitical (in macro and micro sense) readings of rituals, norms, language and behaviours.

To achieve a cultural transformation of schools, in response to technological and social change along with a desire for greater democracy and social justice, we need to give serious attention to *voice and agency*. There are many good models around, including alternative or experimental schools in Europe and North America, where new rituals, relationships and patterns of learning are being developed and evaluated. The small schools movement in the USA, and the internal organization of schools in Scandinavia create different community dynamics which are less needy of constant repair through sanctions and rewards. The Student Voice movement within school self-evaluation (Fielding, 2001) involves students in the transformation and development of their own schools.

All this is central to critical pedagogy, since without a disciplinary reform, students remain trapped in subservience and are unable to assert control of the texts they read and the world they investigate.

3. CURRICULAR IDEOLOGIES: CLOSING GATES TO WORTHWHILE KNOWLEDGE

In the 1980s, the state of Victoria, Australia proposed a vocational alternative to the traditional academic curriculum, and commissioned some academic researchers to report. They came to rather different conclusions, pointing out that the vocational and academic curricula shared the same political *orientation* – of fitting people into an existing social order, albeit for different types of role:

> for some this will be skilled or semi-skilled labour requiring well-known and defined competences; for others, it will be managerial or professional, requiring higher levels of general education and abstract universalized thinking (Kemmis et al, 1983, 9).

According to Kemmis' team, the proponents of both types of curriculum see themselves as 'realists', and implicitly or explicitly share the belief that 'education merely reflects the principles of the wider society'… For both schools of thought, the world appears 'hierarchically ordered, and the best endowed will in any case find their way to the most rewarding positions'. For traditionalists and vocationalists alike, there is considerable certainty about 'what is worth knowing', based on 'time-honoured beliefs' but 'revived and reinterpreted for the modern world'. (Ibid, 9) For working-class communities in particular, there is a denial of both *agency* and *voice* – their history is hidden from view, and teaching is seen as a transmission of a fixed body of facts and skills.

The most obvious alternative, a liberal-progressive orientation, also came in for criticism, as being too individualistic and ahistorical (Ibid, 9). Though it speaks of educating the 'whole person', it chooses to deny the reality of work, a position which most students and their families simply cannot afford to adopt. There are many subtleties here: if it allows of an historical perspective, it sees history as gradual progress. Insofar as it sees society as open to change, it is by creating individuals of good will and sensitivity, with little regard to social forces. Education is placed at a distance from social change:

> This reconstruction can be achieved only through the development of society's future citizens… Education must develop a sense of the good, true and beautiful in every child, and can do this by recognizing these virtues in children and building on them through creative and engaging tasks. (Ibid, 9)

One example would be English lessons where World War I poetry is taught in isolation from historical analysis. Our students learn of the horrors of war, but not of the mass struggle which brought the war to a close – the Bolshevik revolution in 1917, uprisings across Germany in 1918, and growing protests across Britain and elsewhere. This is far better, of course, than a curriculum which glorified war and Empire but denies *agency,* while to some extent privileging *voice.*

We may also see this orientation in versions of multicultural curriculum which celebrates diversity through a superficial focus on features of cultural heritage, without addressing racist oppression. They aestheticize experience, and disempower marginalized groups.

Kemmis identifies a third possible orientation in the *socially-critical curriculum*:

> If changes are to be wrought in our social structure... then individual virtue and
> individual action will be insufficient to bring them about. They must be brought about
> by collective action capable of confronting unjust and irrational social structures.

> The socially-critical orientation sees right knowledge and right action together: it does
> not value only knowledge and leave action to follow. It therefore requires participation
> of the school in the life of its community and of the community in the school. (Ibid, 10)

This orientation is not only about knowledge; it constitutes a challenge at the levels of school discipline, curricular knowledge and pedagogy. However, to focus for a while on the ways in which school curricula might seal off access to key knowledge, I will use a complementary framework by Philip Wexler, who argues that school texts systematically block the very information which students need to make sense of the world and act to change it. Wexler identifies the following aspects of critical understanding which are typically silenced in school texts:

- 'the location of human activity in *history*'
- 'the ability to situate the individual and the immediate within a larger frame, to have a view of the social *totality*'
- '*conflict* rooted in opposing interests' – and particularly exploitation (it can absorb 'differences as cultural pluralism')
- *work*, 'collective human labor as the continuing source of what we are and of what we have', 'the human social making of relations and products' (Wexler, 1982, 287-8).

At the same time, Wexler points to the pedagogical level: the authoritative tone of school texts – and we should add, its reinforcement by teacher voice – conceals from the learner the bias or inadequacies of the text's construction and disables the learner from further enquiry and action (Wexler, 1982, 289-90). Not only are there these blockages, but the texts themselves, in their apparent authority, prevent the learner from questioning their view of the world (see the next section).

These blockages are not all co-present in every text or area of knowledge, but often combine tactically to prevent true understanding. It is here that we must take issue with those liberal-progressive approaches to education which tend to neglect the critique of knowledge in their emphasis on pedagogical style. To take a contemporary example, it is impossible to take a stand on the Israeli government's oppression of Palestinians without some key factual knowledge: for instance:

- the *history* that Israeli Jews returned to their 'homeland' after an absence of nearly 2000 years;
- that Palestinians are now living as a third generation in refugee camps in Gaza and Lebanon;
- that they are largely denied the means to develop the land and engage in productive *work*;
- and that the Israeli state is able to deploy overwhelming force supported by $100 million of American aid each day (the difference between understanding *conflict* laden with *power* and a simple difference of perspective or culture).

This, along with a knowledge of the horrors of the Holocaust which gave impetus to the Zionist solution, are necessary for a critical and responsible understanding. Without this key knowledge, one remains trapped in a vague sense of empathy and 'isn't it terrible but what can one do?' In fact, such empathy prevents the use of voice and blocks political action in a rather suburban 'isn't the violence terrible but one mustn't take sides'.

Other writers point to similar closures. Apple echoes Wexler's point about *totality*:

> The overemphasis on the individual in our educational, emotional, and social lives is ideally suited to both maintain a rather manipulative ethic of consumption and further withering of political and economic sensitivity. It makes it ... nearly impossible for educators to develop a potent analysis of widespread social and economic injustice (Apple 1979, 10).

On conflict, he says:

> There are few serious attempts at dealing with conflict (class conflict, scientific conflict, or other). Instead one 'inquires' into a consensus ideology that bears little resemblance to the complex nexus and contradictions surrounding the control and organization of social life. Hence the selective tradition dictates that we do not teach, or will selectively reinterpret (and hence will soon forget) serious labor or woman's history... It may be rather imperative that urban and working class ... students develop positive perspectives towards conflict and change, ones that will enable them to deal with the complex and often repressive political realities and dynamics of power of their society ... (Apple 1979, 7).

Subject divisions can themselves constitute the closures which Wexler identifies, for example the way science and technology is disconnected from ecology and ethics. Even positive new formations such as Design and Technology – a considerable advance upon earlier models of practical learning in which students just carried out somebody else's design – are open to critique. It is generally individualistic and premised upon a consumer notion of user – we rarely see groups of students investigating and designing a public playground. Sometimes the boundaries are produced by direct political interference, as in the edict that nothing within the last 25 years would count as history (this in a standardized National Curriculum for England that included no contemporary social studies whatsoever).

Particular subject paradigms may have the same effect, such as the 'great men and battles' versions of history, or an English curriculum which is crammed with technical detail. Sometimes teachers may subvert a state's attempt to impose a conservative paradigm; for example, when (again in England) Shakespeare was made compulsory and subject to high-stakes testing for 14-year-olds. The curriculum police clearly intended 'iconic Shakespeare' but teachers have seized the opportunity to develop socially critical responses – the Shakespeare who calls into question kingship, filial obedience and racial prejudice. In other cases, a surreptitious reinterpretation isn't enough; media education in England is deemed worthy of only a few words in the National Curriculum, and educators should be demanding publicly its place as one of the new Basics essential to democratic living in the 21st Century.

The disciplining of schools by high-stakes testing provides a pretext for standardization of the curriculum. Indeed, Tim Brighouse, arguably England's most successful Director of Education, has asserted that high-stakes testing is now more tightly regulated under the National Curriculum than in Stalinist Russia (Brighouse, 2002)! This is not to suggest that statistical performance data is of no value, but it has to be used supportively and intelligently, as Brighouse demonstrated so clearly. The value of having clear data cannot become an excuse for failing to adapt curriculum to real learners, especially those at risk of becoming alienated from school.

> Children whose different talents are developing at different speeds need experiences which will boost their confidence and give them a taste of success – rather than seeing themselves labelled as comparative failures in the 'three R's. (Ibid)

He was determined to overcome the internecine competition which high-stakes testing can generate:

> To have a system which sets out to reward some and not others, where teacher is pitched against teacher, is to plant the seeds of the school's destruction. (Ibid)

Paradoxically, it was Brighouse's critical stance with regard to the macro-environment which helped him to raise Birmingham's test results to nine percentage points above the national average for similar deprivation levels.

As well as questioning the ideological orientation of the state curriculum, we also need to argue for a degree of 'authorship' on the part of the learners. It was a shock and welcome surprise to find the Danish education ministry advising teachers against writing a definitive plan for the year, as this will undermine negotiation with the learners (Ministry of Education, Denmark 1995). It is important to insist on a degree of *authorship* for pupils:

> How can we reconceptualize and reconstruct the curriculum in such a way that pupils, at least for part of the time, have an opportunity for fashioning some time for themselves so that they can pursue their own ideas and studies (Davies and Edwards, 2001, 104)?

Even when tasks are adjusted to meet the needs of different learners, this also tends to be something done to the learner. By contrast, good practice in Denmark consists of the learners, within a broad common theme or task, defining their particular objectives and working methods, and sharing in the evaluation of how well they have achieved their goals and improved.

> The setting of goals and evaluation holds a work process together, both for you and for your pupils. Just as you must formulate a goal for your teaching, so must each pupil formulate a goal which will become a leading thread in the pupil's work (Ministry of Education, Denmark 1995).

It will often happen that the learners' goals are inspired by the framework which your planning provides, and often many pupils will formulate similar objectives. However, the essential point is that each pupil or group of pupils will have ownership of the learning process and will know what they want to teach themselves, so that they can find ways of doing it more effectively (Krogh-Jespersen et al, 1998, 17).

This is easier to manage within the broad architecture known as Project Method (see later section) than when teachers are constantly rushing to cover a detailed content-based syllabus.

4. THE PEDAGOGICAL DENIAL OF VOICE AND AGENCY

Research in the 1970s and 80s clearly identified the asymmetry of language use in the classroom. The teacher's voice dominates. The teacher speaks more than everyone else put together. The teacher asks all the questions, and usually these are phoney questions as she already knows the answers. The frequency of test questions amounts to a subversion of real dialogue by the examination mode of exchange. The questions are rarely invitations to think or contribute, being more frequently closed questions to elicit short factual answers. When my teaching students investigate the extent of 'discussion' in lessons, they often find teachers using the word to mean something else – teacher asking different children questions in turn. After each turn, it is the teacher who validates the response, rather than another child. These well established patterns, to this day largely unchanged, quickly socialize young children into silence.

Despite substantial evidence that discussion, role play and co-operative problem-solving in small groups gives better opportunities for fruitful learning in which more children articulate their ideas, teachers still tend to avoid these arrangements, perhaps for fear of losing direct control. Phillips' (1987) analysis of small group learning identified that children were more likely to express hypotheses, make tentative statements, build theory, and connect with their experience, than in whole class teaching.

Alongside this denial of voice, we can also see the denial of agency as part of the deep grammar of traditional schooling. In a German manual for social studies (Weissenau and Kuhn, 2000), I found as an example of problem-solving – the town hall or hospital coming to the school with a genuine problem, which the students are invited to help solve. The students then discuss and research it before presenting their answers to the local policy makers. What is surprising is not the example itself, but that it should sound so unusual to us!

School is a constant parody or deferral of action. Students are constantly being told 'you'll use this knowledge when you're older'. That is true, of course, but we should note how rarely they are able to follow through on their learning with any kind of immediacy. It is regarded as utterly shocking when, on rare occasions, a minority of young people decide that action cannot be deferred, as when hundreds of young people in my city walked out of their schools to protest against their government's invasion of Iraq. They later produced a film about it which they called 'Old enough to know better'! (There are multiple ironies in the title: conservative politicians had said it was inexcusable they should be so badly behaved as to walk out of school – they were 'old enough to know better'. The young filmmakers countered by saying the politicians were old enough to know better than start the war.)

The economy of school life is characterized by the following pattern of exchange:

- Teacher tells pupils what to produce, and how long they must work at the task.
- Pupils hands it to teacher, who looks hastily at the product
- Teacher hands it back defaced and with it a small token of its worth.
- The product is of no obvious use to anybody.

This is a form of alienated labour, like working in a factory and in some respects more absurd. It is no wonder young people in school need a supplement to this mean reward in the form of other tokens – merit certificates, commendations, etc. – before realizing that they'd earn more in the short term by ignoring school work and focusing on their paper routes.

5. TEXTUALITY AND READERSHIP

The concept that some texts are more 'open' than others focuses on features of the text which give readers more scope to question its message. At the same time, some readers approach texts in a more proactive and critical way. This is not simply an intellectual dynamic, but one which connects text to reader to action.

There are already well established practices designed to develop more open approaches to reading. 'Comprehensions', or texts followed by questions, are probably the most frequent reading activity in schools. It would be foolish to write them off altogether, as skilful questioning can focus readers' attention on stylistic and rhetorical features, ambiguities, ill-founded assertions, and gaps in logic or evidence, thus helping to develop skills of critical literacy. However, they have drawbacks in that the reader remains dependent upon the teacher's questioning, they read and feel like tests, and they don't invite engagement. Alternatives involve an active rather than passive approach to the text. Young readers take control by learning how to do something with a text, through relatively straightforward practices such as:

- predicting how a story will continue
- re-arranging jumbled paragraphs in a narrative or report
- disputing a statement, from someone else's point of view
- comparing two texts on a similar subject. (Simons, c.1986)

Converting textual information into diagrammatic form requires a more proactive struggle to find the holistic meaning offered, and can help to highlight flaws in the logic.

Obviously one must avoid this becoming another set of practice exercises, but such a repertoire of open and active reading practices can generate a consciousness that texts are artefacts structured according to particular conventions and intentions, and that stylistic features exercise rhetorical and ideological power.

Critical literacy should not be seen only as a paper exercise. The technique of 'hot-seating' developed by drama teachers (sit the actor playing Lady Macbeth in the hotseat, so that everybody else can ask her questions) can be extended to many other purposes. For example:

- ask someone to represent the author of a particular text, and subject them to questions about their intentions, motives and evidence;
- role play politicians to ask them to justify their decision to occupy Iraq;

- hotseat an abstract concept such as Imperialism, or more concretely, the British Empire or (dare we say) the American Empire.

This can motivate students into personal research, but key quotations can also stimulate the exchange. For example, we could use Madeleine Albright's infamous television comment that the death of half a million Iraqi children through sanctions had probably been 'worth it' (Pilger, 1998) or Bishop Tutu's summary of the colonization of Africa:

> When the missionaries first came to Africa, they had bibles and we had the land. They said, 'Let us pray.' We closed our eyes. When we opened them, we had the bibles and they had the land (Peterson, in Darder et al, 2003, 379).

It is often assumed that the critical 'deconstruction' of a text amounts to a set of techniques, but a change of perspective is probably more important, as when a particular group of readers are positioned to produce a feminist or anti-racist reading. Pakistani fifteen-year-olds produced the following critique of an apparently 'innocent' television hospital drama in which a Muslim girl runs away with an English boy, and they are pursued by the girl's brother:

> Khalid the big brother strides in through the dark iron gates and stands there with his cigarette in his hands taking a long puff at it. His eyes look big and round with that look of cool anger burning up inside them. He strides in from darkness to light. This atmosphere was very threatening and menacing. He's got shadows cast upon his face, illuminating and menacing. We as viewers are manipulated straight away that this is the bad guy. The only lights in the tunnel were supplied by the car headlights, but there were strange shadows everywhere (Wrigley, 2000, 98).

The youngsters are engaged in media literacy of the best kind, carefully analyzing how dramatic techniques, but also filming and editing techniques, are used to construct a stereotype. Of course, at one level it's 'just a story' but these young Muslims made a very important point in their well-founded claim that 'forced marriage' has become a popular narrative theme on television, but you never see examples of Muslims who are happily married, whether in dramas or documentaries.

Simulations and role-play can be far more effective than open discussion in exposing the perspective from which texts are written. In an open discussion, it is conceivable that students simply reinforce consensus and 'common sense' values. In a role-play, the actors have to take on distinct perspectives arising from specific life experiences, positions within structures of power, and personal choices. Texts appear to be monologic to many young readers, and, even when presented with a collection of different texts, they find it difficult to see that they are written from different viewpoints. They find opening the text difficult because they are socialized into seeing both text and teacher as authoritative. Role-play legitimizes debate about conflict perspectives. The power structures become apparent in, for example, a role-play based on a family polarizing into support for opposing sides during the English or American civil war. A related way of bringing out power and perspective is by using historical documents and writing a personalized account from the position of a key historical figure (e.g. a ruler giving advice to his successor).

One of the best examples of guidance for critical reading has emerged from protracted discussions by teachers at New York's Central Park East Secondary School:

- *Viewpoint*: From whose viewpoint are we hearing this? to who's speaking? Would this look different if she or he were in another place or time?
- *Evidence*: How do we know what we know? What evidence will we accept? How credible will such evidence appear to others? What rules of evidence are appropriate to different tasks?
- *Connections and patterns*: How are things connected together? Have we ever encountered this before? Is there a discernible pattern here? What came first? Is there a clear cause and effect? ...Is this a 'law' of causality, a probability, or a mere correlation?
- *Conjecture*: What if things had been different? Suppose King George had been a very different personality? Suppose Napoleon or Martin Luther King, Jr. or Hitler had not been born? Suppose King's assassin had missed? (Our fourth habit encompassed our belief that a well educated person saw alternatives, other possibilities, and assumed that choices mattered. They could make a difference. The future wasn't, perhaps, inevitable.)
- And finally – who, after all, cares? Does it *matter*? And to whom? Is it of mere 'academic' interest, or might it lead to significant changes in the way we see the world and the world sees us (from Meier, 1998, 607-8)?

This can be applied to all kinds of text, but it is particularly important for critical educators to locate seminal texts – those which offer greatest leverage in key discourses. A recent example would be the use of the phrase 'weapons of mass destruction' in the run-up to war on Iraq. This phrase (parodied as 'words of mass distraction') was neatly upturned by a popular British newspaper.

6. PROJECT METHOD

This approach is to be found in many variants. Developed by Kilpatrick (1918) and Dewey, it has recently become popular in Northern Europe as an architecture for more democratic learning. Essentially, it involves an initial whole-class stage, followed by individual or small-group research, followed by a final plenary stage. It can be carried out across a series of lessons, or in a special block of time (the Project Week).

The theme or issue for a project may be introduced by a teacher or by the students. In the former case, the teacher must stimulate interest to the point where everybody is convinced that this is of interest and importance. If the students, for example, based the project on some current event, the teacher's role may be to draw out key concepts and principles, connecting the particular issue with appropriate academic disciplines.

In a project on refugees with my teaching students, I began with a simulation in which, at some stage in the future, Scottish families experienced a military coup. The scenario proceeds with daily news broadcasts until the family decides to flee. The students then begin to learn, from real examples, how Britain is currently treating asylum seekers using techniques designed to keep them out. By this stage, students are fired up to choose particular aspects to research: Where do most asylum seekers come from? How are their applications processed? How do they survive when not allowed to work?

Another example is a project on Human Rights. I first trialled this at an international conference in the Balkans, involving teachers and students from nine countries in the region and from the USA.

- In mixed groups, they attempted to write specific codes of rights (akin to the Rights of the Child) for particular groups such as teenage girls, old people, religious minorities or parents of young children. This led to more focused thinking than memorization, or even open discussion of the standard lists of human rights, could do. There were surprising discoveries, such as the shock of some Americans to learn about maternity leave.
- The discussion about the research stage emphasized the need to seek out the opinions and experience of real people, as well as looking in books and on the Internet.
- We discussed how such a project might end, and ideas included a Parliament in which each interest group sought to convince the others to include five points in a code of rights. This would lead to engaged debate, some compromise and amendment, the need to justify a position.
- There were also many suggestions for how to develop a sense of agency – for example, by taking the campaign out into the public arena, making posters, approaching local politicians.

Although it is more difficult in contexts where a standardized curriculum is imposed, there are possibilities. Even unlikely topics such as Roman Civilization, normally pursued as a set of content and events, can be re-structured as a project based on problem-based learning. An alternative school in Utah used this method, posing the question: *Were the Romans civilized?* (conversation with school director) This approach opened up many connections, including discussion of America's position in the world today and its claims to extend civilization.

Projects help to make learning more democratic, in a number of important ways.

- They create a foundation of personal and collective engagement with an issue.
- They overcome the standard disciplinary structures of the division of time, space and role.
- They give choice to individuals to pursue particular interests, while maintaining a coherence and space to dialogue.
- They enable students to teach each other, but based on focused research.
- They can create a collective interest and enthusiasm which leads to action.

7. CULTURAL REFLECTION AND REPOSITIONING

When conducting case study research in very successful schools with large numbers of bilingual pupils (mainly South Asia), I discovered an interesting and unusual form of pedagogy which I could only name 'cultural reflection and repositioning'. Focused on an important social issue, it generally used one of the creative or performing arts as the medium (drama, creative writing, painting etc.) It created a space and opportunity for young people to reflect on beliefs from their cultural heritage but in an open way, to consider their own attitudes and often to 'reposition' themselves. It was a form of critical pedagogy which had a necessary foundation of respect for minority cultures.

A good example was the religious education class which studied expressions of belief. Students examined statements in the different religious traditions before writing their own Creed. These typically began with a near quotation from a canonical text, but moved swiftly into contemporary situations.

- I believe in one God because I was brought up that way.
- I believe in the holy book and the prophets.
- I believe in the day of judgement...
- I believe that men and women should be treated equally...
- I believe that disabled people should be treated with the same respect as others, they should not feel like an outsider... (Wrigley, 2000, 68-9).

A similar example consisted of research, in pairs, into what the Bible or Quran said about, for example, global warming or threatened species, and (if it didn't, as was usual) what could be inferred from more general values in those texts. (Ibid, 68) This helped pupils move away from more fundamentalist approaches to texts, whilst recognizing the deeper values they expressed.

A class of girls studying Romeo and Juliet worked in threes to improvize the scene which Shakespeare never wrote: The three female characters Juliet, her nurse and her mother, discuss together how to respond to the father's edict that Juliet will marry the man of his choice or be kicked out of the house (ibid, 66). This carefully avoided the (false) suggestion that such pressure is normal in South Asian families, while enabling these girls to consider the issue in a supportive and unthreatening way.

In these examples, we see a form of 'border pedagogy' in which students can negotiate cultural difference. However, such a pedagogy also has great potential in culturally more homogenous settings. An example from Australia involved young people in a small town studying the local war memorial, and uncovering many local documents relating to the First World War (newspaper cuttings, medals, diaries etc.) They came to realize how distorted the iconic representations are, when matched against personal experiences and expressions. 'Cultural reflection and repositioning' is a pedagogy of relevance in any circumstance where there is a settled ideology and discourse, whether this is patriotism or patriarchy or those most dangerous contemporary fundamentalisms – consumerism, militarism, the belief that our governments make war to bring democracy to the world, or indeed that capitalism is the ultimate stage of human progress. As Dowbor suggests:

> Capitalism requires that free-of-charge happiness be [replaced with] what can be bought and sold (Dowbor, 1997, 26).

8. THE FUTURE

Finally, critical pedagogy and educational leadership requires a re-orientation of schools towards a different and better future. Schools have always dealt very well with the past, but have rarely provided a space for people to articulate their dreams.

This struggle goes on at the level of whole school development. School Improvement typically uses the word 'vision', but without any clear reference. It highlights change processes without any debate about the desired direction of change. In place of improvement, what it delivers is intensification.

> Behind a surface tone of exhortation, the texts are often shadowy. Words such as vision and values are never all they seem. Like ghosts, they disintegrate when we try to take hold of them. Vision so often comes to mean organizational adjustment. Talk about values soon collapses into 'valuing higher attainment' or 'valuing good behaviour', referring back into the schooling process rather than connecting outwards and forwards into the futures we would like to inhabit. Ideas and ideals collapse so easily into the performance outcomes of test scores... What if our schools need a change of direction as much as a boost of capacity? (Wrigley, 2003, 176)

Much of what has already been said about teaching and learning is implicitly future-oriented: project method, critical literacy, cultural repositioning, human rights, and so on. I will only add two particular ideas, a 'futures' website and a 'futures' timeline. The first, building on the older concept of a 'futures workshop', gives young people a space to present and share ideas on the kind of future they would like. It can be generalized (the global future), localized (Imagine Scotland, Imagine New York), or thematized (environment, peace, etc.) A future timeline is rather like those we use for history, but splits into three, with a line going upwards (the future we dream of), one horizontal (the probable future), and one going downhill (the future we fear). Of course, drawing the timeline should serve only as the focus and trigger for discussion and action.

There is widespread acknowledgement that we are living in an era of unprecedented change, which may accelerate unpredictably in the future. It is a reasonable conclusion that schools must also change and prepare young people for change in their own lives. It is an absurd non sequitur to believe that this can be accommodated simply by buying more computers or speeding up instruction.

In the last 20 years, we have seen much officially sponsored change which amounts to little more than intensification, simply speeding up the old structures and processes. The word 'effective' encapsulates this. At the same time, however, we can find some bold attempts to change direction, to set new goals, to develop radically different structures and cultures of education. These involve a challenge to current norms at the three levels referred to earlier in this article – disciplinary, curricular and pedagogical. They offer learners a chance to develop both voice and agency so that they can create a more democratic and just world.

Critical educators need to challenge current norms at all levels. A good model is Rethinking Schools, a teachers' network in the USA, which simultaneously campaigns against government policy and develops practical resources and methods for critical pedagogy.

The project to 'improve' schools just isn't good enough – we need to *rethink* education. We need to challenge school norms and traditions which deny young people voice and agency. We need real vision. We must dare to dream.

REFERENCES

Apple, M. (1979). *Ideology and curriculum*. London: Routledge and Kegan Paul.
Barnes, D. (1976). *From communication to curriculum*. Harmondsworth: Penguin.

Barnes, D., Britton, J. and Rosen, H. (1971). *Language, the learner and the school*. Harmondsworth: Penguin.

Brighouse, T. (2002).British Broadcasting Corporation (BBC) news report of speech made shortly before retirement as Director of Education for Birmingham. http://news.bbc.co.uk/1/hi/education/1924203.stm

Darder, A. et al (eds.) (2003). *The Critical Pedagogy reader*. London: RoutledgeFalmer.

Davies, M. and Edwards, G. (2001). Will the curriculum caterpillar ever learn to fly? In M. Fielding (ed.), *Taking education really seriously: Four years' hard labour*. London: Routledge/Falmer.

Dowbor, L. (1997). Preface: *Pedagogy of the heart*, by Paulo Freire. New York: Continuum.

Fielding, M. (ed.) (2001). Student Voice. *Special issue of Forum* 43(2).

Kemmis, S., Cole, P. and Suggett, D. (1983). *Orientations to curriculum and transition: Towards the socially-critical school*. Melbourne: Victorian Institute of Secondary Education.

Kilpatrick, W. (1918). The project method. *Teachers College Record* 19, pp 319-335.

Krogh-Jespersen, K. et al (1998). *Inspiration til undervisningsdifferentiering*. Copenhagen: Undervisningsministeriet (Folkeskoleafdelingen).

Meier, D. (1998). Authenticity and educational change. In A. Hargreaves et al (eds.), *International handbook of educational change*. Dordrecht: Kluwer.

Phillips, T. (1987). Beyond lip-service: discourse development after the age of nine. In B. Mayor and A. Pugh (eds.), *Language, communication and education*. London: Croom Helm.

Pilger, J. (1998). Killing Iraq. *The Nation*, 14 December.

Sewell, T. (1997). *Black masculinities and schooling: How Black boys survive modern schooling*. Stoke: Trentham.

Simon, B. (1965). *Studies in the history of education: Education and the labour movement, 1870-1920*. London: Lawrence and Wishart.

Simon, B. (1960). *Studies in the history of education, 1780-1870*. London: Lawrence and Wishart.

Simons, M. with Plackett, E. (eds.) (c.1986). *The English curriculum: Reading 1. Comprehension*. London: English and Media Centre.

Slee, R. and Weiner, G. (with Tomlinson, S.) (eds.) (1998). *School effectiveness for whom? Challenges to the school effectiveness and school improvement movements*. London: Falmer.

Weissenau, G. and Kuhn, H-W. (2000). *Lexikon der politischen bildung Band 3*. Schwalbach: Wochenschauverlag.

Wexler, P. (1982). Structure, text and subject: a critical sociology of school knowledge. In M. Apple (ed.), *Cultural and economic reproduction in education*. London: Routledge and Kegan Paul.

Williams, R. (1973). *The country and the city*. London: Chatto and Windus.

Willis, P. (1977). *Learning to labour: How working class kids get working class jobs*. Aldershot: Gower.

Wrigley, T. (2003). *Schools of hope: A new agenda for school improvement*. Stoke: Trentham.

Wrigley, T. (2000). *The power to learn: Stories of success in the education of Asian and other bilingual pupils*. Stoke: Trentham.

EPILOGUE

Literacy, Learning and Leadership: A Critical Focus on Democratic Schooling

1. INTRODUCTION

The selections chosen for this book contain some of the most current thoughts on Critical pedagogy and Critical inquiry to date. The chapters represent a dynamic synthesis of Critical theory, Critical practice and Critical theory-in-practice over the three sections that comprise this work. Each of the three sections of this book represents a central theme that comprises an essential component of the Critical framework of literacy, learning and leadership. Taken together, this work represents an integrated Critical framework that may help to inform teaching, learning and administration within a variety of educational institutions.

Needless to say, aspects of Critical inquiry as they pertain to literacy, learning and leadership are interwoven throughout the pages of this work. While it is necessary to represent these components independently of one another for the sake of clarity, it is also recognized that these divisions are not meant to suggest specifically linear progressions, but merely represent a way to talk about each of the three components from a Critical perspective. Reciprocal learning and transference of skills occur in any learning process, and so render the various processes incorporated here as examples of learning that are serendipitous, simultaneous and subconscious.

At the same time, while it is necessary to identify the three components that maintain the theme of this book, there is also a danger in doing so. To tease literacy from learning and leadership, to envision learning as the only bridge between literacy and leadership, and to view leadership as a natural end product of successful learning and literacy experiences is to do an injustice to the intent of the book. This intent is to recognize that literacy, learning and leadership are free standing but inter-related components, all three of which are essential to the pursuit of an education that is at once democratic, just and inclusive. But literacy, learning and leadership are not sufficient components to ensure that an education of this nature occurs on its own.

It is for this reason that Critical inquiry has been incorporated into this framework and is seen as the overarching reason for these components to support an education that is at once equitable, moral and inclusive. The underlying conceptualization present in this volume is the recognition that the notion of Critical inquiry is necessary for the development of a democratic, moral and socially just curriculum that allows the voices of all to be heard, listened to and acted upon. It is this element of Critical inquiry that unites all three of the sections of this book, literacy, learning and leadership, into an integrated framework. Therefore, as leaders become aware of the various skill sets that they require in order to go about their work, perhaps they will recognize that they need to further their own learning. Perhaps, in order to accomplish this, there may be a need to pick up a new type of literacy. By the same token, a young student may be learning to read. Through his or her learning, literacy is acquired and these skills may serve as building blocks for future leadership opportunities. By any standard, what sets the socially active human agent apart from others is the critical element that their education has been imbued with.

To come full cycle is to recognize that the chapters in this book are not recipes for success, but they chronicle some successes and describe some endeavours that are still in process. One of the most common criticisms of Critical pedagogy is that it has been seen as being unpracticable, impractical and dangerous in terms of upsetting the status quo. The articles on these pages discuss critical theories and underpinnings behind, underlying and superimposed upon the terrain of education. It is in this way that the editors and contributors to this volume have attempted to bridge the perceived gap between Critical theory and educational practice. It is here, on the pages of this book, that the contributors have illustrated and demonstrated that a "Critical practice" can be seen as a completely practicable and practical endeavour.

As this book was in the process of being edited, we were not only actively involved in the process, but were also acted *upon* by the process. As the opening chapter in this volume suggests, the K-W-L learning strategy is a powerful device, and as we progressed through the various stagers of this book, we discovered also that we were experiencing the very strategy that we were writing about. At the outset, we did not have a conceptual framework that clearly tied this volume together. However, as we edited and rewrote our own chapter and were informed by the chapters contributed by the Critical scholars whose work is represented in the pages of this volume, we began to perceive that, while our original view may have been somewhat simplistic and ill-formed, there was a conceptual connection between these various areas of scholarship that was powerful indeed. As we progressed, we began to recognize some of the patterns that Jonathon Hale (1994) has so eloquently commented on.

From the outset, we saw literacy, learning and leadership as being linked somehow. However, it was not until we began to see these three separate fields through the lens of the Critical, that we were able to make meaningful connections. It is in this way that we proceeded, as Paulo Freire so admirably says, from a local to a more universal location.

> The more rooted I am in my own location, the more I extend to other
> places so as to become a citizen of the world. No one becomes local
> from a universal location. (Freire, 1998, 39).

It is here that we introduce the etymology of the word "Critical". While this harbours no surprises, we note that it is related to the word "circus" referring to the circular sense, rather than to the first day of school. As our learning progressed, we found we were moving in evermore widening learning circles that were becoming ever more cognizant of the Critical nature that is required for judicious and democratic teaching and learning.

2. LITERACY, LEARNING AND LEADERSHIP

To begin with, what constitutes "literacy" has changed greatly overt he past number of years. Back in the days of our predecessors, to be literate, or "lettered" meant that you could read and write. Prior to that, literacy meant that you could sign a cheque (whenever that rare opportunity presented itself). In today's world however, not only is the concept of literacy broader, it is also deeper. It seems that one can not be called truly literate unless one has at least one degree or some specialized training, typically in a technologically immersed capacity. Thus the standards for what it means to be "lettered" have risen dramatically. Unfortunately, there are still many individuals the world over, for whom the idea of being literate in even the most archaic sense is but a flight of fancy.

To add to this, there are many more types of literacy available to us nowadays. Numeracy and oracy aside, we cherish our abilities to encode and decode the written word. We also require a technological literacy in order to understand and be able to operate even the simplest of computer programs. The need to be literate in terms of pictograms and logos is a newer form of literacy that will help us operate fax machines effectively by placing the paper in the position indicated by the hieroglyph on the fax tray. Further signs and indicators assist us on our busy way back home. By now, we know which button to punch on the in-dash DVD system, so that we no longer have to decode the symbols that look like so much space jargon. However, the image of the little man sitting in the chair with arrows pointing to various parts of his anatomy, which is supposed to represent something to do with climate control, may remain a mystery. As this discussion seems to indicate, literacy has crossed broad new horizons and, of course, some of us are more literate in any number of these new literacies than others.

In fact, it can be suggested that every discipline has its own form of literacy, since each discipline has its own vocabulary that must be learned in order to be able to communicate with others who maneuver within any given field. Further to this, there are "ways of knowing" peculiar to the discipline at hand that may or may not be shared by other disciplines. Take, for example, the mason who builds chimneys. He uses a refractory mortar since not just any kind of mortar will do. While the trowel that he uses may be a familiar object, his "hod" could present a learning opportunity, and eventually a theoretical knowledge may begin to take shape regarding how a "striker" is used. But these are only vocabulary words. In order to be really literate in the ways of chimney building, one must be able to be conversant with all aspects of the process, including buttering the bricks and lining them up straight and true.

What was amazing about one chimney mason, employed to rebuild the chimney of a 1903 Edwardian homestead, was the skill that he possessed. His literacy in the area of masonry was beautiful – in the way that De Lissovoy and McLaren in Chapter 10 describe as the art of teaching. He used no "sight line" to keep the chimney straight. This was done by eye. He followed the processes and procedures, also from De Lissovoy and McLaren, of the expert by standing in on spot rather than travelling around the chimney to complete the various "courses" of bricks. But his skill in sloughing the mortar on to the top course of brick was beautiful to behold – a flick of the wrist and the mortar moved gracefully from trowel to the brick. It was at this point that it became necessary to realize that true literacy in the art of rebuilding chimneys is not necessarily able to be accessed by everyone. As a skill and an art form, the art of teaching may be similar in many ways to the art of chimney rebuilding, but for some of us, it is much more accessible. That is to say, some of us, the editors of this volume included, are arguably more literate in terms of teaching than in terms of chimney work.

Part of the skill in becoming literate in any discipline or in any given area is the ability with which we are able to decode and encode. Freebody and Luke suggest that successfully literate individuals are code-breakers, meaning-makers, text users, and text analysts (Freebody and Luke, 1990). This is the point at which learning and literacy become connected. In order to understand "the process" of any kind of creative endeavour, and all endeavours are creative in some respect, one must be able to read the code. That is, one must be able to break the code through an understanding, not only of the vocabulary, but also of the techniques, implicit and explicit, that are the "tricks of the trade". Now, it is one thing to *know* the tricks of the trade, but it is quite another to be able to *reproduce* those same skills, codes or hieroglyphs so that an individual may become a practitioner: that is to say, to become one of the "literati".

Imagine literacy, learning and leadership as three points of a triangle. To move to the second prominence of our three-cornered conceptual framework, it can easily be seen that, in order to learn, one must be able to become literate in any particular genre. Learning occurs as we move back and forth between the points of code-breaking and code-making. Success breeds success. As one becomes more adept at mastering literacies in a variety of genres, new genres fall more easily to an inquiring mind. This is precisely because, as one increases one's literacy *within* a particular genre, some rules may apply to other genres. Consequently, the more literate in any areas that an individual may become, the greater their capacity for other literacies becomes. It is this very transference of information that develops learning and produces knowledge. The more experience, the greater the background from which to draw upon in order to learn new things. Each experience becomes a tool in a toolbox that never becomes full. As we are the sum total of all that we have learned, our past learning serves to make our current learning easier. Current learning influences future learning and in many ways, incremental or not, life-long learning becomes a given. This begs the question relating to how language learning is envisioned and structured by a dominant view, particularly as it pertains to "minority groups".

In short, the movement between literacy and learning is multidimensional and multidirectional. As one acts and is acted upon, so learning is informed by growing literacy in specific knowledge areas and, congruently, literacy continues to be informed by further learning. This is reminiscent of M. C. Escher, an artist whose previous incarnation was as an architect, who drew a picture of two hands, each one drawing the other; neither is finished, but the work is always ongoing, always in process.

It is at this point that we come to the third dimension of the three-pointed conceptualization of literacy, learning and leadership. While leadership is not necessarily a natural outgrowth of literacy and learning, we are positing that it *should* be. As an individual demonstrates a facility for learning in any or many genres, a natural offshoot of this would be to instruct others. We are all teachers at one level or another, as witnessed by a youngster at one school teaching his younger sister how to swear more effectively.

What we are trying to say here is that leadership does not have to be formalized in administrative roles. Leadership is often part and parcel of the learning process, or is at least connected to it in very systemic ways. Leadership often arrives in the guise of formalized leadership, such as in the form of principals and school administration, board officials and government bureaucrats. The fact that the roles of these leaders is formalized does not, however, necessarily make them efficient or even effective leaders. This is also true among the ranks of the *informal* leaders, however, it is not our point to say what it is that we think is lacking among our leaders. It is to say that these leaders, be they principals, teachers or students can all become better at what the do by recognizing the impact that both literacy and learning have on leadership.

3. TOWARDS A CONCEPTUAL FRAMEWORK

Further to this, the flow of literacy, learning and leadership is not uni-dimensional. Just as increasing degrees of literacy inform both learning and leadership, and just as learning allows for greater capacity development of both leadership *and* literacies, so, too, does leadership allow additional opportunities to engage existing literacies both more deeply as well as providing means to encounter and explore new literacies. By the same token, leadership, whether formal or informal, also provides opportunities for learning to take place in ever more depth and breadth. Imagine, then, a continuum of literacy, learning and leadership all informing and being informed by one another. Imagine an Escher drawing of *three* hands each drawing one another, rather than the actual image of the Escher drawing of two hands, as each hand acts and is acted upon by the others. The drawing is never complete but is always in the process of becoming complete. Thus it is with literacy, learning and leadership: they are all life-long pursuits.

While we are in the process of imagining the three points of literacy, learning and leadership, let us imagine this as a base upon which another three-pointed conceptualization rotates. This second dimension of the conceptual frame is the lens of Critical inquiry through which literacy, learning and leadership are reflected and refracted. (Please see Figure 1). Clearly, in a world where its citizens have access to literacies of all types, where learning is valued and where leadership is a natural outgrowth of these, to bring this into the realm of Criticality is to create a powerful synthesis. To begin to ask the most difficult questions, the ones that need asking the most, is to begin to question some of the notions that have been taken for granted in the past; that is, to question patterns that are or have been less than helpful for all.

By becoming literate and by learning in order to be a leader is insufficient if we value progress, humankind and education.

Figure 1. The multiple dimensions of Critical literacy, Critical learning and Critical leadership.

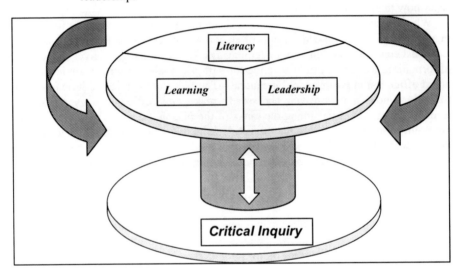

Critical Inquiry is the base for the rotation, in any direction, of literacy, learning and leadership. Literacy, learning and leadership influence and inform one another as each of these constructs are envisioned and re-envisioned through the lens of Critical Inquiry.

We must become Critically literate and indulge in learning to become Critical thinkers in order to become leaders who will examine policies, processes and practices in a Critical manner. As Colleen Capper (1993) suggests, it is not enough to have the ability to be Critical, it is necessary to have the disposition as well. By overlaying the dimension of Critical inquiry on the initial dimensions of literacy, learning and leadership, one can begin to question taken-for-granted practices of hegemony. Why do we agree to accept certain conditions on our freedom? Whose conditions are they? Who benefits from these conditions?

Capitalism is anti-democratic. To simply state this is to offer very little in the way of leadership, learning or even literacy. In order to connect with this in a meaningful way, one must begin at one of the dimensions developed in the conceptual framework. To be literate about the meanings of both capitalism and democracy is necessary, but to *agree* on what is meant by each is pivotal. In order to gain agreement, it may be necessary to create and recreate knowledge surrounding both of these terms. To study both capitalism and democracy is to embark on a study of leadership, albeit none of which is "Critical" in any way. In order to view these events as Critical, one must question the very basis of the notion of capitalism and how it serves to create dominant and subordinate cultures within the same society.

In concert with this, how does hegemony work to manufacture consent among the populace that this consent is as it should be? By viewing these dimensions through the lens of Criticality is to unearth ideas and attitudes that serve to preserve and promote inequitable and unequal practices. To attempt change is to lead.

4. THEORY INTO PRACTICE: SOME PARTING THOUGHTS

What would Critical Literacy, Critical Learning and Critical Leadership look like in a school setting? To consider this question, the following example is a composite of both Karyn and Robert's classes in a Teacher Professional Development Year. Although students crave the "tools of the trade" – the technical survival gimmicks – it takes some time to acquaint students with the notion that a basic grounding in theoretical matters may provide for them a backdrop of attitudes, values and beliefs that will allow these students to view events in the classes they will inherit on a situation-by-situation basis. This is to say that a solid theoretical underpinning, like the understanding of *how* to use the chimney re-builder's tools, is essential in allowing both novice and veteran teachers the opportunity to assess any given situation on its own merits rather than to apply the knee-jerk reaction of "If *that* happens... then do *this!*"

Having provided a place for theory, let us move on to what Critical literacy may look like in our classes. First of all, it is to recognize that there are a multiplicity of literacies available in any situation. The Edelsky and Cherland article in this volume has made this point very well, as has the article by Inglis and Willinsky. The Critical questions that follow are some that we have asked our students to consider as they explore and interrogate their teaching practices.

- Do you think these situations and attitudes still exist in schools? Why?
- Who benefits from it being this way?
- Is this democratic?
- Is there more information you need to help you to understand the situation?
- Is anyone's perspective missing?
- Whose perspective, and why do you think it is missing?
- What does this lived experience not tell you?
- Is there a way to interrupt and rewrite this experience? (Cooper & White, 2004)

Hopefully, by using these questions and reflecting on their practices, both beginning and veteran teachers can begin to question hegemonic practices and work towards producing an atmosphere and a corresponding reality of social justice within their classrooms, and within their schools and their communities. To work towards the recognition of how hegemony operates to counter democratic process requires the formation of linkages between the role of Critical thought and those of hegemony and democracy.

To recognize that a variety of literacies abound and are part and parcel of our students' learning, is to value Howard Gardner's (1999) work on multiple intelligences and to honour individual students learning styles. A Critically literate stance recognizes that, as Cummins (2001) suggests, most of the academic activity that is required of students beyond grade four consists of reading and writing. While listening to others and speaking to large groups, and discussing matters within small groups is more common, viewing and representing through such activities as observation and artwork is much less farther along the frequency continuum. Teachers, both novice and veteran, are urged to consider these aspects of literacy. Teachers of teachers are likewise urged to sensitize themselves and to model approaches that value a multiplicity of literacies that will not only benefit their students, but also the students of their students. What makes this "Critical" is the continuous questioning of Who benefits? Who has the power to decide ? and many other such questions that serve to maintain a Critical stance.

What is the connection between Critical literacies and Critical teaching. While there may be many ways to approach Critical teaching, one of the methods that has often worked is an attempt to "deconstruct" teaching. This means to make the curriculum more about learning and less about teaching. By attempting to neutralize teaching, it allows students space in which to take responsibility for their own learning. Basically, this means to make the teaching process more student centred so that materials and resources, and lesson plans continue to be supplied, but the curriculum is negotiated with the students. As an example, rubrics and/or evaluation sheets can and should be structured and/or negotiated with the students. Even "after-the-fact" negotiation is superior to a completely teacher-centred approach to teaching and learning. By removing the teacher from the centre of attention, students can become free to generate their own knowledge, develop their own patterns of learning and to take greater responsibility for such learning. Terry Wrigley alludes to this in his article in this volume. This approach to learning fits with the ideas of multiple truths, co-existing knowledge frames and interdependent networks of knowledge generation. Student assessment takes the form of projects, presentations and seminars where students can exhibit their own work developed through their own frames of knowledge, literacies and learning. Student presentations and seminars give students opportunities to develop "expert" knowledge and to teach in a way that they are comfortable in learning. Because teaching and learning are inextricably bound together, the old saw, "The best way to learn something is to teach it", has never been more true. Of course, with the forms of knowledge representation being more student-oriented than teacher-centred, this has tremendous implications for assessment and evaluation. This is where authentic assessment really begins to come into its own. While there may be ways to ensure that evaluation maintains certain overall standards, peer-assessment, self-assessment and teacher-based assessment may all be a part of the assessment process for any given project, seminar or presentation.

What does this look like in terms of Critical leadership? By allowing students the freedom to develop curriculum that is relevant to them (even within the bounds of existing curricular demands from central governments), teachers are able to honour their students' voices collectively and individually. One assignment that may be used with pre-service teachers involves having them create a book that tells their future students something important about a theme related to classroom community building. Through this approach, pre-service teachers may learn much about themselves and their fellow students as they also become engaged in thinking about the whole process of community building, both in the pre-service classroom and in their own future classrooms. One of the students produced a touching book about herself and her immigrant experience in Canada, which she now uses to introduce herself to her students. The book is called "To Feel Safe" (Cooper and White, 2004).

To not only hear the student voice, but to listen to it and heed it (Vibert et al, 2002), is empowering. Students tend to become less mark-oriented and envelope themselves in their learning, and yes, in authentic teaching activities that benefit themselves and their peers. This is not to suggest that the teacher just get out of the way and that the kids will be alright, but it is to question the over-control that we often exert over our students that serves to stultify, trivialize and otherwise diminish their own active learning. And this occurs precisely because it is impossible, or at least extremely difficult, to predict how each and every student will best learn on any given day. That is why it is a position of strength to be able to give that decision over to the very individuals who are in the best positions to make that decision – the students themselves.

In another example, introducing oneself to others seems to be an implicit act in the process of community building in the classroom at all levels of education. In beginning any class, instructors often ask students to introduce themselves. Mahawa's story (Cooper and White, 2004), presents a poignant account of an immigrant child whose teacher makes a name change because the child's name is deemed too difficult to pronounce. This important first step in building community has become a ritual with which many may never have been entirely comfortable, either as a student or teacher.

By allowing students to work to their strengths, and to move outside of their comfort zones when they are ready, this allows for a Vigotskian (1986) tradition of progressive learning and the subsequent development of additional knowledge, skills and abilities. This is one of the ways that development of a Critically literate stance can be developed in order to help all students gain access to the curriculum, thus helping to facilitate positive social change through positive educational experiences. Through this, learning is enhanced, allowing a more critical approach to learn that can incorporate issues of social justice. These experiences can build into real leadership opportunities, described by many of the contributors to this volume, as students and their co-researchers, the teachers, cycle backwards and forewards through literacy, learning and leadership which is at once meaningful and critical in the ultimate promotion of positive social critique and Critical activism.

REFERENCES

Capper, C. (1993). Educational administration in a pluralistic society: A multiparadigm approach. In C. Capper (ed.) *Educational Administration in a pluralistic society.* (7-35). New York: SUNY Press.

Cooper, K. and White, R. E. (2004). *Burning Issues: Foundations of Education.* Lanham, Maryland: Rowman and Littlefield.

Cummins, J. (2001). *Language, power, and pedagogy: Bilingual children in the cross-fire.* Clevedon, England: Multicultural Matters.

Escher, M. C. Drawing Hands. Retrieved May 12,2005 http://people.via.ecp.fr/~jm/musee/escher.htm

Freebody, P., & Luke, A. (1990). "Literacies" programs: Debates and demands in cultural context. *Prospect: the Journal of Adult Migrant Education Programs,* 5(30), 7-16.

Freire, P. (1998). *Pedagogy of the Heart.* New York: Continuum.

Frost, W. (Ed.) (1961). *Romantic and Victorian Poetry, Vol. 6, 2ⁿᵈ Edition.* Englewood Cliffs, NJ: Prentice-Hall.

Gardner, H. (1999). *Intelligence reframed: Multiple intelligences for the 21st century.* New York, NY: Basic Books.

Hale, J. (1994). *The old way of seeing.* New York: Houghton Mifflin.

Vibert, A., Portelli, J., Shields, C. and LaRoque, L. (2002). Critical practice in elementary schools: Voice, community and curriculum of life. *Journal of Educational Change,* 3(2), 93-116.

Vygotsky, L. (1986). *Thought and word.* (Trans. Alex Kozulin) Cambridge, MA, London: MIT Press.

INDEX

Action research, 1, 3, 14, 15, 51; methodology loop, 3.

Agency, 5, 8, 14, 43, 67, 69, 91, 105, 106, 133, 135, 151, 179-180, 182, 183, 187, 193, 196.

Art(s), 24-25, 47, 55, 57, 61, 85, 89-90, 99, 191, 197-198, 201; of persuasion, 40, 78.

Authenticity, 69, 81, 84, 133; in education, 75, 153, 154, 202.

Brainstorming, 11.

Buzzwords, 18, 32.

Canadian Charter of Rights and Freedom, 45.

Capacity development, 3, 14, 52, 63, 122, 133-135, 138, 161, 198, 199.

Capitalism, 72, 74-75, 77-86, 88, 90, 91, 111-112, 151, 154, 158, 192, 201.

Citizens and citizenship, 36, 40, 42, 45-47, 58, 76, 80, 105, 124, 134, 151, 155.

Classism, 68, 71, 74, 78, 84-85, 90, 91, 117, 181.

Classroom(s), 8, 12, 24-25, 27, 37, 42, 44-45, 46, 51, 52, 54, 56, 60, 82, 95-110, 118, 154, 157, 161, 174, 179, 181, 182, 187, 201, 203.

Colonization, 81, 82, 154, 189.

Community(ies), 25, 27, 42, 43, 45-46, 54, 56-61, 79, 95-110, 124, 180, 201; of reflective and critical learners, 3, 15, 159, 203.

Community service, democratic inquiry and skill development, 2, 35, 47.

Consensus, 4, 79.

Constitutional democracy, 2, 35, 38, 39, 48.

Consumerism, 78, 80, 111, 192.

Creativity, 24-25, 86, 113, 152, 153.

Critical, 83; awareness, 14, 36, 45, 48, 51, 55, 105; discourse analysis, 53; educators, 2, 14, 42, 48, 54, 67, 71, 74, 82, 85, 91, 154, 160, 161, 179, 180-181; emancipation, 17, 29, 30-31, 105; habitus, 51; inquiry, 1, 35, 195-196; leadership, 1, 2, 14, 67, 133-136, 142, 152, 161, 165-178, 195-205; learning, 1, 2, 14, 67-69, 195-205; literacy, 1-2, 3-16, 17-34, 51-66, 188, 195-205;

and belief structures, 5; capacities, 4; and democratic education, 1-2. in educational institutions, 2; educators, 2, 51; and emancipation, 2, 17; instruction, 17-19, 24; identity, context and teaching practices, 4, 6, 10; and language, 2, 51, 58.

pedagogy, 1-2, 5, 54, 86-87, 133, 134, 151, 154, 157-160, 179, 182, 191, 196; theory, 67, 71-94, 96, 105, 195; thinking, 4, 9, 83, 135; framework, 4; culture and climate, 4.

Cultural, diversity, 7, 8, 56, 63, 67, 68, 97, 117, 191; studies, 10, 97.

Culture, 55, 56, 61, 62, 76, 77, 81, 86, 88, 90, 91, 103-105, 112, 126, 134, 140, 141, 151, 153, 179, 182, 183, 193, 201.

Curriculum, 25, 38, 40, 51, 52, 54, 58, 59, 62, 63, 74, 78, 82, 85-86, 139, 154, 157, 179-180, 181, 183-186, 193, 195, 202-203; guidelines, 11, 112, 135, 154-155, 191; language arts curriculum, 9, 42; theory, 8.

Decoding, 1, 11; and encoding, 1.

Democracy, 35-50, 54, 62, 71, 76, 78, 81-85, 90, 96, 97, 103, 105, 108, 134, 151, 166, 192, 201; constitutional, 35, 36, 38, 39, 48; deliberative, 35, 36, 38 39-40, 45-46, 48; participatory, 18, 74, 82, 147; procedural, 35, 36, 38, 39, 48; representative, 147; rhetorical 35, 36, 38, 40, 48, 134; soup kitchen, 35-50; theories of, 2 35-50, 95-96, 104-105, 108, 146; and social justice, 2, 107, 182, 193.

Democratic, classrooms, 95-110; education, 1-2, 15, 38, 51, 52, 53, 67-69, 71, 106, 133-136, 137-150, 195; inquiry, skill development, and community service, 2, 35; practice, 2, 133; and Critical literacy, Critical learning and Critical leadership, 2; rights, 2, 39; social justice and equity, 8, 17, 39, 195; society, 3, 39, 42, 157; teaching, 2, 71.

Democratization of research, 2; and knowledge producing practices, 2.

Development stage theory, 10.

Discourse(s), 7, 62, 63, 82-85, 87, 104, 105, 138, 139, 153, 154, 192.

Discrimination, 39.

Diversity, 7, 55, 56, 63, 67, 68, 71, 76, 87, 95, 183.

Drama, 22, 27, 47, 188, 191.

Drop Everything and Read, 22.

Economics, 138; political, 71-94.

Educators, 87, 89, 137, 151, 152, 157, 158; Critical, 2, 31, 40, 42, 63, 82, 83, 91, 179, 180-181.

Education, 122, 129, 137, 139, 159, 179, 183, 193, 196, 200; anti-racist, 112; democratic, 15, 53, 71-94, 107, 133-136, 137-150.

Educational, institutions, 51; practices, procedures and policies, 3, 31, 153; systems, 7,8.

Emancipation, 105-106; through Critical literacy, 2.

Empowerment, 52, 67, 71, 76, 80, 86, 87, 90, 105, 135.

Lightning Source UK Ltd.
Milton Keynes UK
11 March 2010

151259UK00002BA/23/A